# CREATING THE SCHOOLS
# OUR CHILDREN NEED

# CREATING THE SCHOOLS OUR CHILDREN NEED

Why What We're Doing Now Won't Help Much

*(And What We Can Do Instead)*

# DYLAN WILIAM

LSi LEARNING® SCIENCES INTERNATIONAL

1400 Centrepark Blvd., Ste 1000
West Palm Beach, FL 33401
717.845.6300
email: pub@learningsciences.com
learningsciences.com

Printed in the United States of America

22   21   20   19   18                    1   2   3   4   5

Library of Congress Control Number: 2018931316

Publisher's Cataloging-in-Publication Data
provided by Five Rainbows Cataloging Services

Names: Wiliam, Dylan, author.

Title: Creating the schools our children need : why what we're doing right now won't work, and what we can do instead / Dylan Wiliam.

Description: West Palm Beach, FL : Learning Sciences, 2018.

Identifiers: LCCN 2018931316 | ISBN 978-1-943920-33-4 (pbk.) | ISBN 978-1-943920-31-0 (ebook)

Subjects: LCSH: School improvement programs--United States. | School management and organization--United States. | School boards--United States--Decision making. | Educational change. | Educational leadership. | BISAC: EDUCATION / Administration / General. | EDUCATION / Educational Policy & Reform / General. | EDUCATION / Leadership.

Classification: LCC LB2822.82 .W558 2018 (print) | LCC LB2822.82 (ebook) | DDC 371.2/07--dc23.

*For Siobhán*

# TABLE OF CONTENTS

# ACKNOWLEDGMENTS

Writing the acknowledgments section of any book is fraught with risk. When individuals are named, there is an implication that the contributions of those who were not named are somehow less important. The alternative—not naming anyone—means that those who have made the greatest contributions get no recognition. However, there is a bigger problem with acknowledgments. The very idea of acknowledging those who have contributed to the book rests on the assumption that the author is able to identify whose ideas, suggestions, conversations, and so on have influenced the author's thinking.

Sometimes, this is true. My collaboration with Paul Black, now well into its third decade, has been the most profound influence on my work as a teacher and researcher, for which I am deeply grateful. It is also clear to me that particular researchers, such as Linda Darling-Hammond, Carol Dweck, Eric Hanushek, Lorrie Shepard, and Lauren Resnick, have powerfully influenced the way I think about education. Most recently, I have become acutely aware that I should have known more about the work of cognitive scientists such as Robert Bjork, John Sweller, and Daniel Willingham much earlier in my career.

However, I am also aware that my thinking about educational issues has been influenced—sometimes dramatically, sometimes more slowly and subtly—in other ways, through reading articles and books, of course, but also through conversations with my students and other researchers, by listening to podcasts, through exchanges with complete strangers on social media, and so on. Again, I am grateful.

Thanks are also due to Mark Combes and his editorial team at Learning Sciences International, and especially Lesley Bolton for her willingness to expedite the production of this book. Harry Fletcher-Wood, Ulrich Boser, and Daniel Willingham provided helpful comments on drafts of the manuscript although, of course, responsibility for any errors in the book remains with me.

Finally, as ever, my greatest thanks go to my partner, Siobhan Leahy, who has supported me in the writing of this book as she has throughout my academic career, providing advice and guidance, keeping my feet on the ground, and sharpening both my arguments and the writing. That is why this book is dedicated to her.

# ABOUT THE AUTHOR

Dylan Wiliam is one of the world's foremost education authorities. He has helped to successfully implement classroom formative assessment in thousands of schools all over the world, including the United States, Singapore, Sweden, Australia, and the United Kingdom. A two-part BBC series, *The Classroom Experiment*, tracked Dr. Wiliam's work at one British middle school, showing how formative assessment strategies empower students, significantly increase engagement, and shift classroom responsibility from teachers to their students so that students become agents of and collaborators in their own learning.

Dylan Wiliam is emeritus professor of educational assessment at University College London. After a first degree in mathematics and physics, he taught in urban schools for seven years, during which time he earned further degrees in mathematics and mathematics education.

Learn more about Wiliam's research, as well as his products and services, at the Learning Sciences Dylan Wiliam Center, www.dylanwiliamcenter.com.

# FOREWORD

Psychologists who study thinking can seem like a gloomy lot, as their research appears to be a catalog of instances in which humans think poorly. Yet these instances of human cognitive frailty do much to help us understand the irrational exuberance for one education policy or another over the last thirty years.

Consider some of the ideas that have come and gone (and usually come back again) over the last fifty years.

- Smart people do any job better than dumb people. So, what we need to do is lure more smart people into teaching.

- Actually, it's too hard to get really smart teachers. What we really need to do is fire the terrible ones.

- Actually, who's to say they are terrible? The real problem is that teachers are overworked; students would learn more in small classes, where they would get more individualized attention.

- Actually, why are we trying to reinvent the wheel? It's easier to steal a good idea than to invent one, and we know which countries are educational leaders; let's just imitate them.

And the most popular (or at least, the most vocally advocated) idea of the last twenty years:

- Actually, we're making this harder than it needs to be. If we just let parents choose among schools, the all-wise invisible hand of the market will inevitably lead to better outcomes for students.

A good deal of research has demonstrated that none of these strategies is a robust method of improving education, yet they are perennial, dying back for a time when they are proven wanting, but then reflowering, often a generation later.

Their hardiness is not attributable to the tough intellectual thinking that has gone into the plans but rather to their fortuitous exploitation of the weakness of human reasoning. Consider some of the factors that make these ideas appealing.

First, the confirmation bias. All of these ideas sound so plausible. The logic behind them is self-evident and relies on assumptions that seem unassailable. But the confirmation bias is defined by our tendency to seek out confirming evidence and to forget to look for disconfirming evidence. So, when we see that some countries do very well on an international test, the most obvious features of that country's education system capture our attention ("Students in Finland have lots of recess!" or "Students in Korea have a no-nonsense curriculum!"), while we ignore the possibility that the high test scores have nothing to do with that feature of schooling or little to do with the educational practice in that country at all. Test-takers may not be a representative sample of students. The factors that lead to good test performance may be cultural. Students from that country may fare much poorer on other tests, for unknown reasons.

Second, consider the difference between statistical and practical significance. When we say that an educational intervention "works," we usually mean the former: in some research setting, the scores of a group of students experiencing some intervention were statistically significantly different than the scores of a comparison group of students. Statistics are a safeguard against being misled by luck; if we simply compared two groups, the odds of the intervention group scoring higher by chance is obviously 50 percent (barring the unlikely event of an exact tie). The backbone of statistical inference is assuring ourselves that the difference between the intervention and comparison group was so big that it was very unlikely to have occurred by chance—the difference is not a fluke. The problem is that "so big" doesn't mean big in practical terms—it means reliable. It means that if you did the research a second time you'd see the same difference again. But reliable is not the same as important. In the right type of experiment, differences that are of no practical significance can be statistically reliable. So it is in the research literature on school choice. The results of comparisons are, in any event, mixed, but even when they seem to show that school choice benefits students, the advantage, although statistically significant, is usually so small as to be of little practical consequence. But it's very hard for people to remember to differentiate between "It worked!" and "It made a difference that matters!"

A third cognitive weakness much in evidence in education policy is overconfidence. The relationship between knowledge and confidence is often shaped like an inverted U. People who know nothing about education policy are ready to admit as much. Press them on how to improve American education, and they'll shrug. People with a great deal of expertise have, overall, only a little more confidence that they know how to make things better. There is a small number of areas of education that they feel are well understood, and for those, they have ready answers and they are confident those answers are right. But their knowledge also sets sharp boundaries regarding what is known, and pressing them beyond those boundaries gets you little more than narrowed eyes and a murmured "well . . . that's a complicated issue." It's the folks with some knowledge who pose the real problem. They are the embodiment of Pope's warning that "a little knowledge is a dangerous thing." Policymakers who've read some research briefings are too often certain they have mastered complex issues, which, in fact, remain poorly understood.

How often I have thought, "If only there were a readable summary of why all these plausible ideas don't work, written by a calm, impartial voice, with simple clarity!" Now someone has created such a summary, and you have it in your hands.

But Wiliam doesn't leave it at explaining which popular ideas sound good but won't work. He tells you what does work. Here again, Wiliam aims straight for the heart of an issue I have long wished someone would tackle. Not all the pie-in-the-sky ideas are bound to fail, but they are unproven. Hearing yet another always prompts me to think, "OK, we could explore that, sure, but meanwhile, why don't we just do what (1) we know works and (2) is practical now?" And again, Wiliam delivers, with proven ways to invest in curriculum and in teachers.

Had I trained in education research, I would have known about Dylan Wiliam early on. Instead (as a mid-career arrival), I found him on Twitter. I quickly perceived that he was a rare voice for high-quality science on that lunatic soapbox, and that led me to his published work. What makes education research so difficult to interpret is that even modest interventions can have wide-ranging, unpredictable impacts— impacts that interact with what you hoped to change. Really effective interpreters of education research not only critique what researchers present, they see beyond what's written, thinking about those unforeseen effects. That's what's behind his comprehensive view. When it comes to putting together research, Wiliam has no peer.

Creating the Schools Our Children Need is a signal work. Amid all of the words and all of the theory, this volume tells what will pay off now. Read, enjoy, profit.

—Daniel T. Willingham

# INTRODUCTION

The argument of this book is simple. In fact, the title says it all. The schools our children attend need to be better; the things we are doing right now to improve our schools won't have much impact; and what we should be doing is both clear and possible.

Those three items in the argument also provide the structure of the book, which may help you decide which parts of the book will be most useful to you. So, if you think our schools are good enough right now, then you need to read section 1 (chapter 1). If you agree that schools need to improve but that the things we are doing right now—such as teacher evaluation, expanding school choice with charter schools and vouchers, or reducing class size—are likely to be enough, then you will probably find it useful to read parts of section 2 (chapters 2 through 7). Each chapter in this section begins with a short summary, so you can decide how much detail you need. If you agree that schools need to improve, and you know why what we are doing now won't help much, you can skip straight ahead to section 3 (chapters 8 through 12).

The main aim of this book is to give parents, school board members, and others who are concerned about education in America the evidence they need to create the schools that will provide our children with the knowledge, skills, and abilities they will need to flourish in the twenty-first century. In particular, it is to help those key decision-makers in school districts become more critical consumers of educational research so that they can make better decisions about where to invest their time and money and how to direct the efforts of those they lead.

Decision-makers in education need to be critical consumers of educational research because they have to navigate a delicate path between two opposing camps in the debates about how we should improve education.

On the one hand are those who call for an evidence based approach to education. We should just find out what works in education and make sure that everyone does it. This argument makes a lot of sense. After all, we spend a lot of money on K–12 education in the United States (over $600 billion each year[1]), and given that most of this is public money, we should make sure that this money is being spent as wisely as possible.

In the other camp are those who—often with justification—decry educational research as providing little more than bland platitudes that tell us only what we already know or, worse, produce research results that might hold true in a laboratory but don't pan out when applied in real schools.

As someone who has been a grade-school teacher, a researcher, a teacher educator, and a dean of a school of education, I sympathize with both of these camps. It seems perverse that we spend so much money on K–12 education in the United States and yet have so little evidence about the best ways to spend this money wisely. Surely we should be able to be more scientific in our approach to teaching—just try different things out and figure out what works. And yet, as a teacher in urban schools, I found most educational research was completely divorced from the reality of trying to ensure that twenty-five, thirty, or thirty-five children in a class made the academic progress I believed was both necessary and possible.

The simple truth is that, in education at least, what works is generally the wrong question, because most ideas that people have had about how to improve education work in some contexts but not others. Put bluntly, everything works somewhere and nothing works everywhere.

That is why school board members and administrators need to become critical consumers of research. They need educational research because as American management guru W. Edwards Deming once said, "Without data you're just another person with an opinion." And people's opinions and intuitions about how to improve education are often completely wrong. One recent example of this, one that has gained particular acceptance in the United States, is the idea that students have preferred learning styles and if we just take these differences into account in planning instruction for our children, they will learn more.

Psychologists have been putting people into boxes for as long as we have been studying people: as introverts and extroverts, in terms of their conscientiousness, in terms of their openness to experience, and so on. While many of these classification systems examine general personality characteristics, a number of classifications look specifically at the way people think—what psychologists call a person's *cognitive style*. When solving problems, for example, some people like to focus on getting the evidence that is most likely to be relevant to the problem at hand, while others have a tendency to think out of the box. Some like to get the big picture first and then look at the details, while others like to get going as quickly as possible and worry about the big picture later. And if people think differently, the argument goes, then they probably learn differently too, so if we can just identify our students' preferred learning styles and make sure we teach them that way, then they will make more progress.

Now this is a perfectly understandable belief. Anyone who spends any time in schools immediately becomes aware of the huge differences in children—in their abilities, their interests, their beliefs, and so on. And we also know that a particular piece of instruction can be effective for some students and not for others. It therefore seems plausible that if the instruction was specifically designed to take into account a particular student's preferred learning style, then it would be more likely to be effective for that student. This is what psychologists call the *meshing hypothesis*: the idea that students will learn more if they receive instruction that specifically matches their learning-style preferences. In other words, visual learners will learn better if they receive instruction that emphasizes visual ways of presenting information, auditory learners will learn best by listening, and kinesthetic learners learn best by doing.

Because of the controversy surrounding these ideas, the Association for Psychological Science decided to investigate the matter and set up a working group composed of some of America's top psychologists and chaired by Harold Pashler, distinguished professor at the University of California San Diego. The group looked for experiments in which students were classified in some way (e.g., visual, auditory, or kinesthetic learners), and then students were given—at random—instruction that either matched or did not match their preferred style, after which they would all take the same test. The researchers were looking for experiments in which the instruction that maximized the performance of one group (e.g., visual learners) was different from the instruction that maximized the performance of another group (e.g., auditory learners).

They found one experiment that partially supported this idea and two experiments that flatly contradicted it. The group's conclusion was stark: "If classification of students' learning styles has practical utility, it remains to be demonstrated."[2]

Put bluntly, there is no good evidence that teaching students in their preferred learning styles has any benefits at all. And yet, in school districts all over the United States, teachers continue to receive professional training that emphasizes the importance of learning styles, continue to be encouraged to plan different kinds of instructional activities for different kinds of learners, and, in some districts, are actually required to take learning styles into account in planning their instruction. It is hard to imagine that school board members who know about the lack of evidence behind learning styles would condone, let alone support, such a policy. The research evidence won't always (or even often) tell you what to do, but it will help you decide whether something is likely to have a chance to be effective in your district. Differentiating instruction on the basis of children's supposed learning styles looks to be a huge waste of teachers' time and may actually be harmful to learning.[3]

Sometimes, even when the data do exist, it is hard to be sure what they mean. In the late 1990s, the Bill and Melinda Gates Foundation started giving money to school districts to help fund the creation of small high schools. The small high schools movement had gained momentum in the 1970s as a reaction to the increased waves of school district consolidation taking place across the whole of America; in 1940, there were over one hundred thousand school districts in America, and now the number is well under fourteen thousand. As districts consolidated, high schools were often merged, and so high schools got larger, which many people believed made the schools depersonalized and alienating. The idea that students would fare better in a school where all the teachers knew all the students was attractive to many.

Initially, most of the arguments in favor of smaller high schools were in terms of the personal benefits for students, about increasing a sense of belonging, which would increase attendance and engagement. However, in the late 1990s, a number of people suggested that smaller high schools were a way of improving student achievement, and the data did look impressive. For example, Howard Wainer and Harris Zwerling collected information on 1,662 schools in Pennsylvania and found that there were four times as many small schools in the top fifty schools than would be expected by chance. Small schools do appear to be more effective than larger schools. Numbers like this appear to have pushed the Gates Foundation to invest massively in the creation of small high schools.[4] By 2001, the Gates Foundation had spent $1.7 billion on small high school programs, and a number of other charities, such as the Annenberg Foundation and the Carnegie Corporation, had joined the push for smaller high schools.

Unfortunately, the idea that converting large high schools into a number of smaller high schools will improve achievement, while attractive, is wrong. To explain why, Wainer and Zwerling use data on the prevalence of kidney cancer in the United States. They found that the counties with the lowest rates of kidney cancer are rural counties. It is easy, from this, to construct a plausible story about healthy lifestyles, lack of pollution in air and water, fresher food, and so on. However, when we look at the counties with the *highest* rates of kidney cancer, we find they are *also* rural counties. The reason that the lowest *and* highest rates of kidney cancer occur in rural counties is because they have fewer people.

In the United States each year, about five out of every one hundred thousand people die from kidney cancer. So, in a rural county of ten thousand people, if no one dies of kidney cancer, the mortality rate is zero, which, of course, is well below the national average. If, on the other hand, one person dies of kidney cancer, the rate is twice the national average: one out of ten thousand is ten out of one hundred thousand. In a county of two hundred thousand people, we would expect ten deaths from kidney cancer each year, and one more person dying increases the rate by only 10 percent. But in a county of twenty thousand, where we would expect just one death, an additional death increases the mortality rate by 100 percent.[5] This is why small counties have both the lowest and highest rates of mortality from kidney cancer. Larger counties cluster around the average much more closely.

The same thing holds for schools. It is true that the highest test scores are more often found in small high schools. But so are the lowest test scores. In fact, there is a slight tendency for larger schools to be *more* effective than smaller schools, because, with more teachers of each subject, teachers can specialize. As one Seattle student observed, in smaller high schools, "There's just one English teacher and one math teacher. They end up teaching things they don't really know."[6]

Now, of course, there are other reasons to prefer small high schools—more neighborhood schools, shorter travel times, less chance for students to fall between the cracks—but increased student achievement is not one of them. And yet, a failure to understand the basic idea—small groups are more variable than big ones—led some of the nation's leading charities to spend literally billions of dollars on initiatives that did no good and may have actually lowered student achievement.

These are just two examples—I could have selected many more—but the important point here is that if citizens are to make informed choices about their own local schools, they need to understand what we know—and don't know—about what is likely to help improve things, and that's where research comes in. Research will never tell school board members exactly what they need to do to improve their schools. Districts are too varied for the same things to work everywhere. Moreover, some things that don't work most places may, because of specific circumstances, be highly effective in a district. But knowing what the research says, and does not say, will help districts avoid some of the things that are clearly unlikely to work, such as getting teachers to take into account the learning styles of their students or creating smaller high schools.

More important, as we shall see in section 2 (chapters 2 through 7), there are things like class size reduction that do help improve student achievement but only under certain circumstances, and so, before adopting class size reduction programs, it is important to be sure that the circumstances necessary for the program to be successful are, in fact, in place. We can also look at what is going on in countries that seem to have more effective education systems, but many of the reasons for those countries' successes are not easy, and perhaps impossible, to implement in the United States. There are also programs that work most anywhere but don't work *enough*. For example, we can try to get smarter people into teaching, we can fire bad teachers, and we can pay good teachers more. We can expand school choice with more charter schools and voucher schemes. All of these are likely to produce improvements in student achievement, but the improvements will be small and nothing like the improvements our children need. Finally, there are things that work almost everywhere and would have a substantial impact on student achievement but are just too expensive to implement. Even if districts have spare cash, there are some things that are just not a good value for the money.

Fortunately, as we shall see in section 3 of this book (chapters 8 through 12), there are concrete suggestions that can help districts increase the odds that their school improvement efforts will be successful. Specifically, there are two things that can improve educational achievement substantially, and with little additional cost. The first is to ensure that the curriculum in each school is content-rich and is focused on developing knowledge. The second is creating an expectation that all teachers in the district, even if they are already the best, continue to improve their classroom practice.

I became convinced that a book such as this, written for nonexperts, was needed only in the last few years. Throughout most of my professional life, I have written articles and books for teachers and for researchers. But as I worked with teachers, administrators, and districts in America, I became more and more convinced that the key to improving American schools is not in knowing what to do—the research is now reasonably clear on that issue—but in creating situations where what we know needs to happen can happen.

To do this, it would be tempting to work at the state level—after all, there are only fifty of them—but as I have worked with teachers and administrators across the country, I have discovered that what states can do is limited. Many, and perhaps most, of the kinds of things that states can do, such as requiring teachers and administrators to hold certain kinds of credentials, placing limits on class sizes, restricting textbook adoptions, and so on, tend to focus on what districts are not allowed to do, rather than on what they should do. Other things that states can do—such as introducing statewide testing programs—have the potential to improve student achievement but are generally implemented in a way that reduces, or even completely negates, the potential benefit.[7] Moreover, most of the things that states can do, even when they do make things better, tend to have a relatively small impact on student achievement. Finally, even where policies are well targeted, such as those that redistribute resources from affluent to less affluent districts, what really matters is what districts do with the money.

That is why improving education in the United States is so challenging. States do have a role to play in improving education, but the policies that are put in place at the state level don't have much impact on what happens in classrooms. What matters most of all is how districts respond to those policies. Improving education in America is hard because it doesn't have an education system. It has 13,491 of them.[8]

Our children need better schools. Whether they get them depends on what school board members, superintendents, other administrators, and teachers do. This book is designed to help them use their time and their talents wisely.

---

1    According to the National Center for Educational Statistics: https://nces.ed.gov/fastfacts/display.asp?id=66.

2    Pashler, McDaniel, Rohrer, and Bjork (2008, p. 117).

3  For a nontechnical summary of how matching instruction to learning styles might be harmful, see Wiliam (2016b).

4  It is also likely that the Bill and Melinda Gates Foundation needed to distribute a large amount of money relatively rapidly. Section 26 USC 492 of the Internal Revenue Code imposes a 30 percent tax on charities that fail to distribute at least 5 percent of their assets in any given year. Given the assets the foundation had at this time, this was a large amount of money to give away, and so large initiatives were needed.

5  Wainer and Zwerling (2006).

6  Geballe (2005).

7  For a discussion of how statewide testing programs can increase student achievement and why they often do not, see Wiliam (2010).

8  Or at least there were in 2014: https://nces.ed.gov/programs/digest/d15/tables/dt15_214.30.asp? current=yes

# SECTION 1

CHAPTER 1

# Why We Need to Improve
# American Education

If someone claimed to have invented a drug that did what education did, no one would believe it. Those with more education live longer—about 1.7 years for every additional year in school.[1] Those with more education have less disability toward the ends of their lives,[2] and they are healthier overall: 75 percent of US high school dropouts report that they are in good health, while the figure for college graduates is 90 percent.[3] More educated people are less likely to be incarcerated, less likely to be teenage parents, less likely to commit suicide, and more tolerant of others.[4] Oh, and they are happier too.[5]

Education also, as is well known, increases wages. In 2015, the average high school dropout earned $493 per week. High school graduates earned 38 percent more, and those with some college credits earned 50 percent more. However, the real financial value of education comes with college graduation. Those with bachelor's degrees earn more than twice as much as high school dropouts ($1,137 per week), and those with advanced degrees earn 20 to 30 percent more than that.[6] Perhaps less obvious, education reduces the chances of being unemployed. Around 8 percent of high school dropouts are unemployed, while the rate for college graduates is only one-third of that. Moreover, education insulates people from shocks in the economy. For example, at the height of the last recession, in June 2009, the unemployment rate for adults without a high school diploma was over 15 percent. For college graduates, it was less than a third of that, at 4.8 percent.[7]

Society also benefits from higher levels of educational achievement. Henry Levin and his colleagues at Columbia University, New York, estimate that preventing one student from dropping out of high school benefits society, over the course of that student's life, by well over $200,000. Most of this (around $139,000) comes because people with more education earn more money over their lifetimes and therefore pay more taxes. People with more education are more likely to get health benefits from their employer and therefore are less likely to receive health and other benefits from the government, saving the taxpayer another $40,000. And because people with more education are less likely to be incarcerated, that saves the taxpayer a further $26,000 in prison and other criminal justice costs.[8]

Perhaps most surprisingly, with a more educated population, the economy grows faster. Estimating how much increased educational achievement increases economic growth obviously requires making a large number of assumptions, but a range of different methods seems to produce reasonably similar estimates. In chapter 6, we will learn more about the Programme for International Student Assessment (PISA), a program run by the Organisation for Economic Co-operation and Development (OECD), a group of thirty-five mostly rich countries. PISA involves testing students from all around the world in reading, math, and science, and ever since the program began in 2000, the United States typically scores just below the international average score of 500. Eric Hanushek and Ludger Woessman estimate that if we could raise the scores of American fifteen-year-olds on this test by twenty-five points (the improvement that Poland made in less than a decade), then over the next fifty to eighty years this would increase US gross domestic product by $62 trillion. In other words, by 2095, the US economy would be 30 percent larger than it would otherwise be, just by increasing the level of educational achievement. And if we could just ensure that every fifteen-year-old reached a level of reading and math that allowed him or her to function in today's complex world, that alone would be worth about $30 trillion.[9] Furthermore, there doesn't seem to be any downside to higher educational achievement at all. In a world where most policies have both winners and losers—think increased international trade, with consumers being better off but manufacturers and their employees being worse off—higher educational achievement seems to be a win-win situation all around. The question, of course, is how we do it.

A good general rule in solving problems is to make sure you understand the problem before you try to solve it. This may seem obvious, but in education, people often argue about which particular way is the best way to improve education when they don't actually agree on what education should do and why they think education is important. It is hardly surprising, therefore, that they then talk past each other. And the fact is that people often differ markedly in their reasons for believing that education is important.

Some people emphasize the role of education in enabling young people to take greater control of their lives, and so they see personal empowerment as the most important goal of education. Others acknowledge that personal empowerment is important but argue that this is best done by making sure that people understand the shared values and culture of their society. For these people, perhaps the most important role of education is, as Matthew Arnold suggested almost a century and a half ago, "to make the best that has been thought and known in the world current everywhere."[10] Others point to the importance of education as a preparation for democratic citizenship, preparing people to play an active part in society and to make a difference in the world. Finally, there is a large group that sees the main purpose of education as ensuring that young people are able to find fulfilling and rewarding employment, perhaps best exemplified by those who want students to leave high school career and college ready (as opposed to, say, life ready).

Much of the time, these different aims do not conflict overmuch and, indeed, can support each other, but there are also undoubtedly tradeoffs that need to be made. For example, employers often complain about skills shortages and blame schools for not preparing students adequately for work, but what employers want is often rather short term. An education system that prepares young people for what employers want right now might not do a very good job of helping young people adapt successfully in a changing world, both inside and outside work. Even if we think the most important role of education is preparing students for the world of work, are we talking about what employers say they want or what they actually need, and is it what employees need now or in fifty years' time? After all, most of today's kindergarten students will still be working in the final quarter of the twenty-first century.

One indication that many young Americans are not well prepared for what lies ahead comes from the OECD's PISA program. As noted above, scores on PISA are reported on a scale where 500 is average, and one year's learning is somewhere between thirty and forty points. The OECD has also established a number of key benchmarks to make the results of the surveys easier to interpret, and one of the most important is what they call level 2, which the OECD describes as "the baseline level of proficiency that is required to participate fully in modern society."[11] In the most recent PISA survey, conducted in 2015, the threshold for level 2 was 407 in reading, 420 in math, and 410 in science, so a student who just reached level 2 would be slightly more than two years behind the average of all the countries participating in PISA.

In 2015, approximately 20 percent of US students failed to reach level 2 in reading and science, and about 30 percent failed to reach it in math. Perhaps more important, 15 percent of American fifteen-year-olds failed to reach this level of achievement in *any* of the three subjects. This suggests that each year well over half a million young Americans leave school without the basic level of literacy and math that they need to participate effectively in modern society.

Because it has to do so many things, any education system will always be a messy compromise, but the rest of this chapter focuses specifically on the changing demands of the world of work, which does seem to merit special attention. This is not because preparing young people for work is more important than the other aims of education but because this is where things are changing most rapidly. Predicting what schools will be teaching in the future is a fool's game, but it does seem highly likely that high school English language arts teachers will still be teaching Shakespeare in fifty years' time. The great things that have been thought and said don't change that quickly. The demands of the workplace do.

## The Changing Nature of Work

In 1900, approximately 10 million Americans worked on the land, which was over 40 percent of the working population at the time.[12] Today, US agriculture employs fewer than 3 million people—only 2 percent of the workforce.[13] Tens of thousands of Americans used to work as carriage and harness makers, cobblers, telegraph operators, and boilermakers, but the number of people doing these jobs today is close to zero. Even when the same work is being done today as it was years ago, the number of people doing the job is often far less. For example, in 1970, approximately 400,000 Americans worked as telephone operators. Today, the figure is around 120,000.[14]

The destruction and creation of jobs has always been with us but is rarely noticed, because when the Bureau of Labor Statistics publishes its monthly jobs report, the figure that gets attention is the *net* number of jobs created: the number of jobs created minus the number of jobs destroyed. On average, the American economy adds over 200,000 jobs every month, but the figures vary a great deal from month to month. In a good month, such as November 2014, as many as 331,000 jobs were added in the US economy, while for May 2015, the figure was only 24,000. But what these figures do not reveal is what is really happening to jobs. For example, in the first quarter of 2016, private sector employment grew by 194,000 jobs overall, but this was the result of 6.8 million private sector jobs being destroyed and 7 million new private sector jobs being created. Even at the depth of the recession, in the first quarter of 2009, although about 8.6 million private sector jobs were lost, about 6 million new private sector jobs were created.

The fact that jobs are constantly being destroyed is a big concern to those who believe that there are only a certain number of jobs in the economy. If jobs disappear, then that means that the people who were doing those jobs will be unemployed. Economists call the idea that there are only a certain number of jobs to go around "the lump of labor fallacy."[15] In fact, the destruction of jobs by automation can actually increase the total number of jobs.

Most people assume that the widespread adoption of ATMs (automated teller machines) by banks in the 1970s resulted in a reduction in the number of tellers employed by banks. In fact, as James Bessen shows in *Learning by Doing*, installing ATMs reduced the cost of running a bank branch and freed tellers to focus on more profitable work. The number of tellers employed by US banks increased from 510,000 in 1980 to 599,000 in 2010.[16]

The general point here is that when automation makes it less expensive to carry out a task, the price of goods and services drops, which in effect makes people richer, which then increases the demand for other goods and services. This is why, even with 7 million fewer agricultural jobs than there were a century ago and with *six times* as many people looking for work in the United States today, most people who want a job can get one. In fact, there have never been so many people employed in the United States as there are now.[17] However, major problems do arise if the changes in the kinds of work that are available happen over a short time period or if the new jobs being created require very different skills from the jobs being lost.

The decline of employment in agriculture occurred fairly steadily over the last hundred years, but in recent years, some sectors of the economy have experienced extraordinarily rapid declines in employment; none more so than manufacturing. According to the Bureau of Labor Statistics, in the year 2000, over 17 million Americans were employed in manufacturing. Ten years later, the figure was fewer than 12 million.[18] In ten years, the United States lost 5 million manufacturing jobs—or to put it another way, in the first decade of the twenty-first century, the United States lost 2,700 manufacturing jobs *every day*.

Evidence of the decline in American manufacturing is everywhere—in the employment numbers produced every month by the Bureau of Labor Statistics, in the shuttered factories and falling population of the so-called rust belt cities of the northeastern United States—everywhere, in fact, except in the actual numbers.

It is common to hear people say "we don't make stuff in America anymore," but that is just not true. Manufacturing output suffered setbacks in the last two recessions, falling by around 10 percent in 2001 and by 25 percent in 2008–2009, but apart from those two declines, the value of goods produced by American manufacturers has grown pretty steadily for as long as people have been measuring it. And in 2016, US manufacturing output surpassed the previous maximum reached in 2008.[19] We now make more stuff than we have ever made in America. We just don't use so many people to do it. And that's a good thing.

As economists are fond of pointing out, increases in the standard of living are driven mainly by increases in productivity, so the fact that we farm more land and make more stuff with fewer people makes us all richer. The use of more sophisticated machines transformed agriculture but reduced employment substantially. With John Deere's CP690 cotton picker, one person can now pick ten acres of cotton in an hour.[20] Similarly, in manufacturing, the work that used to be done by a number of skilled machine operators can now be done to a far higher standard by one person who manages a number of computer numerical control (CNC) machines. A dozen medium-skill jobs are replaced by one high-skill job. Across all US manufacturing between 2002 and 2015, manufacturing output per hour of labor went up by 47 percent,[21] and when we go back to the heyday of American manufacturing, the comparison is even more stark. Per hour, the average American worker employed in manufacturing today is more than *six times* as productive as a worker in 1950. In fact, all over the world in manufacturing there has been a shift from large numbers of low- and medium-skill jobs to smaller numbers of high-skill jobs for the same output.[22]

And that's the real issue. It's not that there aren't jobs. It's that many of the new jobs being created demand a higher level of skill than the jobs that are lost. Almost half of the manufacturing jobs that did not require a high school diploma in 2000 were gone by 2015, while the number of manufacturing jobs that require at least a master's degree rose by 32 percent. And, the jobs look very different. Manufacturing used to involve getting your hands dirty, but today, only two in every five jobs in manufacturing directly involve making things.[23] Today, manufacturing involves a lot of staring at computer screens, as do many other jobs.

For example, in 1984, only 25 percent of American workers used a computer in their job. Just seven years later, it was 50 percent.[24] And it is worth noting that in 1984, someone who worked with a computer was regarded as a specialist and would probably have been paid a premium wage. Now almost everyone entering the world of work needs to work with computers. We are, in the words of Nobel Prize–winning economist Jan Tinbergen, engaged in "a race between education and technology."[25]

In the twentieth century, there is no doubt that, in the United States at least, education was winning the race. In the first half of the twentieth century, most countries in Europe educated children beyond the age of fourteen only if they were likely to go on to some form of higher education. In the United States, between about 1910 and 1940, states and school districts invested massively in high school education for all, rather than just the elite. While some saw this as a grand attempt to produce a more educated populace, others saw it as a way of keeping young people out of a depressed labor market, but whatever the reasons, the effects were dramatic. In 1910, only 10 percent of American eighteen-year-olds completed high school. By 1940, the figure was 50 percent—a level that most European countries did not achieve until the final quarter of the twentieth century.[26]

According to Claudia Goldin and Lawrence Katz, two professors of economics at Harvard University, this investment was essential to America's manufacturing success in the second half of the twentieth century. In recent years, however, while educational achievement has been rising, it has not been rising at the pace needed to keep up with the demands of new technology, and this is probably why employers are unhappy and talk about a skills shortage.

At first sight, the best available data suggest that the employers have a point. Long-term trends in the National Assessment of Educational Progress (NAEP), often described as the nation's report card, show that, with a few ups and downs, the achievement of American seventeen-year-olds in reading and math has not changed much over the last fifty years. That might sound like bad news, but more students stay enrolled in high school than was the case in 1970. Because the students who drop out tend to be those with lower academic achievement, maintaining average NAEP scores for seventeen-year-olds while fewer students are dropping out actually means an increase in educational achievement—these lower achieving students are now being tested, whereas in earlier surveys, they were not because they weren't in school. This is also borne out by the fact that the scores for nine-year-olds and thirteen-year-olds in both reading and math have risen steadily since NAEP began in 1971.[27]

Perhaps even more surprisingly, young people today are more intelligent than their parents and grandparents. Many people find this hard to believe, but as Bernard Baruch said many years ago, "Every man has the right to an opinion but no man has a right to be wrong in his facts."[28] Rising American intelligence is a fact. The people who produce IQ tests have to re-benchmark them every ten years or so because the average American IQ has gone up by about three points a decade for at least the last eighty years.[29]

So, if achievement is not falling, and may even be rising, and young people are smarter than they used to be, why are employers so unhappy? Because the "price of admission" into the job market keeps on going up. Fifty years ago, the average working person didn't need to read or write during the course of a working day. Today, there are very few jobs that do not require these skills. It is as if we have been walking up a down escalator. In the past, we were walking fast enough to make progress, but the escalator keeps on speeding up. And if we cannot raise the achievement of American school leavers, then what is happening in Spain and Greece right now—where the unemployment rate for sixteen- to twenty-four-year-olds is around 50 percent—could happen here.

It is tempting to conclude that it is only low-skill workers that will be affected by the changes in the world of work, but the two main processes at work—offshoring and automation—affect everyone.

In the first few waves of offshoring—sending work to countries with lower labor costs—only low-skill jobs, such as food packaging and data entry, were exported. But in recent years, the increasing availability of technology has allowed high-skill jobs to be offshored as well. For example, if you are involved in an automobile accident in Manhattan at 3 a.m., it is likely that your x-rays will be viewed by a radiographer in Bangalore, India.[30] And it has been seventeen years since the first transatlantic telesurgery procedure, in which two surgeons in Manhattan, using robot scalpels, removed the gall bladder of a sixty-eight-year-old woman in Strasbourg, France, over 3,800 miles away.[31]

In a similar way, the first waves of automation replaced mostly low-skill jobs, but in recent years, as the work of David Autor and his colleagues at the Massachusetts Institute of Technology has shown, the skill level is irrelevant. What matters for automation is how routine the job is.[32]

A dramatic example of this is the use of artificial neural nets—computer programs that can learn from their previous experiences—in predicting the results of biopsies in men at risk of prostate cancer. Given standard diagnostic information about a patient, expert urologists correctly predict the result of a biopsy for prostate cancer 34 percent of the time. Twenty years ago, the computer program got it right 77 percent of the time.[33] Interpreting diagnostic information requires a high level of skill, but the task is routine, and that is why the performance of machines is so much better than that of humans. We will, of course, need doctors in the future, but perhaps not so many as we do now. As the accuracy of computer diagnosis systems improve, it seems likely that more and more of the routine tasks involved in medical diagnosis will be automated. But it also seems likely that people will want to discuss their treatment options with a human.

In fact, this illustrates the really important trend in the development of work in the future. Very few jobs will be completely replaced by machines. Only one of the 270 job categories used in the 1950 US Census has been eliminated—elevator operator.[34]

The future will belong to those who can use technology to become more productive. In many US cities, trash is collected by a single person operating a truck with arms that can pick up trash cans and empty their contents into the truck. The job used to be done by a three- or four-person team, but now it's one person with a higher skill level and a machine. The best chess player in the world isn't a computer, but it isn't a human either. The best chess player in the world is a team of humans using a number of computers to try out different moves. The game is called *freestyle chess*.[35]

Whether the trends we have seen to date will continue is impossible to say, although, as Erik Brynjolfsson and Andrew McAfee argue in *The Second Machine Age*, it seems likely that existing trends will not only continue but accelerate. In 2012, many people were saying that self-driving cars were at least twenty-five years away, but just six years later, they are here. And while they are not perfect, they are probably already safer than human drivers. The major impediment to their wider use seems to be concern about who gets prosecuted when things go wrong rather than any inherent problem in the technology.

Of course, not all jobs will be offshored or automated. According to Princeton economist Alan Blinder, around 25 to 30 percent of the jobs being done in the US economy right now could, in principle, be moved offshore within the next thirty years.[36] However, it is worth noting that for the last ten years or so, many jobs that had been offshored are being returned to the United States for a variety of reasons, including concerns about quality and the desire to cut delivery times. But, apart from government incentives, the main reason given by companies for bringing jobs back is the skill level of workers.[37] In most cases, the jobs coming back are not the same as the jobs that left. They require higher levels of skill.

While much of the talk in the United States is about stopping jobs from being sent overseas, far more jobs are likely to be destroyed through automation, with careful analyses suggesting that around half of all the work currently being done in the US economy could be automated over the next twenty to thirty years with *existing* technology.[38]

What this means for what our children should be learning is explored further in chapter 10, but there seems to be little doubt that what Joseph Schumpeter called "creative destruction"[39] will continue to be a major feature of the world of work, particularly in the United States. Millions of jobs will be lost to offshoring and automation each month, but millions will also be created.

And it is important to realize that some of these will not require much in the way of education. The Bureau of Labor Statistics projects that between 2012 and 2022, the US economy will create just over 4 million new jobs for those with college degrees, but it will also create 4 million jobs that do not even require a high school diploma, another 4 million that require just a high school diploma, and another 3 million that require some education beyond high school but not a college degree. As far as we can tell, there will be jobs for people whatever their level of education in the United States. It is therefore probably not accurate to say to young people that they need to get a good education to get a job. But it does seem that education will be important to getting a *good* job.

We have already seen this in the changes that have occurred in the last twenty years. As noted earlier, the greatest job destruction has not been for the lowest-skilled workers. It has been for those doing routine jobs, whatever the skill level. And because computers are simpler and less expensive than robots, things like routine office work—what economists call *routine cognitive* jobs—have been easier to automate than manual work. We think playing chess is an amazing human achievement, but for a few dollars, you can now buy a smartphone app that will beat most humans on the planet. What we haven't been able to do yet is use robots to stock shelves in Walmart in a cost-effective way, which is why right now, the job is done by humans. But the message of the last 250 years has been that as soon as a job can be done cost-effectively by a machine, it will be.

No country is immune from this. In many parts of China, for example, factory workers cost less than $2 per hour, while robot labor, including the initial outlay for the purchase of the robot, costs around $4 per hour. This is why at the moment, in most Chinese factories, complex electronic devices are assembled by hand. But the costs of labor are going up, and costs of robots are coming down. As a result, Foxconn, which currently employs around 1 million people in mainland China making iPhones and other electronic devices, plans to automate 70 percent of its workforce by 2018.[40]

A similar trend can be seen in the United States, although starting from a higher baseline. As more states increase their minimum wage, where the extra costs cannot be passed on to customers, employers are likely to make greater and greater use of technology. Hadrian X, developed by Fastbrick Robotics in Australia, is a robot that can lay one thousand concrete blocks an hour, which is more than ten times as fast as a human.[41] Completely automated milking parlors allow cows to be milked when they please and appear to be less stressful for the cows.[42] Ed Rensi, former CEO of McDonald's, points out that from the point of view of an employer, for many of the jobs in a fast-food restaurant, a $35,000 robotic arm is less expensive in the long run than a worker earning $15 per hour.[43] And, of course, the price of the robot arm will come down steadily over the coming years.

For this reason, promises made by politicians to revitalize manufacturing jobs by bringing them back to the United States ring hollow. Even if manufacturing is brought back to the United States, it isn't going to have a major impact on the number of people employed in manufacturing. Rather, the question is only whether things are made by Chinese or American robots. If iPhones are made by American robots, then that will create a few more jobs making and servicing the robots, but the total number of people so employed will be negligible in terms of the total US economy. And while people seem to be aware of these trends in a general sense, they do not think they will be affected personally. For example, two-thirds of Americans believe that within fifty years robots and computers will do much of the work currently being done by humans. And yet 80 percent of American workers believe that their *own* job will continue to exist for at least that long.[44]

In many ways, what is happening now is very similar to what has happened over and over again in the US economy. Jobs are destroyed, new jobs are created, and most people are more productive in their new jobs than they were in their old jobs, so their wages go up and their standard of living increases. However, there is one way that what is happening now is different from previous waves of creative destruction, and it is changing the relationship between education and earnings.

As noted above, many middle-skill jobs have been offshored or automated. Some of the workers doing those jobs were able to increase their skills to gain higher-skill jobs. For example, some machinists became programmers of CNC machines and thus enjoyed increases in their standard of living. However, other workers were not able or willing to increase their skills. As a result, they are now competing with lower-skilled workers for lower-skilled and lower-paid jobs. Economists call this hollowing out of middle-skill jobs *job polarization*, but the reality is more immediately conveyed by Martin Goos and Alan Manning's phrase *lousy and lovely jobs*.[45]

This is the key idea that economist Tyler Cowen wrote about in *Average Is Over*.[46] In previous waves of technological innovation, technology made most people more productive so earnings tended to increase across the board. What we have seen in the United States over the last forty or so years is that those who have the skills to harness the power of technology become richer and the earnings of others stagnate or decline. The same argument is made by Thomas Piketty in his book *Capital in the Twenty-First Century*."[47] The real-terms income of the lowest-earning 50 percent of Americans of working age has been basically flat for over thirty years.[48]

Moreover, these trends are likely to continue and even accelerate. Those who are able to work with what Erik Brynjolfsson and Andrew McAfee call *brilliant machines* will garner a disproportionate share of the new wealth. Those who own the factories where robots make other robots will become wealthier, as will their personal chefs and fitness coaches. But those without high levels of skill will find themselves competing for more generic jobs, and the competition will put downward pressure on wages. There will be jobs, but for the less skilled, the jobs won't be well paid.

Now, of course, it could be that in the future, we distribute the new wealth more broadly, but, in the United States at least, that does not seem likely. Higher levels of educational achievement will be the key to empowering young people to take greater control of their lives.

## Conclusion

People have been calling for higher educational achievement for many years. In 1957, when the Soviet Union launched the Sputnik satellite, there was widespread concern that the United States was falling behind in science and technology.[49] In 1983, the National Commission on Excellence in Education said, in its report *A Nation at Risk*, that "If an unfriendly foreign power had attempted to impose on America the mediocre educational performance that exists today, we might well have viewed it as an act of war."[50]

In 1994, Bill Clinton, in his first presidential term, signed into law The Goals 2000: Educate America Act, which, among other things, aimed, by the end of the decade, to have American students first in the world in mathematics and science achievement, with all citizens with a level of achievement to be globally competitive in work and prepared for the rights and responsibilities of citizenship. This, in turn, was superseded in 2002 by the No Child Left Behind Act, which was intended "to ensure that all children have a fair, equal, and significant opportunity to obtain a high-quality education and reach, at a minimum, proficiency on challenging state academic achievement standards and state academic assessments."[51] The specific target for this was that by 2014, all students would reach proficiency on their state's standards. Needless to say, none of these targets were achieved.

Some people have argued that things really aren't that bad. Since 1974, the Phi Delta Kappa organization has been conducting annual surveys of public attitudes toward public education by asking adults to give American schools a grade of A, B, C, D, or Fail. Of the 1,221 people who participated in the 2016 survey, only 24 percent gave American schools an A or a B. However, when people were asked about the schools in their own neighborhoods, 48 percent gave their local schools an A or a B. And for parents who had a child in public school, the figure was 70 percent.[52] In other words, the vast majority of American parents think their child goes to a good or excellent school, but they believe that they must be lucky, because most American schools are, at best, average.

Indeed, some have suggested that talk about inadequacies in American education amount to a manufactured crisis.[53] As we shall see in chapter 6, even making reasonable comparisons between the performance of schools in the United States and that of schools in other countries is difficult, let alone whether we can learn anything from such comparisons, but the main argument here is not whether the performance of our students is good enough to compete with those in other countries. It is that higher levels of achievement will be needed in the future just to live empowered, productive, fulfilled lives.

The next six chapters, which form section 2 of the book, look at the main solutions that are currently being proposed and implemented as ways of improving education. The first three look at ways of improving the quality of the American teaching force by getting smarter people into teaching, by firing bad teachers, and by paying good teachers more. The next three chapters look at reducing class size, emulating the policies of our industrial competitors, and expanding school choice. While each of these ideas has a role to play in improving American education, none, either individually or collectively, will produce enough change to give our children what they need.

That's why the third and final section of the book looks at what we should be doing to improve American education. It provides a general framework for thinking about the costs, benefits, and feasibility of different possible reforms and, in particular, looks in detail at two things—reemphasizing the role of knowledge in the curriculum and improving the teachers we already have—that show the greatest promise to improve our schools and help our children flourish.

---

1   Graduates actually live about nine years longer than nongraduates, but of course, this could be because those with health issues drop out of education. We need studies in which some people were forced to get more education whether they wanted it or not, and changes in the school leaving ages in the United States provide a natural experiment because students born a day later than other students are forced to get one more year's schooling. Between 1915 and 1939, at least thirty US states increased their school leaving ages and Adriana Lleras-Muney (2005) investigated the impact on life expectancy. This is where the figure of 1.7 years comes from.

2   Jagger, Matthews, Melzer, Matthews, Brayne, and Medical Research Council Cognitive Functioning Aging Study (2007).

3   Organisation for Economic Co-operation and Development (2010).

4   For a summary of the noneconomic benefits of education, see Centre for Research on the Wider Benefits of Learning (2006).

5   Oreopoulos and Salvanes (2011).

6   United States Bureau of Labor Statistics (2016b).

7   United States Bureau of Labor Statistics (2015).

8   Levin, Belfield, Muennig, and Rouse (2007).

9   Hanushek and Woessman (2015).

10  Arnold (1869, p. 70).

11  Organisation for Economic Co-operation and Development (2016a, p. 38).

12  Lebergott (1957).

13  Cox and Alm (2008).

14  Ibid.

15  The phrase *lump of labor* seems to have been used first by Schloss (1891).

16  Bessen (2015, 2016).

17  The website of the Bureau of Labor Statistics (www.bls.gov) indicates that at the end of 2016, non-farm employment stood at 145 million, which is well above the previous peak of 138 million reached just before the last recession.

18  United States Bureau of Labor Statistics (2016a).

19  Federal Reserve Bank of St. Louis (2016).

20  John Deere (2014).

21  Levinson (2017).

22  Timmer, Azeez, Los, Stehrer, and de Vries (2014).

23  Levinson (2016).

24  Autor, Katz, and Krueger (1998).

25  Jan Tinbergen was awarded the Nobel Memorial Prize in Economic Sciences in 1969, and his memorable phrase was used as the title of a book on education and employment by Goldin and Katz (2008, p. 30).

26  Goldin and Katz (2008).

27  National Assessment of Educational Progress (2013).

28  Quoted in the *Toledo Blade* (1946).

29  Flynn (2007).

30  Burute and Jankharia (2009).

31  Heyman (2001). The patient left the hospital forty-eight hours after the surgery with no complications.

32  Autor, Levy, and Murnane (2003).

33  The estimate of the accuracy of expert urologists comes from Catalona, Smith, Ratliff, and Basler (1993). The investigation of the performance of the neural net can be found in Snow, Smith, and Catalona (1994).

34  Bessen (2016).

35  There is an extensive discussion of freestyle chess in Tyler Cowen's book *Average Is Over* (2013).

36  Blinder (2009).

37  Reshoring Initiative (2016).

38  Frey and Osborne (2013).

39  Schumpeter (1942).

40  Kan (2015).

41  FastBrick Robotics (2017).

42  Amelinckx (2016).

43  Limitone (2016).

44  A. Smith (2016).

45  Goos and Manning (2007).

46  Cowen (2013).

47  Piketty (2014).

48  Piketty, Saez, and Zucman (2016, p. 42).

49  It is often claimed that the launch of the Sputnik 1 satellite shocked American scientists, but in fact, it was expected, and welcome. In the mid-1950s, the United States had a well-developed rocket program let by German scientist Werner von Braun, who was pushing to launch a rocket into Earth's orbit but was told repeatedly not to do so, for fear that the Soviet Union would regard an orbiting satellite as an invasion of air space. The Eisenhower administration had been advocating an "open skies" policy in which any country could fly satellites over any other country but wanted the Soviet Union to be the first to do so, so that they could not object when the United States followed suit (Begley, 2007).

50  National Commission on Excellence in Education (1983, p. 5).

51  "No Child Left Behind Act" (2002, p. 1440).

52  The raw data for the 2016 poll can be found at Langer Research Associates (2016).

53  Berliner and Biddle (1995).

# SECTION 2

CHAPTER 2

# Getting Smarter
# People Into Teaching

For most of the last century, it was assumed that teachers were basically interchangeable. Any teacher who went through an approved course of training would be as good as any other teacher, or at least the differences would be so small as to be unimportant. However, toward the end of the last century, there was steadily accumulating evidence that some teachers were more effective than others. Moreover, the differences in effectiveness were significant, with students in some classrooms making twice as much progress as in other classrooms. Some researchers claimed that these differences were caused largely by the way that teachers were assigned—it wasn't that the teachers were better, but rather that they were assigned to teach higher-achieving students. However, as researchers looked at how much progress students made in different classrooms rather than just the final test scores, it became clear that it was quite common to find that some teachers were at least twice as effective as others—students in some classrooms were learning twice as much in the same time as students in other classrooms.

Perhaps not surprisingly, attention focused on teacher qualifications. By hiring only the best-qualified teachers, districts assumed they could produce a rapid improvement in student learning. Unfortunately, it turns out that most teacher qualifications tell us nothing about how good a teacher is likely to be. Teachers' scores on college entrance tests like the SAT, the courses they have taken in college, and even their grades on those courses tell us almost nothing about how much their students will learn.

Because performance on traditional teacher preparation programs bore little relation to teacher quality, a number of states explored alternative routes into teaching. Some of these were designed to reduce the time teachers would need to spend on teacher preparation programs, thus reducing the cost to prospective teachers. Others, like Teach for America, hoped to appeal to those who might not consider school teaching for their whole career but would be willing to spend a number of years teaching in hard-to-staff schools.

While teachers produced by some of these alternative programs are slightly more effective than teachers following traditional teacher preparation programs, the differences are small, and most of these programs are on such a small scale that their impact on student achievement nationwide, even if they are successful, will be too small to be noticeable.

A number of states require teachers to pass tests that assess the particular knowledge teachers will need in teaching, but even the best of these tell us little about how good teachers are going to be once they get into the classroom. Attractive though the idea may be, improving education by getting smarter people into teaching will have little or no effect on how much our children learn.

For as long as governments have been involved in education, whether at the local, state, or federal level, they have tried to regulate who may and who may not be teachers. The logic seems sound. Just as we want assurances that those who fly planes and perform surgical procedures can be trusted, we want to ensure that those who are teaching our children know what they are doing.

In most professions—and, over recent years, in a large number of other occupations[1]—the way we do this is to require people to get a certificate before they can work. Of course, the standards for these licenses could be pitched at an absolute minimum level, certifying nothing more than the person holding the license will do no harm, but in most cases, the standards for the occupational license are pitched a lot higher than this. The result is that people assume that the person holding a license will actually be good at the job.

For example, in a nationwide poll conducted in 2000, 89 percent of Americans thought that ensuring a well-qualified teacher in every classroom was important to improving schools. The only thing ranked higher, at 90 percent, was ensuring that schools were safe and free from violence.[2] The idea is popular with politicians too. In a Senate discussion on higher education in 2002, Senator Edward Kennedy said, "We want a well-qualified teacher in every classroom."[3]

While such occupational licensing can be helpful, and is often essential in many jobs, there are two potential problems. The first is that we need to be careful how high we set the bar, because no system of qualifications gets it right in every case. Set the bar too low, and many people who really aren't good enough end up getting qualified. Set the bar too high, and many people who could do the job perfectly well are not allowed to do the job.

The second problem is that once we have a system of qualifications and certificates, there is a tendency to assume that all those who possess the right certificates are equally good and are therefore essentially interchangeable—what Daniel Weisberg and his colleagues called the *widget effect*.[4] If people really are interchangeable, then no damage is done, but if people with the same qualifications vary greatly in how good they are, then significant problems arise. In particular, policies such as class size reduction make sense if all teachers are equally good. But the same policies turn out to be disastrous if people with the same qualifications are very different in their capabilities (see chapter 5 on *reducing class size* for more on this).

One of the first people to study the question of whether some teachers are more effective than others—what is often called *teacher quality*—was Eric Hanushek, now a scholar at the Hoover Institution at Stanford University. In 1969, Hanushek collected data on 2,445 elementary school students in a school district in California. He looked in particular at the 1,061 cases where, for a particular child, there was a test score both at the beginning and at the end of the year (so that the progress made over a school year could be ascertained), and where the teacher who had taught the student could be identified. It turned out that the amount of progress students were making varied a lot from classroom to classroom. In some classrooms, students were making up to five months' more progress than in others.[5]

Of course, as Hanushek acknowledged in his paper, this was just one sample of students in one district in the United States. But in the forty-five years since this groundbreaking study, Hanushek's basic result—that some teachers are much more effective than others—has been confirmed over and over again.

For example, Daniel Aaronson looked at the effectiveness of ninth-grade teachers in Chicago Public Schools and, on the basis of the progress made by their students, classified teachers into three categories: more effective, average, and less effective. Students taught by more effective teachers made 40 percent more progress than those taught by average teachers, and students taught by less effective teachers made 30 percent less progress than average. In other words, the progress made by students in the most effective teachers' classrooms was twice as great as that made by those in the classrooms of the least effective teachers (140 percent versus 70 percent).[6]

The researchers were aware that such differences might be just the result of random variations from year to year in how effective teachers were, so they looked at whether teachers who were effective in a particular year were more effective the following year. When they divided teachers into four equally sized categories—most effective, above average, below average, least effective—they found that well over half the teachers who were rated as least effective in one year were likely to receive the same rating the following year. However, for the other categories, things were less clear-cut. Across all the categories, only 37 percent of the teachers got the same rating two years running. Now, of course, this could just be the result of teachers making more effort in one year than another, but the most likely explanation is that how much progress students make depends to a significant extent on things that are outside the teacher's control.

So, one year's data might not tell you much because next year's data might be very different. However, when we look at data over a longer period, we find that some teachers are consistently more effective than others. Jonah Rockoff looked at reading and math scores over a twelve-year period in elementary schools in two neighboring districts in New Jersey.[7] Students taught by good teachers (i.e., in the top one-third of effectiveness) made around 50 percent more progress in math and 40 percent more progress in reading when compared with average teachers.

Of course, these differences might not be due to the teachers themselves. It could be that some teachers get to work in better conditions than others, or they get their pick of the best students. To check this out, Thomas Kane, an economics professor at Harvard University, and his colleagues recently conducted an experiment in six urban school districts in which teachers who were found to be effective in one school were moved, the following year, to a different school. Even though they were teaching in a different school, teaching students from different socioeconomic groups, and often teaching a different grade, the teachers who were more effective in the first school were more effective in the second.[8]

While any one of these studies might be faulted for not taking into account particular details, the balance of the research evidence on this question is now clear. Which teachers you have teaching you makes a big difference in how much progress you make in school. As noted above, if we group teachers into three groups—more effective, average, and less effective—then you will learn twice as much if you are taught by a more effective teacher compared with the progress you would have made with a less effective teacher. However, at the extremes, the differences are even greater. For example, if we took a group of fifty teachers across a district teaching fifth-grade math, students taught by the most effective teacher in that group would learn math at four times the rate of those taught by the least effective teacher. What students would take one year to learn in an average teacher's classroom would take six months in the classroom of the most effective teacher in the group of fifty and two years in the classroom of the least effective teacher.

Moreover, the teachers who are most effective overall seem to be much more effective for students at the lower end of the achievement range. All students benefit from having a good teacher, but disadvantaged students benefit more than others. The result of this is that what people sometimes call *achievement gaps*—differences in achievement between more and less affluent students—are much smaller, and often do not arise at all, in the classrooms of the most effective teachers.[9] This is why the issue of teacher quality is so firmly on the education agenda in the United States. As well as improving the achievement of all students, higher teacher quality seems to result in more equitable outcomes for all students.

At this stage in the argument, one might assume that if we know that teachers make such a difference, it would be easy to identify exactly how effective teachers are, but this turns out to be far from straightforward. To understand why, an analogy with baseball might be helpful.

We know that a batter averaging .300 at the All-Star break is, if he stays healthy, almost certainly going to end the season with a higher batting average than one who is averaging .250. He is, for that season at least, the better batter. On a given day, the .250 player might go five for five, while the .300 batter is hitless, but over a period of time, the chance variations average out. In the same way, a teacher might appear to be good one year and much less effective the next. Over the long term, we know that some teachers are more effective than others, but we can only establish this with hindsight.

In the remainder of this chapter, we will look at whether we can improve student achievement by improving teacher selection procedures. In the two subsequent chapters, we will look at ways of improving teacher quality by firing bad teachers and paying good teachers more.

## Teacher Selection

In many, perhaps most, lines of work, employers look at the biographical data of potential employees to help them make decisions about who to hire. What most people find surprising is these biographical data are not very good at predicting how well someone will do a job. Thomas Bliesener analyzed a large number of studies that explored the relationship between biographical data and actual performance on the job in a range of different occupations. Examples of biographical data include high school or college grade-point average, the number of times a student made the honor roll, length of service in the most recent job, recent training received, and so on. He found that by using biographical data it was possible to improve personnel selection but not by much. For example, if you had two candidates for a single post, then flipping a coin would get you the better employee (i.e., the person who, two years later, turned out to be the better employee) half the time. Averaged over 116 different research studies, using biographical data would improve your odds of choosing the better employee from the 50 percent you would get from flipping a coin to 57 percent.[10] This is an improvement, but you would still end up choosing the less effective employee 43 percent of the time. Another way to look at this is that using biographical data would enable you to make a better choice just once in every fourteen hires.

Getting the right person for the job seems to be hard everywhere, but what about teaching? An article by Malcolm Gladwell in the *New Yorker* magazine in 2008 compared selecting teachers to picking quarterbacks for the National Football League (NFL). Professional football teams have found that how well a player plays at college predicts performance in the NFL pretty well at most positions but not at quarterback. Some people thought that this might be because the professional game was more complex than college football—perhaps defenses were harder to read, perhaps the playbooks were more difficult to learn. So now, players entering the draft are given the Wonderlic Cognitive Abilities test. However, as a number of studies have found, those with high scores on the Wonderlic do no better or worse, on average, than those with low scores.[11] Clearly, being an effective NFL player involves a lot more than just smarts, so some have suggested using the Wonderlic in combination with other biographical data. One popular rule of thumb is that college quarterbacks should only be considered if they have at least twenty-seven starts at college level, a completion percentage of at least 60 percent, and a score of at least 27 out of 50 on the Wonderlic. This sounds reasonable, until you realize this would have you passing on Brett Favre (Wonderlic score of 22), Terry Bradshaw (16), Dan Marino (15), Jim Kelly (15), and Donovan McNabb (14). As Yogi Berra once said, "Prediction is hard, especially about the future."[12]

Many of the standard qualifications that are used for selecting teachers do not appear any more effective than the Wonderlic test used in the NFL. Doug Harris and Tim Sass made use of a rich set of data on students in third through tenth grades in a medium-sized Florida public school district over a six-year period (from 1999–2000 to 2004–2005). As with the dataset used by Hanushek many years earlier, it was possible, for all students, to identify the teacher who had been teaching them each year. And, because they had details on teacher qualifications, they could examine the relationship between teacher qualification and student progress. What they found was rather surprising.

- If teachers had followed general theory of education courses, then for most students, it made no difference to the students' progress. The exception to this was for middle school English language arts, where students taught by teachers who had studied general theory of education courses at college actually made *less* progress than other students.

- If the teachers had followed teaching practice courses at college, it made no difference to math scores, but for reading, these courses lowered student achievement in the elementary grades but raised them in the middle school grades (and had no effect in high school).

- Where teachers had followed courses that focused specifically on the content they would be teaching (what is called in the educational jargon *pedagogical content knowledge*), then students made more progress in math in elementary and middle schools but not at high school and not at all in reading.

- Whether teachers had attended advanced university courses in the subjects they were teaching had no impact for elementary and middle school students. For high school students, their scores were higher in reading but *lower* in math if their teacher had attended advanced university courses.

- Perhaps more surprisingly, there seemed to be no relationship between a teacher's own aptitude test scores (such as the SAT or the ACT) and how much progress students made, except in high school math, where students made *less* progress in classes taught by teachers with higher aptitude test scores.[13]

Perhaps the best description of these results is that they are basically just noise.

This general picture—that there is no clear relationship between academic credentials and teacher effectiveness—has been confirmed many times.[14] All states require teachers to have credentials, but the evidence that people with credentials are more effective is rather hard to find.

Some people are not surprised by this, because most teacher credentials are awarded on the basis of an academic program of study at a university, and what student teachers learn varies considerably from college to college. Moreover, some critics allege that trainee teachers are taught more about sociology than they are about how to manage an unruly class. Whether this is true or not, it might be more effective to ignore general credentials and instead focus specifically on the skills that are needed for teaching.

In California, for example, anyone wishing to teach in the state's public schools is required to pass tests to demonstrate competence for his or her chosen assignment. All teachers have to pass the California Basic Educational Skills Test (CBEST) and the California Subject Examinations for Teachers (CSET) in the subjects they are teaching. In addition, anyone teaching in the elementary grades is required to pass the Reading Instruction Competence Assessment (RICA).

These tests certainly look as if they are testing the kinds of things that teachers ought to know (what is sometimes called *face validity*). For example, the practice paper provided in the preparation materials produced by Pearson, the tests' publisher, includes the following question:[15]

> 1. A sixth grader who is advanced in most areas of reading has difficulty completing assigned reading selections. He appears motivated when he begins reading, but he has

difficulty keeping his attention on the task at hand. Which of the following would be his teacher's best initial strategy for addressing this difficulty?

A. adapting the student's reading assignments to reduce their complexity and level of cognitive challenge

B. telling the student that his grades will be based in part on his ability to improve his concentration when he works on reading assignments

C. breaking down the student's reading assignments into small steps and helping him learn to monitor his own attention and progress

D. managing the student's reading assignments so that he generally has only one to work on at any given time

This seems to be the kind of thing we would want anyone teaching in the elementary grades to know. However, when Richard Buddin and Gema Zamarro looked at the progress made by students in elementary schools in the Los Angeles Unified School District from 2000 to 2004, they found that there was no relationship between students' progress in reading and their teachers' scores on any of the credentialing tests, although, oddly, students taught by teachers with high scores on the RICA did make more progress in math.[16] Perhaps even more oddly, the higher a teacher's score on the CBEST or the CSET, the *less* progress students made in mathematics.

Now, none of this should be taken as evidence that subject knowledge doesn't matter. It is clearly impossible to be a good teacher of something you don't know anything about, and the older the students are, the more important subject knowledge seems to be. However, even in high school, what seems to matter most is knowing the subject really well at the level you are teaching it, not advanced knowledge of the subject. For example, a study of German math teachers found that their in-depth knowledge of the content they were teaching was strongly linked to the progress of their students but how much advanced math they had studied at university was not.[17]

At elementary school, content knowledge matters too, but the relationship seems to be less strong. Deborah Ball and her colleagues at the University of Michigan have developed sophisticated ways of assessing what they call *mathematical knowledge for teaching*. The tests they have developed assess teachers' knowledge of math but also assess teachers' understanding of the best way to teach math. One question from their sample materials is shown below.

To introduce the idea of grouping by tens and ones with young learners, which of the following materials or tools would be most appropriate? (Circle ONE answer.)

A. A number line

B. Plastic counting chips

C. Pennies and dimes

D.  Straws and rubber bands

E.  Any of these would be equally appropriate for introducing the idea of grouping by tens and ones [18]

Students taught by teachers who score higher on mathematical knowledge for teaching—unlike the RICA test mentioned earlier—do make more progress, but the difference is smaller than most people imagine. If you are taught by a teacher who scores in the top one-third on the test, then compared with an average teacher, you will make two weeks' more progress per year—an increase in the rate of learning of around 4 percent.[19]

To put this into context, recall that, compared with average teachers, the most effective math teachers (say the top one-third) are 50 percent more effective. If good teacher subject knowledge increases the rate of student learning by only 4 percent, then it is clear that subject knowledge in elementary math teaching is only a small part of what makes a teacher effective.

Of course, all things being equal, it would be better to have more knowledgeable teachers, but recruiting teachers with better subject knowledge and enhancing the subject knowledge of existing teachers won't have a big impact on student achievement nationally. Whatever it is that differentiates good teachers from those who are less effective, it isn't just subject knowledge, particularly in the elementary grades.

An alternative approach to improving the quality of those training to be teachers has been to offer different ways into teaching. The logic of these *alternative routes* as they are sometimes called is that there may be people who would be highly effective teachers but are deterred by the length and the cost of traditional teacher preparation programs. The largest of these alternative routes, and certainly the one that has been the subject of most research, is Teach for America.

## Teach for America

Teach for America (TFA) was founded in 1990 with the explicit aim of closing achievement gaps between students from rich and poor backgrounds by encouraging high-achieving college graduates to spend at least two years teaching in low-income and rural schools. Rather than a formal qualification, Teach for America corps members (as they are known) receive an intensive five-week crash course in instruction and classroom management, and then they assume a regular teacher's workload, supported by regular meetings with other corps members and supervisors.

Teach for America has been criticized on many grounds, although some of the criticisms do not stand up to scrutiny. High-need students, some people argue, need stability and consistency in the classroom, but since most American students get new teachers every year, it is hard to see how the number of years a teacher has taught in a building makes much difference. Others claim that removing the need for formal qualifications de-professionalizes teaching, although given the lack of evidence about the benefit of formal educational qualifications, this too seems a difficult argument to sustain.

A third claim, and one that has some merit, is that many of those who begin as TFA corps members fail to complete their two-year commitment. Typically, around seven out of every eight TFA corps members honor their commitment to stay for at least two years in their assigned school, and 60 percent stay in teaching for a third year. However, after that, the retention rate drops quickly, with only around one-third teaching for four years, and only around one-fourth still in teaching after five years.[20] For comparison, over 80 percent of traditionally trained teachers who began teaching in 2007 were still teaching in 2012.[21]

However, the most common argument leveled against Teach for America is that without formal training, TFA teachers will be less effective than traditionally trained teachers. This claim is almost certainly *not* true.

For the first few years of Teach for America's operation, there were a number of claims that TFA teachers were less effective than traditionally prepared teachers.[22] However, many of these claims were based on comparing TFA teachers with those who had prepared by following a traditional teacher preparation program. This was not really an apples-to-apples comparison, since many of those who were traditionally credentialed had spent five years in preparation (a four-year bachelor's degree plus a one-year teacher prep program) while most of the TFA teachers had just completed a four-year bachelor's degree program and the five-week TFA preparation program. Now, the district might not care how the teachers were trained—what matters is how good they are. From the teacher's point of view, however, the fact that TFA teachers are earning a salary in their first year of teaching while those in the teacher prep programs are generally not means that TFA is a much more attractive option even for those who would have considered a traditional teacher preparation program. After one year in the classroom, most studies find that TFA teachers are at least as good as traditionally prepared teachers, and many find that TFA teachers are substantially more effective than traditionally prepared teachers, especially in teaching math.[23] While most studies of TFA teachers have focused on reading and math scores, some studies have looked at other outcomes, and when they have, TFA teachers seem to have the edge here too. For example, one study found that students taught by TFA teachers were less likely to miss school due to unexcused absences or suspensions.[24]

However, while TFA teachers may be at least as effective as traditionally trained teachers, they are less effective than the average teacher, because most teachers have more than two years' experience, and as we shall see in chapter 4, teachers with three or more years' experience are, on average, much more effective than teachers in their first or second year. If TFA teachers are employed in jobs that otherwise would be filled by more experienced teachers, then they are likely to be, on average, *lowering* student achievement.

Moreover, TFA teachers do not seem to have any benefit beyond their own classrooms. One study in Miami-Dade's public schools found that concentrating TFA teachers in a smaller number of schools had the same effect as distributing them across all the county's schools. On average, you learn more if you are taught by a TFA teacher than if you are taught by an equally experienced but traditionally trained teacher, but the number of TFA teachers in your school doesn't matter.[25] And you will learn more if your teacher has at least three years' teaching experience no matter how she or he was trained.

The real problem with Teach for America is not that the teachers are worse than teachers from other preparation programs; they really aren't, and they are often better. The real problem is that there will never be many of them, because it is an elite program that would be very expensive—and perhaps impossible—to expand.

Teach for America often publishes statistics on the number of TFA alumni—those who were once TFA corps members but are no longer teaching. As of 2014, TFA had 37,200 alumni, and some of these people occupy important positions of influence within American education. Moreover, they are effective advocates for talking up teaching as a profession. By making teaching a job that is seen to be done by the smartest people, Teach for America may well raise the quality of those applying to traditional teacher preparation routes. But the number of TFA teachers in American schools is small, and attempts to expand the program have met with only limited success.

This may be, in part, due to the cost of Teach for America. Interviewed by Rachel Cohen for *American Prospect* magazine, Takirra Winfield, TFA's national spokesperson, said that the organization spends $16,400 to recruit each corps member, $7,000 on the initial training program, and $14,000 each year in supporting each corps member. That's over $25,000 per year for the first two years. Much of the cost of TFA comes from charitable organizations, but schools that employ TFA corps members are expected to contribute to these recruitment, training, and support costs. In 2013, Cleveland Metropolitan School District signed a contract with TFA that would require the district to pay $4,000 for each first-year recruit employed in the district and an additional $5,000 if the teacher stayed for a second year.[26] While other districts have negotiated lower costs with Teach for America, there remains a real question about whether the extra costs of TFA corps members are worth it in terms of any marginal, and short term, benefits that TFA teachers bring.[27]

In fact, even if the costs are ignored, it may be hard to scale up Teach for America. In 2010, Teach for America was awarded a $50 million grant from the United States Department of Education in order to help it scale up the program by 80 percent to provide a total of 13,500 first- and second-year corps members by September 2014.[28] In the event, there were only a total of 10,500 TFA corps members in American schools, and that figure includes those who had stayed beyond their two-year commitment. Even if TFA continues to expand at its current rate for the next forty years, TFA corps members would be fewer than 1 percent of the teachers employed in US public schools. And even if every single one of these TFA teachers were as good as the very best traditionally trained teachers, the impact on the American education system would be too small to detect.

None of this is intended as a criticism of the main idea behind Teach for America. The value of good teachers is so great that we should do everything we can to get the best teachers into our schools. TFA teachers are almost always more effective than uncertified and emergency teachers, and especially in hard-to-staff schools, they may well represent the best short-term option. But in terms of having an impact on the wider system, TFA teachers will have a negligible impact on student achievement. And the danger with any short-term fix is that districts come to depend on a series of short-term fixes, rather than attempting to recruit and invest in teachers who are in it for the long haul.

## Improving Teacher Selection

Because qualifications, certificates, biographical data, and other such objective measures aren't of much help for selecting the right teachers, a number of districts have explored the use of standardized interview procedures, but the improvement in teacher selection gained by such measures is usually small.

For example, one moderately large north Texas school district uses a commercial web-based questionnaire to screen potential applicants. The questionnaire responses are used to calculate a score between 0 and 100 for each candidate, and the publisher of the questionnaire recommends that only those with scores of at least 67 should be hired. During the 2006–2007 school year, the district hired a total of 527 teachers, but 47 percent had questionnaire scores below the recommended cutoff. This might be a cause for concern, except that those making the hiring decisions were probably right to ignore the questionnaire scores because they bore little relationship to the teachers' performance when they were observed subsequently.

We know this because at the time Texas had adopted a standardized Professional Development and Appraisal System (PDAS) for schools to use in evaluating teachers and determining their training needs. The PDAS included fifty-one criteria organized into eight domains as listed below.

1. Active successful student participation in the learning process
2. Learner-centered instruction
3. Evaluation and feedback on student progress
4. Management of student discipline, instructional strategies, time, and materials
5. Professional communication
6. Professional development
7. Compliance with policies, operating procedures, and requirements
8. Improvement of the academic performance of all students on the campus[29]

Teachers' scores on each of these eight domains are the result of teacher self-reports and observations by supervisors (each teacher has to be observed for at least forty-five minutes each year). All teachers in their first year of teaching had to be evaluated using the PDAS, while others were evaluated every three years, or using some other system adopted by the district.

As might be expected, teachers who scored high on one of these domains tended to score high on other domains too, but there was no relationship with the questionnaire scores. The screening questionnaire was simply of no use in helping the district identify who would be effective teachers and who would not.

What has been successful, in some districts, is combining information from a number of sources to make hiring decisions. For example, those involved in hiring teachers for the public schools in Spokane, Washington, use a three-stage procedure. First, human resource specialists rate applicants on experience, depth of skills, and quality of recommendations (the first two are rated on a 1 to 6 scale, the last is rated 1 to 9), resulting in a score between 3 and 21 for each applicant.

In the second stage, a principal specifies a threshold for applicants (e.g., a score of at least 17 out of 21) and is given a list of applicants reaching the threshold. The principal will then give each person on the list a rating from 1 to 6 on ten different attributes: education and certification, additional relevant training, experience, classroom management, flexibility, instructional skills, interpersonal skills, cultural competency, specific qualifications for the particular post, and recommendations, resulting in a score from 10 to 60. The highest scorers are then invited for the third stage: formal interview.

Dan Goldhaber and his colleagues compared the test scores of students taught by teachers selected to work in Spokane Public Schools with those taught by other teachers who applied but were unsuccessful and ended up teaching somewhere else in the state. This gives a good comparison because it compares those who wanted to teach in Spokane and were selected with those who wanted to teach in Spokane but were not selected.[30] They found that using the three-stage procedure in Spokane increased the chance of hiring the best teacher from the 50 percent that would be the result of selecting candidates by flipping a coin to 62 percent for reading specialists and 67 percent for math specialists. This would result in a better decision once in every seven or eight hires. This is about twice as good as the figure found by Bliesener for the average across all occupations, so it is clear that we can improve teacher hiring decisions. However, we can't get it right all the time. The simple truth is that it is very difficult—bordering on impossible, in fact—to determine who will and will not be good teachers until we can get them into classrooms. And even then, as we shall see, it is still pretty hard to distinguish between more effective and less effective teachers.

---

1   Carpenter II, Knepper, Erickson, and Ross (2012) note that while in 1950, only 5% of American workers required government licenses to do their job, today, the figure is around 30%.

2   Haselkorn and Harris (2001).

3   Kennedy (2002).

4   Weisberg, Sexton, Mulhern, and Keeling (2008).

5   Hanushek (1971).

6   Aaronson, Barrow, and Sander (2007); "more effective" and "less effective" teachers were those in the top and bottom one-third of effectiveness, respectively.

7   Rockoff (2004); the data included test scores from first through fifth grade and covered the period from the 1989–1990 school year through to 2000–2001.

8   Kane, McCaffrey, Miller, and Staiger (2013).

9   This comes from the work of Hamre and Pianta (2005) for students in the elementary grades and Slater, Davies, and Burgess (2008) for secondary grade students.

10   Bliesener (1996).

11   See for example, Mirabile (2005) or Lyons, Hoffman, and Michel (2009).

12   This quotation, or something like it, is variously attributed to Mark Twain, the Danish physicist Niels Bohr, and Samuel Goldwyn, as well as Yogi Berra. For a thorough analysis of the provenance of this quotation, see O'Toole (2016).

13   Harris and Sass (2007).

14    See, for example, Harris (2009).

15   Sample assessments can be found in the preparation materials for each of the tests at http://www.ctc exams.nesinc.com. The sample test for the Reading Instruction Competency Test is at http://www .ctcexams.nesinc.com/content/docs/RICA_Practice_Test.pdf. The correct response for this question is option C.

16   Buddin and Zamarro (2010).

17   Baumert et al. (2009).

18  Sample questions on mathematical knowledge for teaching can be found at http://www.umich.edu /~lmtweb/files/lmt_sample_items.pdf. The correct answer to this question is option C. Using a number line, plastic counters, or pennies and dimes are too abstract for young children just learning about place value. Moreover, the idea of bundles of straws extends naturally to hundreds (ten bundles of ten), thousands, and so on.

19  The true relationship between mathematical knowledge and a teacher's effectiveness is likely to be stronger than this, but because our measurements of teacher knowledge and their effectiveness have some margin of error, teachers who have reasonable knowledge may look as if they know little and, conversely, the measurement of their effectiveness might be unrepresentatively high. However, because these margins of error are real, and unavoidable, the argument here stands. We can't figure out who the good teachers are by looking at how much they know.

20  Donaldson and Johnson (2011).

21  Gray and Taie (2015).

22  See, for example, Darling-Hammond, Holtzman, Gatlin, and Vasquez Heilig (2005).

23  See Henry et al. (2014) for a reasonably recent review of the research of the effectiveness of Teach for America trained teachers.

24  Backes and Hansen (2015).

25  Hansen, Backes, Brady, and Xu (2014).

26  Cohen (2015).

27  There is, in addition, of course, the issue of the cost of traditional teacher preparation programs. However, since these are generally borne by the teacher, rather than the district, these costs are ignored here.

28  Clark, Isenberg, Liu, Makowsky, and Zukiewicz (2015).

29  Texas Education Agency (2005).

30  See discussion of "intention to treat" studies in the chapter "Expanding School Choice."

CHAPTER 3

# Firing Bad Teachers

The idea that we can improve the education our children receive by firing bad teachers is attractive—obvious even. We just figure out who the bad teachers are and stop employing them. However, it turns out that reliably identifying the teachers who contribute least to our children's education is much harder than it looks.

In my experience, most people find this hard to believe. Most people, whether they are education experts or concerned citizens, believe that it is possible to distinguish between effective and ineffective teaching by just observing classrooms. However, there are three problems with using classroom observations as a guide to student learning.

1.  Teacher performance is variable. Good teachers have bad days, and bad teachers have good days.

2.  Context matters. The same teacher will appear to be a better teacher when teaching a class of highly motivated, well-prepared students from affluent homes. It is very hard, if not impossible, to distinguish between motivated students being badly taught and less motivated students being well taught.

3.  Performance is not learning. Research on human memory shows that the more that students struggle in the lesson, the more they are likely to remember in the long-term. What looks like a very effective, clear lesson might result in no long-term learning, while one that looks confusing may be highly effective.

Because of this, many people have suggested just calculating how much progress students make. Test the students at the beginning of the school year and again at the end and see which teachers have students making the least progress. However, this necessarily involves making a lot of assumptions, which radically affect teachers' ratings. Using the same data, a teacher could be rated as outstanding with one set of assumptions and inadequate with another, equally valid, set of assumptions. Worse, in most states, the tests used are not taken at the beginning and the end of the year but in April, so part of the progress depends on the teacher who taught the students from April to June the previous year and how much students forget over the summer.

Even if we combine classroom observations, measures of student progress, and student surveys, the ratings of individual teachers are still not very accurate unless we use data over a number of years. In fact, to get data as reliable as the tests we use for college entrance, such as the ACT and the SAT, we would need to collect data on each teacher for eleven years.

Because of this unreliability, if we play safe and remove only those we are sure really are ineffective, we won't end up removing many teachers. And if we reduce the burden of proof so we remove those teachers who appear to be, on balance, the least effective, then we end up removing some good, and maybe even some excellent, teachers. Firing really bad teachers is a good idea, but the impact it will have on student achievement is minimal.

In the previous chapter, we saw that some teachers are a lot more effective than others, but we also saw that it is difficult, if not impossible, to predict, from their qualifications, which teachers will be most effective. One alternative, therefore, is to deselect the least effective teachers once we have evidence about their performance as teachers. For example, if we could remove the least effective 8 percent of teachers each year and replace them with average teachers, then the academic achievement of students in the United States would match that of students in Finland.[1]

Unfortunately, these projections depend on being able to identify the least effective teachers accurately, and it turns out that whether we use classroom observations, test scores, or student perception surveys, our ability to identify less and more effective teachers is limited. Of course, removing ineffective teachers could be very good for the morale of other teachers, so there may be good reasons to remove teachers where there is clear evidence of their ineffectiveness. However, these teachers are relatively limited in number. So limited, in fact, that removing the weakest teachers probably won't have any measurable impact on student achievement.

## Classroom Observations

Ask any teacher who teaches multiple sections in a class (e.g., a seventh-grade science teacher who teaches the same lesson to four different seventh-grade classes each day). Unless a special track has been created, these four classes will, on average, have similar levels of achievement, similar background knowledge, and so on. The classes are, at least in terms of science achievement, indistinguishable. And yet, as just about every teacher has experienced, the same lesson can go superbly with one group, disastrously with another, and OK with the other two. It's the same teacher teaching the same lesson to the four groups, but an observer's rating of the teacher would depend on which of the four lessons was observed. Moreover, two different observers watching the *same* lesson are likely to reach different conclusions about what they saw.

Heather Hill, a professor of education at Harvard University, and her colleagues investigated how many observations of a teacher you would need to conduct to get a reliable rating of that teacher. Just to be clear, this does not mean that we are, in fact, measuring the right things about the teacher and whether the students are learning anything. This is just to get a rating of the teacher that different observers would agree on and doesn't depend on whether the lesson, by chance, happens to go especially well or especially badly. Before we can do this, we have to decide on what we mean by *reliable* because an evaluation isn't just reliable or unreliable—reliability is measured on a continuum from completely unreliable to completely reliable.

One obvious benchmark is the College Board's SAT, used by many colleges to determine a student's readiness for higher education. After all, if we are thinking of firing a teacher based on observations of his or her teaching performance, it seems reasonable that this should be based on at least as reliable an evaluation as we would use to decide which students to admit to a university. In order to get a rating of a teacher as reliable as the SAT, it turns out that you would need to see each teacher teaching six different classes and have each lesson rated by five independent judges. In other words, you would need thirty independent ratings of a teacher's performance to get a reliable rating of how good he or she is, and even that doesn't tell us whether the teacher is actually any good or not. We need thirty ratings just to get a *reliable* rating.[2]

Teacher ratings based on classroom observations are also strongly influenced by the kind of students they are teaching. One study by Matthew Steinberg and Rachel Garrett looked at a representative sample of 834 teachers from six large US school districts over a period of two years.[3] The study focused on teachers assigned to teach students in fourth through ninth grades, so standardized test scores were available for students from the previous year and the current year. What Steinberg and Garrett found was that teachers were more likely to be rated as outstanding if they were assigned to teach the highest-achieving students. In English language arts, teachers were two and a half times more likely to be evaluated as an outstanding teacher if they were teaching the highest-achieving students versus the lowest-achieving students. And math teachers were *six* times more likely to be rated in the top category (out of four) if assigned to teach the highest-achieving students.[4] In many districts, teachers with seniority have considerable say in which classes they teach, and they often get to pick classes of gifted students. Because teachers are rarely assigned to classes at random, there is simply no way that observations can provide a fair basis for evaluating teachers and determining who are the most effective and who are the least effective.

Classroom observations are a poor guide to instructional quality for another reason: what looks like good teaching may not be effective in the longer term. If a teacher teaches students something today in a way that results in the students forgetting it all within a week or two, then most people would agree that the instruction is ineffective. As Paul Kirschner and his colleagues point out, "The aim of all instruction is to alter long-term memory. If nothing has changed in long-term memory, nothing has been learned."[5] So what we are trying to do in evaluating effective teaching is figure out how much of what is happening in the classroom right now will be remembered in, say, six weeks' time. And it turns out that our intuitions about how we learn things, and therefore what makes for good teaching, are, for the most part, wide of the mark. Most people seem to believe that if the teacher explains things in a clear way, and students are motivated and attentive, then the students will learn what they are being taught. However, it turns out that this is not how our memories work. Robert Bjork, a psychology professor at UCLA and one of the world's leading researchers of human memory, has shown that learning is more effective when students struggle to make sense of what they are being told—when there are, in his words, "desirable difficulties" in learning.[6] In particular, the more that students struggle in the learning task, the more likely they are to remember what they have learned in six weeks' time.

So, teaching that looks clear—where the teacher breaks down complex material into a sequence of easy-to-follow stages and where students are led through the material step-by-step—may actually be less effective than teaching that makes students struggle. As Daniel Willingham, a professor of psychology at the University of Virginia, points out, "Memory is the residue of thought."[7] Students remember what they have been thinking about, so instruction that does not make students think is less likely to be remembered in the long term. To understand what this means in practice, it is useful to look at one of the most commonly used systems for evaluating teachers in the United States: Charlotte Danielson's Framework for Teaching.

At the outset, I think it is important to acknowledge that the Danielson framework is an impressive achievement. Before the Danielson framework, we had no way of relating what teachers did to how much students learned. While systems for evaluating teaching did exist, students who were taught by teachers with high ratings didn't seem to learn any more than students taught by teachers with low ratings. With the Danielson framework, however, students taught by higher-rated teachers do make more progress than students taught by lower-rated teachers. A study in Chicago Public Schools found that students who were taught by teachers who were rated as *distinguished* (the highest rating on the four-point scale) made 30 percent more progress than students taught by teachers rated as *below basic* (the lowest rating on the scale).[8] This is an important difference. What average teachers accomplish in a year is accomplished in ten months by teachers with the highest rating on the four-point Danielson framework, and for the lowest-rated teachers, the same learning takes fourteen months. But we saw in chapter 2 that the very best teachers achieve a year's learning in six months, and for the least effective, a year's learning takes two years to achieve. Having a teacher with a higher rating on the Danielson scale is better than having a teacher with a low rating. But having an outstanding teacher is much, much better.

The important conclusion from these research findings is that even the best teacher evaluation systems are unreliable, biased, and capture only a small part of teacher quality. If we paid attention to them, we would end up giving bonuses to many teachers who didn't deserve them and firing many teachers who were really quite good. But there is a deeper problem, which is that the use of such systems distorts the incentives for teachers.

All teacher evaluation systems, by definition, have to be comprehensive. They include all the things that teachers do—the things teachers do that really help their students learn and things teachers do that don't have much impact one way or the other. Where the consequences of getting low ratings on a teacher evaluation system include getting fired—or getting a substantial bonus for a high rating, as they do, for example, in Washington, DC's IMPACT system—there is a real incentive for teachers to improve their ratings in the easiest way possible. For example, the Danielson framework reports on teacher performance under four broad categories, or domains.

1. Planning and preparation
2. Classroom environment
3. Instruction
4. Professional responsibilities

While all of these would appear to be important, it turns out that some teacher characteristics are much more important to student success than others. Students taught by teachers who were rated high on *planning and preparation* or on *professional responsibilities* actually made no more progress than students taught by teachers who received low ratings on these aspects of their teaching. The aspects of teaching that made a difference were, not surprisingly, *classroom environment* and *instruction*. The important point here is that teachers can improve their ratings by improving *any* aspect of their practice. Many teachers would find it easier to improve their ratings on *planning and preparation* or *professional responsibilities* than they would on *classroom environment* or *instruction*. Their ratings would improve, but their students would not learn any more.

Rewards and sanctions for teachers based on their ratings can push them to get better ratings on things that don't help their students much or, indeed, at all. Worse, the teachers may actually stop doing the things that they were doing that were highly effective but which didn't show up in the evaluation because the framework didn't include them. As a way of improving student learning, evaluation frameworks are at best ineffective and may actually be counterproductive.

One response to these problems with teacher observations is to give up on such evaluations entirely and just evaluate teachers on the basis of their students' test scores, at least for those who teach math and English language arts. Since teachers are rarely allocated to students at random, it would be unfair to evaluate teachers solely on their students' scores, but we can look at the progress made by students. Test the students at the beginning of the year, test them again at the end of the year, and identify the classrooms where students are making the most progress.

## Using Test Scores to Measure Teachers' Effectiveness

Such an approach feels much more scientific than teacher observation, which inevitably, being based on human judgment, seems more subjective, but there are at least as many problems with what are called "value-added" approaches to teacher evaluation as there are with observation.

First, most state tests are taken in the spring, rather than at the end of the school year. So, if we try to estimate the value added by a fourth-grade teacher by looking at the difference between her students' third-grade test scores and their fourth-grade test scores, as much as one-third of the increase in achievement will be due to the third-grade teacher.

Second, because the period over which student progress is measured includes the summer vacation, a teacher's rating will depend on how much students regress over the summer—what is sometimes called *summer learning loss*. This is an important issue because students from affluent homes tend to read more over the summer than those from less affluent homes. If we estimate the progress made by students by comparing this year's test scores with those from last year, a teacher who teaches students from affluent homes will look better simply because her students did more reading over the summer.[9]

The third problem with value-added approaches to evaluating teachers is that we need to make some statistical calculations in order to adjust for differences in students' achievement at the beginning of the year. These calculations are complex and require making assumptions that have a substantial impact on the ratings of teachers. In one study, Dan Goldhaber and his colleagues studied over two hundred high school teachers and their students' scores on the ACT college admissions test.[10] For each student, the researchers looked at how well students scored on the ACT college admissions test, taking into account the achievement of the students at the start of the school year. They then placed teachers into five equal-sized categories—excellent, good, average, below average, least effective—based on how much progress their students had made over the course of the year (i.e., the teacher's value-added).

Goldhaber and his colleagues did this in two ways, using two different statistical approaches.[11] As might be expected, most teachers were ranked similarly using the two different approaches. Just under half of the teachers (47 percent) who were rated as least effective in one approach were also rated as least effective in the other approach, and about two-thirds of the teachers got ratings that differed by only one category in the two models. However, four of the teachers who were rated as excellent teachers in one approach were rated as the least effective in the other approach, even though there is no way of choosing between the two approaches—they are both equally valid ways of analyzing the data. So, were these four teachers excellent or terrible? We just don't know. They could be either or somewhere in between.

The fourth problem with value-added estimates of teacher effectiveness is that the ratings given to teachers seem to vary quite a lot from year to year. In *Weapons of Math Destruction*, Cathy O'Neil tells the story of Tim Clifford, a fifth-grade English language arts teacher in a New York City middle school with twenty-six years' teaching experience.[12] When the district introduced a teacher value-added rating system, Clifford was given a score of 6 out of 100—a score that would probably have gotten him fired if he didn't have tenure. However, since the score came with no explanation of why his score was so low or how he might improve his score, the next year, Clifford taught the same way as he had before, and got a score of 96. Same teacher, same school, same curriculum, similar students, different result.

In fact, the results of value-added modeling are so unreliable that they are almost useless as a guide to how good an individual teacher is. Clifford's experience is unusual—not many teachers would see their results swing so much from one year to the next—but it is common to find teachers who are in reality better than average getting ratings that suggest they are terrible and some teachers who are in reality terrible getting above average ratings.

The issues with value-added approaches raised above are serious and mean that right now value-added modeling cannot give us reliable indications of how good individual teachers are, although it is always possible that the reliability of such evaluations can be improved. But there is a fifth problem with value-added measures that means that value-added approaches to teacher evaluation will *never* be able to tell us how good teachers are: the measures that we use in the value-added calculations cannot capture all the things that good teachers contribute to their students' learning.

For example, in Florida, where I now live, the state standards for English language arts require teachers to teach both reading and writing from third grade on. However, the state tests for third grade assess only reading; writing is tested from fourth grade up. A third-grade teacher should therefore be teaching her students to read and to write, but of course, if she is being evaluated on the basis of her students' test scores, there is a strong incentive for her to place greater emphasis on reading than on writing or maybe even to ignore writing altogether. Any fourth-grade teacher, however, hopes that the teacher who had her students in third grade spent a lot of time on writing because if the students arrive in fourth grade with little writing experience, that fourth-grade teacher is going to have her work cut out to get her students to grade level. This kind of thing happens in every grade. Every teacher lays foundations for subsequent learning that are not captured in the tests that students take at the end of the year. In fact, a study of over sixty thousand students in North Carolina by Jesse Rothstein found that some teachers benefitted students for at least three years after they stopped teaching them.[13] In other words, some teachers make the teachers who teach their students in the future appear to be better teachers than they really are because they lay such strong foundations for future learning. What this means in practice is that it is quite simply impossible to take the progress a child makes in school and apportion it to different teachers. In this context, it is worth noting that value-added ratings can give us useful data on student achievement at the building level, because for every teacher who gets a rating higher than they merit, there will be another who will get a lower one, just by chance. And if the whole building is evaluated, then there is less incentive for teachers to make themselves look good at their colleagues' expense. But the main conclusion here is very simple. Value-added modeling cannot tell us how effective individual teachers are with any degree of accuracy and will never be able to do so in the future.

One response to this is, so what? Even if the value-added ratings aren't perfect, they do, on average, tell us who the good teachers are. So, if we fire the teachers with low value-added ratings, we will, to be sure, be getting rid of some teachers who are in fact very good but will, at the same time, be getting rid of more bad teachers. The net effect of such policies will then be to improve teacher quality.

This is true, but because our evaluations of teachers are so inaccurate, the benefits are minimal, as is shown by a study of Florida teachers by Marcus Winters and Joshua Cowen.[14] They used a dataset that included the reading scores of all the students who were in fourth and fifth grade in public schools in Florida over five school years (2004–2005 to 2008–2009) and managed to link the records of 96 percent of the students to the teachers who were teaching them. For each teacher, they calculated a value-added score and then looked at what would have happened if, each year, the lower-performing teachers had been removed, and, in subsequent years, replaced with average teachers.

Since a teacher's value-added rating can vary so much from year to year (as we saw with the case of Tim Clifford), they assumed that a policy that relied on a single year's data would be open to legal challenge, so they looked at a couple of policy options that used two years' worth of data. One policy option was to remove teachers if they received a low rating in *each* of two consecutive years, and the other was to remove teachers if their *average* rating over two years was low.

They also looked at three different definitions of *low-performing*—the lowest 5 percent of all teachers, the lowest 10 percent of all teachers, and the lowest 25 percent of all teachers. The results are shown in table 3.1 below.

**Table 3.1: Effects of Removing Ineffective Teachers in Florida (Winters & Cowen, 2013)**

| Policy option | Removal threshold | Extra days of learning per year |
|---|---|---|
| Removing teachers based on poor performance in each of two consecutive years | Lowest 5% | 0.0 |
|  | Lowest 10% | 0.0 |
|  | Lowest 25% | 1.5 |
| Removing teachers based on poor performance averaged over two consecutive years | Lowest 5% | 1.5 |
|  | Lowest 10% | 2.0 |
|  | Lowest 25% | 3.5 |

In other words, even if we adopted the most aggressive policy—firing teachers who are, over a two-year period, in the lowest performing 25 percent—we would get only an extra three and a half days' learning for our children each year, and we would only get that if the replacement teachers were as good as average. If they were worse, we would get even less. Given the political cost of such a policy, not least because it would entail removing a large number of effective and popular teachers, it is hard to see any benefit at all in using value-added approaches to identify and remove ineffective teachers.

So far in this chapter, we have seen that it is simply not possible to identify ineffective teachers with any reliability either by observing them or on the basis of their students' test scores. However, if we use a combination of approaches, could that work? That is exactly the approach adopted by the Measures of Effective Teaching (MET) project funded by the Bill and Melinda Gates Foundation.[15]

## Combining Observations, Value-Added Data, and Student Surveys

The MET project examined whether it was possible to predict which teachers would be the most effective using a combination of classroom observations, value-added measures, and student surveys. It found that the best way to predict students' scores on standardized tests was to calculate, for each teacher, a composite score in which

81 percent of the weight was given to the teacher's value-added score, 17 percent to the results of classroom observation, and 2 percent to surveys of students' perceptions of their teachers. The resulting teacher rating did allow them to predict, on average, which teachers would be more effective the following year—the teachers with a higher composite rating were, on average, the teachers whose students did better the following year. However, the prediction was far from perfect.[16] For example, if we used the composite measure to remove the least effective twenty teachers out of a group of one hundred, then we would get it right more often than we would get it wrong. But not much more. Of the twenty teachers we identified for removal, twelve would deserve to be removed, but eight would not. And of course, eight teachers who really belonged in the least effective group would get a pass. Of course, if we used more years of data, we would get more accurate results. But to get a rating for a teacher that is as accurate as the SAT (the benchmark we used earlier with classroom observations), we would need to collect data on each teacher over an eleven-year-period.[17] More important, even when we get it right, we are only identifying the teachers who are most or least effective in terms of the students' scores on standard-ized tests. When we use the composite measure to predict which teachers are the most effective in getting students to write extended pieces, we would actually get it wrong more often than we would get it right. Only seven out of the twenty teachers identified as being in the bottom 20 percent would belong there. The other thirteen would not, and of course, there are another thirteen teachers who should have been placed in the bottom twenty but were not.

Unpalatable and implausible though it may be, the conclusion of this chapter is simple. Improving schools by firing bad teachers simply will not have much impact on student achievement. If we adopt a cautious approach and fire only the teachers we are sure really are ineffective, we will remove very few teachers from our schools, and the impact on our children's achievement will be negligible, if not actually zero. A more aggressive approach will not be any more effective, because of the inherent unreliability in the process. If we remove more teachers, we end up removing many effective teachers as well as the less effective ones. Not only that, but in many parts of the country, because of the difficulties of recruiting teachers, those teachers who are removed would be replaced by teachers who are even less effective.

But it's even worse than that, because attempting to improve education by firing bad teachers may actually make things worse, for two reasons. First, we create incentives for teachers to focus on the short term rather than the long term. We may get higher standardized test scores, but our children will be less well prepared for what comes next. Second, we undermine teachers' support for each other. When teachers are compared and ranked, there is no incentive for teachers to support each other. Quite the reverse, in fact—teachers who want to keep their jobs would be well-advised not to help their colleagues in any way and thus increase the likelihood that a colleague gets a lower ranking.

Moreover, these are not just problems of implementation that we can fix by paying more attention to the details. They are fundamental limitations of the approach. Any district that thinks it can improve education by firing ineffective teachers is likely to spend a lot of time, and a lot of money, on something that, at best, will produce a negligible benefit for our children and, at worst, could significantly lower our children's educational achievement. Now, as I argued above, this does not mean that we should not fire bad teachers. There are undoubtedly some teachers who are so ineffective that they should be removed, not least because the failure to address such issues can sap the morale of other teachers. The lesson of this chapter is that doing so is not going to have much of an impact on student achievement.

---

1   Hanushek (2010).

2   Hill, Charalambous, and Kraft (2012).

3   These were the same six districts that featured in the research conducted by Thomas Kane and his colleagues that was cited in the previous chapter: Charlotte-Mecklenburg Schools (NC), Dallas Independent School District (TX), Denver Public Schools (CO), Hillsborough County Public Schools (FL), Memphis City Schools (TN), and the New York City Department of Education (NY).

4   Steinberg and Garrett (2016).

5   Kirschner, Sweller, and Clark (2006, p. 77)

6   Bjork (2011).

7   Willingham (2009, p. 54).

8   Sartain et al. (2011).

9   Gershenson and Hayes (2016).

10  Goldhaber, Goldschmidt, and Tseng (2013).

11  For those who are interested, they were a random-effects model and a fixed-effects model.

12  O'Neil (2016).

13  Rothstein (2010).

14  Winters and Cowen (2013).

15  Bill and Melinda Gates Foundation (2012).

16  The correlation between the prediction and the teacher's actual performance the following year was 0.69.

17  This is a straightforward application of the Spearman-Brown prophecy formula to determine by how many times the length of a test would need to be increased to increase the reliability of an assessment from 0.51 (the reliability of the MET teacher effectiveness measure) to 0.92 (the reliability of the SAT).

# CHAPTER 4

# Paying Good Teachers More

In most countries, and especially in the United States, there is a widespread belief that if people do a job better than others do the same job, then they should be paid more, for several reasons. If some people create more value for their employers, then it is only fair that they should receive some of that value, and by paying more effective employees more, we encourage them to stay in their jobs. Paying more effective employees more may also persuade less effective employees to look for other kinds of work. And of course, paying people for better performance may encourage people to put in more effort in their jobs, thus improving performance further.

Whatever the rights and wrongs of performance-based pay, or differentiated compensation as such an arrangement is often called, it appears that paying good teachers more will have little, if any, impact on student achievement in the United States.

It does seem likely that if all teachers were paid more—for example, paying teachers at the same level as other graduates, such as engineers—then, over time, the quality of teachers would rise appreciably, and increased student achievement would follow. However, identifying the individual teachers who are most effective in increasing student achievement, as we saw in the previous chapter, appears to be extremely difficult and perhaps impossible. Every teacher builds on the work of a student's previous teachers, so it is impossible to work out how much each teacher has contributed to the increase in a student's achievement over time at school. Observations of teaching performance are subjective and are generally poor indicators of the amount of learning that takes place.

Despite the problems with performance-related pay, a number of districts have explored such schemes, and, perhaps predictably, the results have been disappointing. Some of these schemes were abandoned because the evidence that they were ineffective was clear before they were completed. Most of the completed schemes found no impact on student achievement, and the few that did find some impact on student achievement were extremely expensive to implement.

Because of the difficulties of establishing how much each teacher contributes to a student's learning, US school districts use proxies for teacher quality in their compensation schemes. All districts pay higher salaries to teachers with more experience, which seems reasonable given that more experienced teachers are more effective. However, most districts also pay teachers for having postgraduate qualifications such as master's degrees and PhDs, which is harder to justify, since there appears to be no evidence that teachers with such advanced degrees are any more effective than teachers without them. Paying good teachers more seems like a good idea, but it can't be done fairly, generally doesn't work, and, when it does work, is very expensive. There are better ways for a district to spend its money.

We saw in the previous chapter that trying to improve education by removing ineffective teachers has, at best, a very small impact on student achievement. Perhaps not surprisingly, therefore, many US school districts have looked at the other end of the scale. Could we raise educational achievement by paying teachers more to keep the very best of them in the classroom?

It turns out the answer may well be yes, provided we pay *all* teachers more. In 2010, Peter Dolton and Oscar Marcenaro-Gutierrez looked at teacher salaries in thirty-nine countries, most of which were members of the OECD. They also looked at the scores that fifteen-year-old students in those countries achieved on math, reading, and science tests administered every three years as part of PISA. To get a fairer comparison, they compared salaries in terms of what is called *purchasing power parity* rather than the standard dollar exchange rate, so that they were comparing salaries in terms of what they could purchase in each country. As might be expected, the correlation was not perfect. If we look at countries where salaries for teachers with fifteen years' experience were close to those in the United States (around $35,000 per year in 2007 dollars), some, such as Finland, had very high test scores, and others, such as Spain, had relatively low test scores. However, overall, there was a strong tendency for scores to be higher in countries where teachers were paid more.[1]

Now, of course, this does not mean that the higher salaries were the *cause* of the higher achievement. There are many possible reasons for the association between teacher salaries and educational achievement. For example, it is possible that what really matters is the public's attitudes toward teachers, and where teachers are held in high regard, then teacher salaries are higher and more talented people want to be teachers. Teachers' salaries may also influence the size of classes. For a given amount of money and a certain number of children who need teachers, higher pay will lead to larger classes. It could be that the conclusions depend on which countries are included in the analysis, and a different selection of countries would lead to different conclusions. However, by tackling the analysis in a number of different ways, with different assumptions, they found similar results—a 10 percent increase in teacher salaries would appear to produce an increase in student achievement of somewhere between 5 and 10 percent.

Intuitively, it does make sense that countries that pay teachers more would have more effective education systems. Very few people go into teaching to make money, but the way teacher salaries compare to salaries of equally qualified workers is bound to have an impact on the quality of the teaching force. When teacher salaries are too low, many of those who would be highly effective teachers are likely to choose other jobs in order to have enough money to buy a home and raise a family. Or teachers may have to take on second jobs, which reduces the time and energy they can give to their teaching.

Of course, it could be argued that those who go into teaching would do so anyway, whatever the salary, but the evidence on trends in teacher recruitment suggests this is not true. For example, Marie Bacolod looked at trends in the academic qualifications of those entering teaching from the 1960s on. She found that in the early 1960s, 50 percent of all females entering teaching were high-achievers (defined as those with standardized test scores in the top one-fifth of the population). Twenty years later, only 10 percent of females going into teaching were high-achievers (for males the figure was 6 percent, down from 18 percent in the early 1960s). And these women were not staying home; over the same time period, the proportion of high-achievers in other professions (engineering, medicine, law) rose from 30 percent to 60 percent.[2] As Marie Bacolod concluded:

> Results show that the lower teachers were paid relative to professionals, the less likely high-quality educated women were to choose to teach. High-quality teachers are particularly more sensitive to changes in relative teacher wages. (p. 749)

For many people, the idea of paying all teachers more seems wasteful. Given the range in teacher quality that we know from chapter 2 exists in American schools, if we raise salaries for all teachers, we will certainly end up paying both effective and ineffective teachers more. It seems to make much more sense to pay more effective teachers more than less effective ones, for at least three reasons.

First, it just seems right. Students learn more in the classes of more effective teachers, earn more money, and as a result, pay more taxes. Raj Chetty and his colleagues estimate an above-average kindergarten teacher increases the lifetime earnings of a class of twenty students by $320,000.[3] It seems only fair that the teachers who produce that benefit get a share.

Second, the most effective teachers are also likely to have other skills. While they may have a passion for teaching, if the salary differential between teaching and other things they might do for a living is too great, no matter how much passion they have for teaching, there must come a point at which they would leave teaching and use their talents elsewhere. In this regard, it is worth noting that teaching probably suffers from what William Baumol calls *cost disease*.[4] It is widely accepted by economists that increases in wealth are driven primarily by increases in productivity. There is no doubt that productivity in many jobs, such as automobile manufacturing, has increased. But it still takes the same amount of time to play a Mozart string quartet as it did two hundred years ago (and you still need the same number of musicians). To be competitive, teachers' compensation has to be linked to increases in earnings in other professions, which almost always rise faster than prices of goods. Education, like opera and live music, is likely to increase in cost faster than the rate of inflation.

Third, it seems plausible that paying the most effective teachers more would create incentives for all teachers to become more effective. This seems to be the most widely cited reason for paying good teachers more. If we pay all teachers more, then there is no incentive for teachers to improve. Indeed, Greg Mankiw, author of the most widely used economics textbook in the United States, suggests that the idea that people respond to incentives is one of the ten big ideas in economics.[5] People do respond to incentives. The question is, of course, how do they respond, and, in particular, do they respond in the way we want?

Most countries have always paid some teachers more than others for doing very similar jobs. Every country in the OECD pays teachers more if they have more teaching experience. In some countries, such as England, a teacher reaches the maximum of the main professional pay scale after six years, while in Greece, for example, teachers get (small) annual pay raises every year for forty-five years.[6] The size of salary differentials between novices and more experienced teachers also varies greatly from country to country. In some countries, particularly in Scandinavia, teachers with fifteen years' experience are paid about only 10 to 15 percent more than those at the beginning of their careers, while in others, such as Korea, Japan, and the Netherlands, those with fifteen years' experience earn over 70 percent more than novices.[7]

Countries also vary dramatically in the extent to which they pay teachers more for their qualifications. Denmark does not pay teachers any more no matter how many educational qualifications they have, while in Mexico, a well-qualified teacher can earn two and a half times as much as a fifteen-year veteran who has just the minimum credentials for teaching.

Across the United States, on average, teachers with fifteen years' experience are paid 25 percent to 30 percent more than novices, which is just slightly below the international average. But well-qualified teachers earn about 38 percent more than teachers with equivalent experience but with only the minimal certification necessary for teaching. So, does this make sense? Are teachers with more experience or more qualifications more effective?

The answer to the first question is a definite yes. Many research studies have shown that teachers become much more effective in their first two or three years. On average, in the United States, students make around three months' less progress each year if they are taught by a novice teacher than if they are taught by a teacher with at least three years' experience.[8] Beyond that, the picture is less clear. Many, indeed probably most, teachers continue to improve after three years, but the improvement is less rapid, so it is harder to measure accurately. Many studies have concluded that there is effectively no improvement after five years, but that could be because the improvements beyond that point are smaller and therefore more difficult to detect. Also, very few studies have tracked individual teachers and looked at improvements in effectiveness over ten or twenty years (what economists call *panel data*). Instead, most studies look at how effective different teachers are when they have five, ten, fifteen, or twenty years' experience (cross-sectional data). The reason this is potentially misleading is that, particularly in the United States, good teachers are regularly taken out of the classroom to become coaches or administrators. By constantly removing some of the best teachers from the classroom, and looking only at those who are left, we may be underestimating the improvement of teachers with experience. This may also go some way toward explaining the apparent drop in teacher effectiveness after about twenty years that has been found by some researchers.[9] It could be that those who move into coaching and administration are also more effective teachers and so the sample of teachers still teaching after twenty years is not representative of how good all teachers with twenty years' experience would be.

Looking across all the available research, the broad finding is that teachers improve rapidly in their first three years of teaching, and while the rate of improvement slows down, American teachers continue to improve for at least the first ten years of their careers and perhaps, at least in mathematics, beyond that.[10] However, when we look in more detail at the available evidence, something rather interesting emerges.

Allison Atteberry and her colleagues looked at the improvements in effectiveness during the first five years of the careers of over two thousand fourth- and fifth-grade teachers who started teaching in New York between 2000 and 2006.[11] They found that while, as might be expected, teachers improved on average, some teachers improved much more than others. They classified teachers into five equal-sized categories on the basis of how effective they were in their first year: most effective (top 20 percent), above average (next 20 percent), average (middle 20 percent), below average (next 20 percent), and least effective (bottom 20 percent). Over the first five years of their careers, the most effective teachers didn't improve at all—they were no more effective after five years than they were at the start of their careers. The above average teachers improved slightly, as did the average and the below average teachers. The least effective teachers, on the other hand, improved dramatically. In fact, half of the total improvement gain of all the teachers in the study was produced by just the teachers who, in their first year, were the least effective.

When we look at the second question—whether better qualified teachers are more effective—the answer is just as clear. Unfortunately, the finding is that they are not. John Schacter and Yeow Meng Thum reviewed studies going back to the 1970s that examined the relationship between teachers' postgraduate qualifications (e.g., masters' degrees, doctorates, and other professional qualifications) and their students' achievement. They identified 217 relevant, well-designed studies. Eight of the studies found a positive relationship—i.e., students taught by better qualified teachers made more progress. But seven studies found a negative relationship; students taught by teachers with more qualifications actually made *less* progress. And the rest of the studies—202 out of the 217—found no relationship either way.[12]

To teachers who already have master's degrees or PhDs in education, this probably does not come as a surprise. Most master's degrees in education are not designed to improve classroom practice—rather, they serve as an introduction to the academic study of education. Following such a program might make teachers more thoughtful about their practice, but there is little in most master's degrees that is specifically designed to improve teaching. What does seem odd, therefore, is that many, and perhaps most, school districts in the United States pay teachers more for gaining qualifications that have little or no benefit for their students.

When we look at programs specifically designed to improve teacher practice, the news is more positive. For example, studies of teachers who have been certified by the National Board for Professional Teaching Standards (NBPTS) have found that they are more effective than other teachers.[13] Moreover, the effects are substantial. Students taught by NBPTS certified teachers make, on average, an additional two months' progress each year, although the effects vary across grades and subjects. It is important to realize that the lengthy process that teachers go through to gain NBPTS certification does not appear to make teachers any more effective; what NBPTS certification does is provide a signal to districts that teachers who hold such certification are likely to be more effective.

The real problem here, of course, is that schools, districts, and states are using qualifications and experience as proxies for what they are really interested in, which is how good the teachers are, and the evidence discussed above suggests that while some of the proxies are better than others, none of them are particularly good. Surely it would be better to measure teacher quality directly. Rather than relying on input measures for teachers, perhaps we would be better looking at output measures.

## Performance-Related Pay

In the United States, and indeed in most of the world, people who do a job more effectively tend to get paid more. For athletes, hedge-fund managers, chief executives, lawyers, or surgeons, the law of supply and demand means that those who are regarded as more effective are paid more.

In individual sports, such as tennis or golf, it does seem pretty easy to work out who is best. If you consistently beat your opponents, then it seems fairly clear that you are better and deserve more money, although, as Michael Mauboussin has pointed out, people consistently underrate the value of luck in their success.[14]

Where success depends on teams, it is much more difficult to figure out who is contributing what. For example, it is widely known that the more times a surgeon has performed a surgical procedure, the greater the likelihood of success. Robert Huckman and Gary Pisano looked at the performance of 203 cardiac surgeons who performed coronary artery bypass surgeries in forty-three Pennsylvania hospitals in 1994 and 1995. Where surgeons performed only one such procedure a month, the mortality rate was 3.3 percent but only 2.5 percent when the surgeon carried out at least twenty procedures a month. But what was surprising is that when Huckman and Pisano looked at the data more closely, it turned out that what really mattered was not the number of procedures that a surgeon performed per month but how many she or he performed *in a particular hospital*. When a surgeon performed more surgeries in different hospitals, the mortality rate was the same as if the surgeon only carried out one procedure a month.[15] It was the surgical *team* that produced the improvement in mortality, not the experience of the individual surgeon.

Despite the difficulties of figuring out the individual contributions of people who work in teams, there is a widespread belief that teachers do not have incentives to work harder, and if they did, they would do so, and their students would learn more.

This idea was tested in the Project on Incentives in Teaching (POINT) conducted in Nashville, Tennessee, from 2006–2007 to 2008–2009.[16] Middle school math teachers in Nashville Public Schools were invited to volunteer for the project in which half of them, at random, would be paid bonuses if their students met certain targets, while the other half would just be paid as usual.

In order to ensure that teachers were not competing against each other, the targets were set so that theoretically every teacher eligible for bonuses could get them if their students did well enough. If a teacher's performance, judged on the basis of her or his students' test scores, was at a level that had only been achieved in the past by the highest-performing 5 percent of teachers, then the teacher would receive a bonus of $15,000. Bonuses of $5,000 and $10,000 were given if the teacher's performance was in the top 20 percent or 10 percent.

This would appear to be a well-designed incentive scheme. As noted above, the scheme did not pit one teacher against another. All teachers who reached one of the targets would get a bonus. Moreover, the targets seemed reasonable and achievable. Approximately half of the teachers in the group eligible for bonuses could achieve at least one of the bonuses if their students answered two or three more items correctly on a fifty-five-item test. However, when they looked at the results of the students taught by teachers eligible for bonuses, on average they scored the same as teachers not eligible for bonuses.

There was one exception to this, and this was in the fifth grade, where students taught by teachers eligible for bonuses did score higher. But a year later, when these students had been taught by different teachers in sixth grade, their scores were the same as those taught by the teachers not eligible for bonuses. Whatever benefit the bonuses produced in fifth grade was gone within a year.

The reasons for this are not clear, but the two most likely reasons are changes in teachers' time allocation and teaching to the test. In Nashville schools, teachers who teach math in fifth grade are more likely to teach the same students at least one other subject (e.g., science). It is plausible that the fifth-grade teachers who were eligible for bonuses spent less time teaching other subjects in order to spend more time on math. The other possibility is that these teachers focused to a greater extent than others on teaching only those things that were likely to be tested. Either way, the remarkable thing about the POINT study is that the substantial bonuses offered to teachers for getting higher test scores produced absolutely no long-term benefit for their students.

There are a few studies of performance-related pay that have been more successful. Perhaps the most successful of all is the IMPACT scheme operated in Washington, DC's public schools, which began in September 2009. At the end of each school year, teachers in Washington's public schools are given a score that ranges from 100 to 400. For teachers teaching mathematics and reading, the score is a weighted average of the performance of their students on standardized tests (50 percent), the results of observations of the teacher by administrators (35 percent), an evaluation of their contribution to the work of the school (10 percent), and the performance of the school as a whole (5 percent). For teachers not teaching mathematics or reading, the weighting of the observations is increased to 75 percent, and the student test scores are replaced by an administrator's rating of goals set by the teacher (10 percent).

A rating below 175 results in immediate dismissal. A rating of 176 to 249 results in a warning to improve, followed by dismissal the following year if the teacher scores below 250 a second time. A score of between 250 and 349 results in a designation of the teacher as *effective* with no sanction and no bonus. Teachers who score at least 350 are given a bonus of $5,000, with an additional $5,000 if their score is based on student test data (i.e., if they are teaching math or English) and a further $2,500 if the teacher teaches a high-need subject. Moreover, these bonuses are doubled if the teacher works in a high-poverty school. Teachers who score at least 350 in two consecutive years are automatically paid as if they had earned a master's degree; their salary is further increased by the equivalent of three years' normal progression (five if they work in high-poverty schools).

Clearly these are substantial benefits. A teacher scoring at least 350 for two years running would, over the next fifteen years, receive a total benefit of $185,000.[17] Over the first three years of the scheme, the impact of the scheme was significant. Approximately half of the teachers receiving scores between 176 and 249, and who were therefore under threat of dismissal the following year if they did not improve, voluntarily left Washington's public schools. The teachers who remained became more effective, by an amount equivalent to the improvement made by a typical teacher in his or her first year and a half of teaching, or an additional month of progress each year. Moreover, the teachers receiving *highly effective* ratings improved by a similar amount in the following year. However, we don't know whether these improvements in the teachers rated as highly effective were maintained in subsequent years, when there were no further incentives.

Perhaps the clearest evidence about the potential of incentive pay for teachers comes from a four-year evaluation of the Teacher Incentive Fund (TIF), established by the US Congress in 2006 to provide grants to districts to support the development of performance-based compensation schemes for teachers and principals working in high-need schools. Ten of the 130 districts receiving funding in 2010 agreed to participate in a randomized-control trial in which half the schools would offer teachers and principals bonuses of up to $9,000 per year for good student progress and half would not.

An evaluation of the impact of TIF in these ten districts over a four-year period (2011–2012 to 2014–2015) found that the incentives increased student achievement by the equivalent of three or four weeks per year after the first year. However, the differences in test scores between the schools with incentives and the schools without incentives were the same in years 3 and 4 as they had been in year 2.[18] In other words, even though the incentives were in place for four years, there was only a one off bump in the second year. If the incentives were improving the quality of instruction of those teachers offered incentives, we would expect additional improvements, relative to the other schools, in years 3 and 4. Furthermore, fewer than half of the 130 participating districts planned to continue to offer teacher incentives once the grant funding ended, because of the cost.

So where does that leave us? Many of the teacher incentive schemes that have been conducted in the United States over the last few decades have either been abandoned before being properly evaluated, as was the case with New York City's bonus program,[19] or have found little or no impact on student achievement (e.g., Nashville). On the other hand, it does seem that a well-designed performance-related pay system such as Washington's IMPACT scheme can raise achievement, but the gains are modest, and the costs are high. And the largest study of incentive programs conducted in the United States to date found that incentives for teachers produced small, one-off improvements in achievement that were, in the judgment of most districts, not sustainable.

One response to these findings is that we just haven't found the right combination of incentives yet, and of course, it is possible that different kinds of incentives may be more effective. However, the fact that so many different kinds of incentive programs for teachers have failed to produce large, sustainable benefits suggests that it is very hard to get such programs to work—if incentive programs did produce sizeable effects, we would probably have found them by now.

To some people, these findings are surprising. How can it be that paying people more to do their jobs better does not improve performance? It may depend on the kinds of work you want people to do. As Daniel Pink explains in *Drive: The Surprising Truth About What Motivates Us*, paying people more to complete tasks quickly does, at least in the laboratory, seem to improve performance where the task is straight-forward and requires little creativity.[20] For example, if I have a stack of boxes that I need moved from one room to another, telling those who are doing the job that they will be paid $20 more if they finish the job within the hour may well improve performance (or at least how quickly the job gets done). However, offering people rewards that depend on performance can actually make things worse when the work is complex or requires creativity, because people pursue ineffective strategies more aggressively in pursuit of the reward.

This was neatly illustrated by a study of professional artists that was conducted by Teresa Amabile, director of research at Harvard Business School, and her colleagues Eileen Phillips and Mary Ann Collins. They asked twenty-three professional visual artists to identify twenty pieces of work for an art exhibition—ten commissioned pieces (i.e., where they were being paid by a specific patron for a piece of work) and ten noncommissioned pieces (those where the artist had no specific client). The works were displayed with just the artists' names, so that whether the work was commissioned or not was not apparent. Independent art experts were asked to judge the pieces of work, both in terms of their technical competence and in terms of their overall value as works of art. The results were, in the researchers' own words, "startling." Although the commissioned works were rated similarly to the noncommissioned works in terms of technical quality, they were rated as much less good as works of art.[21]

What the research shows therefore is that extrinsic rewards can improve performance on tasks that are simple and do not require creativity but may make performance worse for complex tasks or where creativity is required. This distinction—between tasks that are complex and require creativity on the one hand and those that are straightforward and simple on the other—goes a long way to explaining the research on performance-related pay for teachers. There are, in fact, a few studies that have found that bonus pay for teachers improves students' test scores, but these studies involved solutions to problems that American schools don't have.

For example, Esther Duflo and her colleagues evaluated the impact of an incentive scheme in India carried out by a nongovernmental organization named Seva Mandir, which runs a number of what are called *non-formal education centers* in rural parts of Rajasthan, India. These centers typically enroll about twenty students and are open six hours a day. Although children of any age can attend, most are between seven and ten years old.

Despite the fact that teachers are regularly threatened with dismissal if they are absent from work too frequently, on any given day, upward of a third of the teachers regularly fail to show up for work.

To try to address this, from 2003 to 2006, Seva Mandir ran an experiment in 113 of their centers. In fifty-six centers, teachers were paid a fixed rate of Rs.1,000 per month (around $23 at the time of the experiment in 2003). In the other fifty-seven centers, selected at random, teachers were paid according to their attendance.

Each teacher working in one of the fifty-seven centers operating attendance-related pay was given a camera, which a student used to take a photograph of the teacher and the other students at the beginning and end of each school day. The cameras were tamper-proof and incorporated a time-stamp mechanism that recorded the time and date of the photograph. A full day was defined as a day in which the teacher submitted two photographs, time-stamped five hours apart, with at least eight students in each photograph. If the teacher attended ten or fewer days, the teacher was paid Rs.500. For each additional day over the ten-day threshold, the teachers were paid an additional Rs.50.

The results were dramatic. There was an immediate improvement in teacher attendance in the fifty-seven schools paying teachers by attendance. At the start of the experiment, the average teacher absentee rate across all the schools was 42 percent, and it continued at that level over the two and a half years of the experiment in the fifty-six schools where teachers were paid a fixed salary. Where teachers' pay depended on attendance, there was an immediate drop in absenteeism, to 21 percent, and teachers seemed to work just as hard while at school.[22] The effect of this was that students attending centers where the teachers were paid by attendance received 30 percent more instructional time per month, which resulted in approximately 25 percent more progress over a year.[23]

The important point here is that these findings are entirely consistent with the conclusions reached by Daniel Pink described above. Turning up for work is a low-complexity task. Where teachers are not turning up for work, paying teachers for doing so is likely to have an immediate and substantial effect. However, if teachers are already turning up for work and we want them to work more effectively, then paying teachers for results is likely to produce small, transient benefits, at high cost.

## Conclusion

Paying more money to people who do a job more effectively than their colleagues seems like an obvious way to improve performance. Even if those who aren't very good don't improve (perhaps because they can't) at least the best are more likely to stay. There are countries, such as Finland, where the social status of teaching is so high that high salaries are not needed to recruit the best and brightest into the profession, but in general, high-performing countries tend to pay teachers at a level comparable to salaries earned by other graduates, such as engineers or nurses. In the United States, however, on average, teachers are paid 30 percent less than engineers or nurses.[24] Now that might not be too much of an issue if the social status of teachers was high in the United States, but the evidence is clear that it's not. While American parents have a lot of trust in their children's teachers, the social status of teachers in the United States is similar to that of other countries.[25] Of course, it does not make sense to increase teacher salaries too quickly. Giving all teachers a 20 percent pay raise would simply pay our existing teachers—effective and less effective—more, but systematically raising teachers' salaries over time would probably help a district recruit and retain good teachers.

Moreover, it makes sense to pay teachers more for their experience. Teachers improve rapidly in their first few years, and recent evidence suggests that this may continue for at least ten years, so it makes sense to adopt a *step and lane* salary schedule in which teachers get annual increases in salary for at least ten years. What makes less sense, however, is to have different lanes in a step and lane schedule on the basis of the level of education the teacher has achieved, as is the case in many US districts.[26] Paying teachers more for experience, when we know this benefits students, is a good idea. Paying teachers more for gaining qualifications that have no impact on how much their children learn is harder to justify. Quite apart from the waste of money, such schemes encourage teachers to spend time doing things that don't help their students (like getting advanced degrees) when that time could be spent on things that do benefit students (like improving classroom practice).

Whether teacher compensation should be based on that teacher's individual performance is a much more difficult question. Some people are implacably opposed to performance-related pay for teachers. On the other hand, many policymakers argue that limited public funds should be used carefully and targeted at only the most effective teachers, both to retain the best and to provide incentives for others to improve.

Whether something is a good idea in principle and whether it can be made to work in practice are, of course, completely different things, and the difficulty of implementing effective performance-related pay systems should make even the most ardent supporters of the idea think twice, for at least four reasons.

First, performance-related compensation can't be done fairly. All teachers build on what previous teachers have done. Paying good teachers more creates incentives for teachers to focus on the short term rather than the child's best interests (think teaching writing in third grade in Florida). It can also undermine teachers' support for one another—if there's only a limited number of bonuses, teachers are in competition with each other and so are unlikely to help each other improve.

Second, performance-related schemes may actually lower student achievement overall. As we saw in the previous chapter, most systems for evaluating teachers capture only 10 to 30 percent of the variation in teacher quality. Creating incentives for teachers to increase their ratings on the system may result in teachers focusing on aspects of the rating system that are easiest to improve and becoming less effective teachers as a result, even though they get higher ratings.

Third, many of the systems of performance-related compensation have either been abandoned as expensive failures (New York) or completed and finding no impact on student achievement (Nashville).

Fourth, those systems that have shown effects, such as Washington, DC's IMPACT system, are extremely expensive. Paying good teachers more seems like a simple solution, but as H. L. Mencken said many years ago, "there is always a well-known solution to every human problem—neat, plausible, and wrong."[27]

---

1    Dolton and Marcenaro-Gutierrez (2011).

2    Bacolod (2007).

3    Chetty, Friedman, Hilger, Saez, Schanzenbach, and Yagan (2010) defined an "above average" teacher as one at the 75th percentile, and a "below average" teacher as one at the 25th percentile.

4    See, for example, Heilbrun (2003) for an explanation.

5    Mankiw (2014).

6  Organisation for Economic Co-operation and Development (2014, p. 459).

7  Organisation for Economic Co-operation and Development (2014, Chart D3.2).

8  See the analysis in Rivkin, Hanushek, and Kain (2005). The conversion into months of learning has been done on the basis that one year's growth for students in the sample used by Rivkin et al. is 0.4 standard deviations.

9  See, for example, Sass, Hannaway, Xu, Figlio, and Feng (2012).

10  Papay and Kraft (2015).

11  Atteberry, Loeb, and Wyckoff (2013).

12  Schacter and Thum (2004, p. 413).

13  Goldhaber and Anthony (2007).

14  Mauboussin (2012).

15  Huckman and Pisano (2006).

16  Springer et al. (2010).

17  Dee and Wyckoff (2015). The figure of $185,000 assumes a discount rate of 5% per year.

18  Chiang, Speroni, Hermann, Hallgren, Burkander, and Wellington (2017, p. 99).

19  Otterman (2011).

20  Pink (2009).

21  Amabile, Phillips, and Collins (1994).

22  Duflo, Hanna, and Ryan (2012).

23  The actual increase in test scores reported by Duflo et al. was 0.17 standard deviations. Since reliable age norms are not available for schoolchildren in India, I have used the norms for American seven- to ten-year-olds provided by Bloom, Hill, Black, and Lipsey (2008). While this is far from ideal, the norms provided by Bloom et al. do seem similar to those found in other countries—see, for example, Wiliam (1992).

24  Average salaries for engineers and nurses from www.glassdoor.com were, respectively, $66,200 and $67,500. High school teachers earn on average $47,600, while middle school teachers earn $45,600, and elementary school teachers earn $44,800.

25  Dolton and Marcenaro-Gutierrez (2013) surveyed people in a number of countries and asked people to rank the following fourteen professions in order of how much they were respected: elementary school teacher, secondary (i.e., middle or high) school teacher, school principal, doctor, nurse, librarian, local government manager, social worker, website designer, police officer, engineer, lawyer, accountant, and management consultant. The average ranking of teachers and principals in the US was just above average (7.5 for elementary school teachers, 7.9 for secondary school teachers, and 8.2 for principals, where 1 is low and 14 is high).

26  For example, teachers in Chicago's public schools are paid about $4,000 more per year if they have a master's degree and over $10,000 more per year if they have a doctoral level qualification (Dabrowski & Klingner, 2016).

27  Mencken (1917, p. 158).

CHAPTER 5

# Reducing Class Size

Reducing class size is an attractive route to improving educational achievement, not least because it is popular with both parents and teachers. However, class size reduction programs are typically a lot more expensive to implement than other educational reforms, so we need good estimates of the likely benefits to weigh against the costs.

The most widely cited experiment on the benefits of class size reduction programs—conducted from 1985 to 1989 in Tennessee—is widely known as Project STAR (Student-Teacher Achievement Ratio). In the experiment, kindergarten students were placed either into classes of seventeen or twenty-five and their progress was followed up both during the experiment and over subsequent years as they moved to middle and high school.

The results show that being placed in a smaller class was advantageous for all students but seemed to be especially effective for minority students and those from less advantaged homes. The benefits of being in a smaller class also persisted when these students moved back into regular-sized classes in upper elementary school and even into secondary schools.

However, a number of other studies have found little increase in achievement for students assigned to smaller classes or that benefits faded out when students returned to larger classes. While the reasons for the differences are not well understood, one important factor is that the Tennessee STAR study required hiring only an additional fifty teachers. Where studies have been done on a larger scale, the additional teachers hired may well have been less effective than those already working in schools, thus weakening the benefits of class size reduction. Studies also tend to find that class size reduction programs are more effective with younger children. Again, the reasons for this are not entirely clear, but it seems likely that teachers of younger children tend to work with individual students or small groups, so the benefits of class size reduction are immediate: fewer students means more time with each student. Teachers of older students, on the other hand, tend to work with whole classes of students; the benefits of smaller classes materialize only when teachers change the way they teach.

Class size reduction may be a way of increasing student achievement, but there are several important issues for districts to note before embarking on such a program. First, the benefits are relatively small, and the costs are high, often requiring increasing education expenditure by 30 to 40 percent per year (plus the cost of building additional classrooms). Second, unless teachers are given training on how to take advantage of their smaller classes, then reducing class size may have little or no effect. Third, where teacher recruitment is difficult, hiring additional teachers may result in a lowering of average teacher quality, thus weakening, or completely negating, the benefits of smaller classes.

Few educational reforms generate as much debate and controversy as class size reduction programs. The National Education Association describes it as a "proven reform strategy,"[1] and a number of other education advocacy groups have claimed that it represents one of the best ways, if not the single best way, of increasing student achievement. Others, such as Eric Hanushek, argue that the relationship between class size and educational achievement is weak or nonexistent.[2] The problem, as with many educational innovations, is that class size reduction works sometimes and not at other times. And again, like most other educational innovations, the important question is "Under what conditions does class size reduction work?"

The best-researched class size reduction program is probably the Tennessee STAR study, described by Frederick Mosteller—one of America's greatest statisticians—as "one of the most important educational investigations ever carried out."[3]

In the experiment, teachers and students in kindergarten were assigned at random to one of three kinds of classes:

1. Small classes (thirteen to seventeen students)
2. Large classes (twenty-two to twenty-six students)
3. Large classes with a teacher's aide

By the end of kindergarten, students taught in smaller classes were about one month ahead of their peers taught in larger classes,[4] while the presence of teachers' aides seemed to have little impact one way or the other. The experiment continued for three more years, with students being taught in whatever kind of class they had been allocated in kindergarten. By the end of second grade, students in smaller classess were three months ahead, and by the end of fourth grade (one year after the experiment had ended), they were six months ahead,[5] with gains of up to twice as much for students from poorer homes and minorities. More important, although some of the advantage of the smaller classes diminished when the students returned to larger classes, students who had been placed in the smaller classes were less likely to need to repeat a grade.[6] They were also more likely, once they got to high school, to take the SAT,[7] which suggests that the educational aspirations of the students had been raised, and they were more likely to graduate high school. Henry Levin and his colleagues estimated that the smaller classes of the STAR study in kindergarten through third grade resulted in an additional eleven out of every one hundred students graduating high school.[8] The fact that the improvements were maintained over such a long period of time is significant, since so many educational interventions, such as Head Start, seem to be successful at first, but then the initial improvements fade out, or even disappear entirely, when the program ends.[9]

For many people, the Tennessee STAR study is conclusive proof of the benefits of class size reduction programs. Unlike many other studies of class size, teachers were randomly allocated to classes, so there was no way that teachers with seniority got to choose their students. And although the results may have been skewed to some extent by the fact that some pushy parents found out about the experiment and managed to get their children moved to the smaller classes, it seems that this did not distort the findings much.

However, in many ways, the Tennessee STAR is an outlier—most other studies of class size reduction programs have found the benefits of reduced class size to be smaller or even nonexistent.[10] So why were the effects of the Tennessee STAR study so different from other class size reduction programs?

Perhaps the most important thing to bear in mind in looking at the Tennessee STAR study, especially in comparison to other similar programs, is that it was relatively small in scale. When class size is reduced, more teachers are needed, and what is important, especially in view of what we saw in chapter 2 about the importance of teacher quality, is how good these extra teachers are. Specifically, were the extra teachers employed as a result of the class size reduction program as good as the ones who were already employed? The Tennessee STAR study involved 76 schools, 330 classrooms, and 6,500 students. Since one-third of the students were placed in standard-sized classes with a teacher's aide, one-third of the students were placed in a standard-sized class with just the teacher, and one-third of the students were placed in smaller classes, only fifty extra teachers were needed for the experiment. It seems plausible that it would be possible to hire an extra fifty teachers who were as good as those already employed.

However, if such a program were implemented across a large district, or a state, it is not at all clear that it would be possible to find sufficient additional teachers who are as good as the ones already teaching. That's why what happened in California in the 1990s provides a valuable lesson.

In 1996, partly as a result of the Tennessee STAR study, the California state legislature enacted legislation that reduced the typical class in the early elementary grades from thirty students to twenty students, at a cost of approximately $1 billion per year (mostly teacher salaries). At each grade where the policy was implemented, the effect was to increase the number of teachers needed by 50 percent (because, for example, a school with 120 students in first grade would previously need only four first-grade teachers and would now need six).

Obviously, this required training a large number of new teachers rapidly. Many new teacher preparation programs were set up, and others were expanded, but even so, it was still necessary to employ a large number of uncertified teachers. In 1990 about one in every two hundred teachers working in California's schools lacked full certification. In 1997, one year after the class size reduction policy was introduced, the figure was one in eight.[11] This is probably the main reason that the benefit of class size reduction in California was only around half as great as was found in the Tennessee STAR study.[12]

Moreover, new and uncertified teachers were not allocated randomly across the state. As Randy Ross pointed out in *Education Week*, many experienced teachers left urban schools to take up newly created positions in more affluent areas.[13] The net effect of class size reduction in California was to reduce average teacher quality across the state and to concentrate those reductions in the schools serving the most disadvantaged students.

This is perhaps the major problem with class-size reduction as a way of improving educational achievement across an educational system—you need a lot more teachers. And unless there are many high-quality teachers not currently working, increasing the number of teachers employed will inevitably reduce the average quality of the teaching force, at least temporarily. This is rather like trying to fill a sink without the plug in. The success of the program depends on whether the extra achievement produced by having smaller classes is more or less than the lower achievement caused by the fact that students will be taught by teachers who are, on average, less effective.

To estimate the impact of class size reduction programs, we need to make assumptions about two things: the increase in student achievement caused by reducing class size and how much teacher quality varies. For the effects of class size reduction, it seems reasonable to assume that the result of having smaller classes would be similar to what was found in the Tennessee STAR study. As for the variability of teacher quality, we can use the estimates from chapter 2.

To describe the effects, it is helpful to categorize our existing teachers into five equal-sized groups: most effective, above average, average, below average, and least effective. When we do the math, we find that if the new teachers are only as good as those in the bottom two categories, then the reduction in teacher quality cancels out the benefits of class size reduction. Where the teachers we are adding are only as good as the least effective teachers, then class size reduction actually lowers student achievement.

On the other hand, if the new teachers hired to staff the extra classes are better than those already working, then the benefits of class size reduction policies will be even greater than found in the Tennessee STAR study. Unfortunately, while there may be some excellent teachers who can't get work, there aren't that many of them. This is why, when class size reduction programs are implemented across a large district or state, the effects are generally small, negligible, or even negative.

There are two further problems with class size reduction programs that suggest they will only ever play a limited role in improving educational achievement. The first is that while the benefits can be substantial for younger children, most studies of class size reduction programs find much smaller and sometimes no effect for older students. The consistent finding across the research studies that have been done on class size reduction is that effects are strongest in grades K to 2, much weaker in grades 3 to 8, and practically nonexistent in grades 9 to 12.

Why this is might not be clear, but there are two reasonably plausible explanations. The first is that the smaller impact of class size reduction programs for older students may just be an artifact of the data. Researchers often report the results of educational interventions in terms of percentiles, as when a new math program is described as moving a student from the 50th percentile to, say, the 56th percentile. This means that if we had one hundred students getting each of the old and the new programs, the average student getting the new program would be better than fifty-six of the students getting the old program. Because children learn at different speeds, as they get older, the range of achievement in a grade gets larger. The amount of extra learning that would be needed to get a student from the 50th percentile to the 60th percentile is therefore greater for older students than younger students. Or, put another way, the same amount of extra learning will produce a smaller percentile increase for older students. While this may partially explain why the benefits of smaller classes are greater for younger children, it is not enough to explain it all. A more convincing explanation has to do with the way that teachers teach.

In elementary schools, particularly in the early grades, teachers work with individual children for much of the time, listening to them read, for example, or working with small groups. It is easy to see that with smaller classes, each individual teacher will be able to spend more time with each student, which will lead to better progress. The Tennessee STAR study found that the teachers assigned to teach smaller classes tended to teach the way they had when they were assigned larger classes, but clearly the extra attention students received was beneficial. In middle schools and high schools, however, teachers spend a much greater proportion of the time standing at the front of the classroom, presenting information and leading whole-class discussions. A teacher standing at the front of the class and talking to a group of twenty isn't going to be very different from a teacher talking to a group of thirty.

As a result, some have argued that, at least for older students, class size reduction programs should be combined with teacher development programs so that teachers can take better advantage of smaller classes, but the evidence here is not particularly convincing. The main conclusion of all the research in this area is that smaller class sizes in kindergarten through first or second grade might get one extra year's achievement across K–12 education but only if the extra teachers being employed are as good as the ones already employed.

The second problem with class size reduction is the cost. As noted above, reducing class size from thirty down to twenty increases the number of teachers needed by 50 percent. If the policy were applied only in kindergarten through second grade, then that would increase the cost of education in the United States by around 12 percent (i.e., an increase of around $60 billion a year). In addition, across the United States, we would need to build an additional two hundred thousand classrooms, at a cost of at least $100,000 each.[14] As a result, many districts and states have tried to keep the costs of class size reduction lower by implementing smaller class size reductions (e.g., from thirty to twenty-five rather than twenty or fifteen). However, evidence from Florida suggests that modest class size reductions of this kind have little or no effect.[15]

Another way to lower the cost of class size reduction programs is to make greater use of teachers' aides. In the Tennessee STAR study, students in standard-sized classrooms (i.e., twenty-two to twenty-five students) made no more progress when the teacher had an assistant than when the teacher was working on his or her own. Since the Tennessee STAR study, a number of other studies have confirmed this finding. For example, a large study of teaching assistants in England found that despite the large sums of money expended on teaching assistants across the country, there was no evidence of increased achievement. Indeed, the study found that students who were assigned to receive one-to-one support from a teaching assistant made less progress than if teaching assistants were not employed.[16]

However, a closer look at what was happening in schools showed that teaching assistants were often being assigned to students with special educational needs. In other words, the people with the least amount of training were being assigned to work with the students with the most profound and complex needs. It is not, therefore, too surprising that, in such circumstances, teaching assistants had little impact on student achievement.

In recent years, a number of studies have explored the use of teaching assistants in more thoughtful ways, and they have produced more promising results. For example, one program in which teaching assistants worked with groups of three to five kindergarten students on basic reading activities found that students made two to three months' more progress than other students.[17] Most recently, a 2016 study of elementary schools in North Carolina found that smaller classes improved student achievement in third-, fourth-, and fifth-grade classrooms. And while teaching assistants were not as effective as fully certified teachers, given their lower cost, they provided good value for the money, especially in reading instruction.[18]

## Conclusion

Taking all these findings together, the cost of reducing class size to fifteen students may well be justified in kindergarten through second grade, even with the additional construction costs that would be incurred, provided that any additional staff recruited are as effective as existing staff. The research also suggests that rather than reducing class size for all activities, it may be beneficial to employ teaching assistants, especially for reading instruction.

It's too soon to estimate the impact of the latest studies on student achievement across the whole of schooling, but it seems that smaller classes in early elementary school could produce an extra year of progress by the time students graduate high school. More important, because smaller classes appear to be especially effective for students from disadvantaged backgrounds and minorities, class size reduction programs can help in closing the gap in achievement between the most advantaged students and their less advantaged peers. Smaller classes would also probably improve teacher morale.[19] It is worth noting, however, that this approach seems to suffer from diminishing returns. We would be increasing our educational expenditure by around 12 percent (ignoring the construction costs) for a 4 to 8 percent increase in the rate of learning. Class size reduction programs have a role to play in increasing student achievement but on their own will not be anything near enough.

---

1   National Education Association (2008).

2   Hanushek (1999).

3   Mosteller (1995, p. 113).

4   The estimates of the effects of class-size reduction quoted here are based on Mosteller (1995) and have been converted into months of learning using the estimates of annual growth provided in Bloom et al. (2008).

5   Grissmer (1999); Molnar, Smith, Zahorik, Palmer, Halbach, and Ehrle (1999).

6   Pate-Bain, Boyd-Zaharias, Cain, Word, and Binkley (1997).

7   Krueger and Whitmore (2001).

8    Levin et al. (2007).

9    Puma et al. (2012).

10   Hanushek (1999).

11   Jepsen and Rivkin (2002).

12   Stecher and Bohrnstedt (2002).

13   Ross (1999).

14   This is based on estimates provided by Abramson (2016), which suggest a cost of $29,629 per student for elementary school construction.

15   Nyhan and Alkadry (1999).

16   Blatchford, Basset, Brown, Martin, Russell, and Webster (2009).

17   McNally, Ruiz-Valenzuela, and Rolfe (2016).

18   Clotfelter, Hemelt, and Ladd (2016).

19   See, for example, Glass, Cahen, Smith, and Filby (1982, p. 65).

CHAPTER 6

# Copying Other Countries

In January 1965, Admiral Hyman G. Rickover, who had directed the development of nuclear propulsion for the US Navy, published a widely syndicated newspaper article questioning the value of education in US schools. In the article, he claimed that "the educational value of a school year in Europe is at least a third higher than in America."[1] Although he published no evidence in support of this claim, at the time he wrote the article, the analysis of the results from the first international comparison of student achievement in mathematics had just begun.[2] Fifty years later, the idea of comparing the achievement of students from different countries has grown into a multimillion-dollar industry.

From the outset, these studies did more than just provide rankings of the relative success of students in different countries in mathematics, science, and reading. They also sought to find explanations for differences, by looking at differences in how countries funded, organized, and ran their schools.

While such studies certainly provide lots of data for researchers to analyze, whether they can provide sound guidance for improving education systems is not clear, for at least four reasons.

First, different tests produce very different results. While performance of the United States on the PISA tests developed by the OECD is modest, American students do much better on tests developed by the International Association for the Evaluation of Educational Achievement (IEA).

Second, some countries perform very well in these international comparisons because the sample of students who take the test is not representative of the whole country.

Third, even when countries do select representative samples of students to participate, if they do well, it is very hard to figure out which particular factors about the education system of that country were responsible for the success.

Fourth, even when we can be clear about the reasons for a particular country's success, it is far from clear whether the same solutions could be implemented effectively in the United States.

Comparisons of the performances of US students with those of other countries can provide useful insights into the challenges we face. However, simple pronouncements that we should be copying Finland, or China, or Singapore, or whatever country leads the latest international survey will do nothing to help American children learn more in schools.

Hardly a week goes by without some newspaper report claiming that the performance of US students lags behind that of other countries. Many implications are drawn from such comparisons including claims that we need to match or even surpass the educational achievements of our industrial competitors, that the reasons for other countries' successes are obvious, and that if we don't do what these other countries are doing, then the United States will become a poorer country.

Such claims certainly contain some elements of truth, but in this chapter, I want to try to tease out what is true and what is false—or at least wildly speculative—about such claims. And to do that, we need to be clear about whether performance in other countries really is higher than that in the United States, whether we can identify the reasons for the higher achievement in other countries, and whether the things that are working in other countries would work if they were implemented in the United States.

## Are Other Countries Doing Better Than the United States?

The first thing to say is that the picture of American education that is provided by international comparisons depends a lot on which international comparisons are used. Probably the best known is the Programme for International Student Assessment, or PISA, which administers tests of reading, math, and science to students every three years in a range of countries. While the earliest survey in 2000 involved only twenty-eight countries, the latest survey, in 2015, had students from around seventy countries participating (depending on what you count as a country).[3]

A quick look at the United States' scores on PISA is rather depressing, with scores stagnant or declining over the last fifteen years. The international average score in each of the three subjects tested (math, reading, science) is 500. Over the last fifteen years, US scores are down from 504 to 497 in reading, down from 493 to 470 in math, and approximately flat in science, with scores just below the international average. However, there is another series of international comparisons that focuses on math and science, called Trends in Mathematics and Science Study, or TIMSS,[4] and the United States' results on TIMSS tell a rather different story.

Unlike PISA, which focuses exclusively on fifteen-year-olds, TIMSS looks at student achievement in math and science at fourth and eighth grades. There is also a survey for twelfth graders, but that is less useful for international comparisons, because in many countries, enrollment beyond tenth grade is much lower than it is in the United States.

The big-picture story from TIMSS is that performance in math and science in the United States is good and getting steadily better, at both fourth grade and eighth grade. If we compare the United States' performance in 2015 with its performance in 2003, then at fourth grade, students are now performing six months higher in math and three months higher in science.[5] At eighth grade, the improvement is smaller—three extra months in math and one extra month in science—but things are definitely getting better.

In a similar vein, the Progress in International Reading Literacy Study (PIRLS), which is administered by the same organization as TIMSS, paints a broadly positive story about student achievement in reading in the United States. To date, there have been four administrations of PIRLS, in 2001, 2006, 2011, and 2016. US fourth graders have performed well above the international average during that period, scoring 542 in 2001 and 549 in the most recent round. PIRLS includes more developing countries than PISA, so the international average of 500 does not represent the same standard in reading achievement in the two programs.

Many journalists report rankings rather than scores, which makes little sense, because the number of countries participating changes over time—being tenth out of seventy countries is a lot better than being tenth out of twenty countries. As far as TIMSS is concerned, the big picture is that the United States' scores are improving at about the same rate as other countries, so the rank has stayed roughly the same. In PIRLS, the trend is flat—in 2011, US fourth graders scored 541 (eleventh out of forty-eight participating countries) and in 2016 scored 549 (fifteenth out of fifty).

In an interesting aside, in 2011, the State of Florida participated in PIRLS as part of a separate benchmarking exercise, and the average score of fourth graders in Florida's public schools was 569, which was not significantly different from Hong Kong, the highest-performing system in PIRLS. In other words, fourth graders in Florida, which is one jurisdiction in the United States, performed at the same level as fourth graders in Hong Kong, which is one jurisdiction within China.

Those who want to claim that things are getting worse will focus on the PISA results, and those who want to claim that things are good or getting better will choose the TIMSS or PIRLS results as being more representative. But which is correct? Steady improvement or stagnation?

The answer is both, or neither, depending on your perspective. The tests used in TIMSS and PIRLS tend to focus on the basics of the subjects students are learning (algorithms and facts in math, decoding in reading) while the PISA tests focus on students' ability to apply their skills in real-world contexts. The United States may be doing relatively well on TIMSS and PIRLS because those tests are a better match for the kinds of learning that is emphasized in American schools. American students do less well when they are tested on things that require background knowledge and conceptual understanding.

For example, one of the sample science questions released by the OECD for the 2015 survey is shown below:[6]

> Most migratory birds gather in one area and then migrate in large groups rather than individually.
>
> This behaviour is a result of evolution.
>
> Which of the following is the best scientific explanation for the evolution of this behaviour in most migratory birds?
>
> > A. Birds that migrated individually or in small groups were less likely to survive and have offspring.
> >
> > B. Birds that migrated individually or in small groups were more likely to find adequate food.
> >
> > C. Flying in large groups allowed other bird species to join the migration.
> >
> > D. Flying in large groups allowed each bird to have a better chance of finding a nesting site.

Although this looks like a question on a scientific topic—evolution—students who are well-read have a good chance of answering the question even if they haven't actually studied the topic. You don't have to know anything about bird migration to realize that option (B) is arguing for the opposite of the correct conclusion and option (D) makes no sense, given that the larger the group, the less likely the group would be to find a nesting place for all the birds. You probably need to know a little bit about bird migration to know that birds tend not to have multiple species in the same flock, but even if you know nothing about bird migration, just using reading ability and basic reasoning has increased the chance of a guess getting you the right answer from 25 percent to 50 percent.

It is likely the OECD realizes this, because they describe their tests as tests of reading literacy, mathematical literacy, and scientific literacy, but the fact remains that items such as this are not testing the kind of disciplinary knowledge of science and mathematics that are assessed in the more traditional tests used in TIMSS. In this context, it is interesting to note that in 2005, professors of mathematics in

Finland were complaining that although Finnish students were getting high scores in PISA, the performance of Finnish eighteen-year-olds in the university entrance examinations in mathematics were declining, and universities were having to run remedial classes for college students.[7]

Ultimately, of course we want high scores on both TIMSS and PISA. We want students to learn the mathematics and science they are being taught in school, and we want them to be able to apply this knowledge to solve novel problems. But as we shall see in chapter 9, it may well be that it is better to start with strong disciplinary knowledge and then learn to apply it, rather than trying to learn content matter while applying it to real-world problems.

So, the United States may not be doing as badly as many people claim and may, in fact, be doing quite well, but of course, the argument of this book is that no matter how well we are doing, even if our students are the best in the world, they still need to be even better. The question then is can we learn how to improve our education system by looking at other countries? The answer is yes, but only if we are very careful.

One reason to be cautious about international comparisons of reading performance is that the relationship between written and spoken words is very simple in some languages and very complex in others. Obviously, character-based languages such as Chinese or Japanese have a very complex relationship between what is written and how it is spoken, but even alphabet-based languages vary greatly in the relationship between letters and sounds. If you come across the word *quay* in a text, you may think that you do not know what it means, unless you realize that the word is pronounced *key* in many parts of the United States. This kind of thing never happens in Finnish, where once you know the sounds of the letters, you pretty much know how any word is pronounced. In other words, even the basic process of reading is harder in some languages and easier in others.

A second problem that arises in making comparisons across countries is that it is very difficult to ensure that test questions are the same in different languages. One way to ensure that translated tests are equivalent to the original is through *back translation*: translate the test, then translate the translation back into the original language. If you get the same as where you started from, then you can be pretty sure that the translation is faithful to the original. However, this does not prove the items are equivalent.

For example, the word *similar* is used in math to describe two triangles that have the same angles but not necessarily the same length sides. The problem is that the word *similar* is used in English to describe things that merely resemble each other. Many English-speaking students, when asked whether two triangles are similar, respond on the basis of whether they resemble each other, without looking at whether the angles are identical. In many other languages, the word used in math classrooms to describe this relationship is only ever encountered in math classrooms, so students know that they are being asked a mathematical question and therefore respond mathematically. Students taking the test in English tend to get lower scores on questions about similar triangles because the word means more things in English.[8] And yet, a back translation of this item from one language to another, and then back again, would suggest that the two versions are perfectly equivalent.

A third problem in comparing students' performance in different countries comes from the fact that in some countries, it is often difficult to get a representative sample of students. In many countries, students who are not successful at school are able to leave before the age of fifteen, so when samples of school students are taken, the lowest achievers are missing. Even when students are in school, getting a representative sample of students is still challenging. For example, the first international surveys looked at students in particular grades, but this leads to difficulties in making sense of the results for countries that make students repeat a grade if they haven't made enough progress to be ready for the next grade (a practice sometimes called *grade retention*). By the age of fifteen, in France, Germany, and many other countries, up to 25 percent will have repeated a grade by the time they finish middle school. If we survey all the students in eighth grade in France or Germany, we would not get a representative sample of fourteen-year-olds because the lowest-achieving fourteen-year-olds will still be in seventh or even sixth grade. Countries that practice social promotion—moving students on to the next grade irrespective of their achievement—will therefore appear to have lower achievement. The earliest international comparisons focused on sampling students from particular grades, so countries that retained students, like Germany, appeared to be highly effective. When later surveys sampled students from a particular age group (e.g., all fourteen-year-olds), the results were much lower and resulted, in Germany at least, in a phenomenon that was labeled *PISA shock* and prompted much national debate and soul-searching.

Whether samples are representative is a particular issue when looking at the performance of students in China. In 2012, the province of Shanghai posted the best results in the world in reading, math, and science (570, 613, and 580, respectively). Why the OECD allowed these scores to be published in the country rankings is somewhat of a mystery. The state of Massachusetts had enough students participating in PISA to allow a reliable score to be calculated for the state and, with a population of around 6.7 million, is larger than many countries participating in PISA, such as Finland (5.5 million), Scotland (5.3 million), and New Zealand (4.4 million). Had it been listed separately, Massachusetts would have ranked ninth in the world. Moreover, Chinese students outside Shanghai participated in PISA.[9] Had these results been published, the results for Shanghai could have been placed in some kind of context, but the Chinese authorities have never allowed the results to be released. Whatever the reason, since 2009, results for Shanghai have been published as if Shanghai were a country rather than a rather unrepresentative region of China. The real problem, however, is that the posted results are not even representative of Shanghai, let alone the rest of China.

All citizens in mainland China are required by law to be registered as residents of a particular area, and the record of this registration is called a *hukou*. One of the most important consequences of the *hukou* system in modern China[10] is that it restricts internal migration and particularly migration from rural to urban areas, since it is difficult—and quite often impossible—to obtain government services in a province other than that of one's *hukou*, which generally does not change throughout one's life, no matter where one lives (although some provinces are trying to introduce some changes to the system).

This puts parents from rural areas who move to Shanghai for better jobs in a difficult situation. If they bring their children with them, they will not be able to take the national university entrance examination, called the *gaokao*. The result is that many manual laborers who move to Shanghai for work do not bring their children with them—they remain in the home province living with grandparents. If migrant workers do bring their children with them, they will either have to pay often unaffordable fees for their children to attend government schools (and that's only if you can get a school to agree to admit the children) or find places in private schools, which are more affordable but generally of low quality. According to the OECD's own statistics, only around 73 percent of the fifteen-year-olds in Shanghai were sampled for the 2012 PISA survey. If those who were missing scored around 400 (which is reasonable given that, even if they are attending schools, they are likely to be of rather poor quality), then Shanghai's real score would be over fifty points lower. It is also worth noting that Shanghai may not even be representative of other large metropolitan regions in China, let alone the whole country. In the 2015 PISA survey, mainland China was represented by Beijing, Jiangsu, and Guangdong in addition to Shanghai, and the average score across these four provinces was 514—a creditable performance, but seventy-four points lower than Shanghai's average across reading, math, and science three years earlier (for comparison, the gap between the United States and Mexico is also around seventy-four points).

The main conclusion here is that while the results from countries like Singapore, the Republic of Korea, Finland, and other rich countries can probably be trusted as being reliable guides to the achievement of fifteen-year-olds, for other countries—and China, in particular—there are real doubts about the meaningfulness of results on survey tests such as PISA. Unless we can be sure that all fifteen-year-olds have an equal chance of being asked to take the test—whether they are in school or not—we should be skeptical. Moreover, even when the results of a particular country can be trusted, even when it is clear that student achievement in that country is high, it is really hard to determine the reasons for that success.

## If Other Countries Are Doing Better, Can We Figure Out Why?

Whenever a new set of international results is published, there is no shortage of people claiming they know exactly why certain countries get high scores and other countries get low scores. The problem is that these claims are little more than speculation, and many are just plain wrong.

Perhaps the most common mistake that people make is assuming that the reason for a country's success (or lack of it) can be determined by looking at what is currently happening in the country. Students taking the PISA tests are fifteen years old, so the tests are assessing the cumulative impact of eight to ten years of education. The quality of that education will be influenced by policy decisions made much earlier—possibly as many as twenty years ago. If we want to learn from the countries that are currently successful, we should be looking at what those countries were doing twenty years ago, not what they are doing now. In this regard, Finland is a particularly instructive example.

In the first PISA survey in 2000, Finland topped the international league table with a score of 546 in reading and did pretty well in math (536) and science (538). Averaged across the three subjects, they were the highest-performing country in the West (540), outscored only by Japan (543), Hong Kong (542), and Korea (541).[11]

In the second survey in 2003, Finland did even better, posting the highest scores of any country in reading (543), scoring 544 in math (only Hong Kong with 550 scored higher), and tying Japan for the highest scores in science (548).[12] Averaged across the three subjects, Finland scored higher than every single other country participating in PISA.

When, in 2006, Finland managed to improve even further on these already impressive levels of performance, politicians all over the world began to take notice. Finland's average achievement across reading, math, and science was again the highest in the world (553), outscoring every country in science (563), joint top with Korea in math (548), and second only to Korea in reading (547 and 556, respectively).

However, just as people were traveling to Finland to understand the reasons behind what many people were calling the *Finnish miracle*,[13] things began to unravel in Finland. Over the last ten years, Finland's performance across reading, math, and science has gone down steadily. A lot. In the next three PISA surveys, Finland's scores went down from a high of 553 in 2006 to 539, then to 529, and most recently, to 523 (in 2015).

I have chosen to focus on Finland not out of any sense of delight at their declining scores. Indeed, despite these declining scores, Finland may well still have the most efficient education system in the world, because each week, their fifteen-year-olds get only around twenty-four hours of instruction and spend only twelve hours on out-of-school studying (i.e., homework), whereas in many Pacific Rim countries, they spend over 45 forty-five hours studying each week.[14] The reason I draw attention to the decline in results is to point out that the extremely high levels of achievement that Finland demonstrated in 2003 and 2006 were probably the result of policy decisions made in the late 1980s and early 1990s. Anyone who visited Finland in 2006 was learning about things that were probably lowering student achievement, not raising it.

Another kind of problem is caused by focusing only on companies or systems that are successful, as is often the case in management books such as Jim Collins's *From Good to Great*. As Jay Greene, professor of education reform at the University of Arkansas, points out, this doesn't really help us identify what, exactly, is causing that success.

> The fundamental flaw of a "best practices" approach, as any student in a half-decent research-design course would know, is that it suffers from what is called "selection on the dependent variable." If you only look at successful organizations, then you have no variation in the dependent variable: they all have good outcomes. When you look at the things that successful organizations are doing, you have no idea whether each one of those things caused the good outcomes, had no effect on success, or was actually an impediment that held organizations back from being even more successful. An appropriate research design would have variation in the dependent variable; some have good outcomes and some have bad ones. To identify factors that contribute to good outcomes, you would, at a minimum, want to see those factors more likely to be present where there was success and less so where there was not.[15]

A related problem is cherry-picking the data—including the cases that support your argument and ignoring those that don't. In many of the countries that score well on international comparisons, teaching is a highly esteemed profession, and competition to get into teacher preparation programs is intense. In both Singapore and Finland, there are ten applicants for every place in a teacher preparation program. The smartest people in the country want to be teachers, so, the argument goes, that must be the reason their results are so good.

Except that there are countries that don't fit. Getting into a teacher preparation program in Ireland is as tough as it is in Finland or Singapore. There are universities in Ireland where it is tougher to get into the teacher preparation program than it is to get into medical school. They really do have people who end up as doctors because they weren't good enough to be elementary school teachers. And yet while Ireland's results are above average, they are nothing like what you would expect if the key to improving education was getting the smartest people in the country to want to be teachers, which is often the claim that is made about Finland and Singapore.

In a similar vein, some commentators claim that the most successful countries group students by ability (Singapore), while others claim that they do not (Finland). We are told that the key to a high-performing education system is teacher autonomy (the Netherlands), while others point to the importance of central control (Singapore). Those who like high-stakes testing will claim that Canada, and specifically Alberta, is the system to copy, while those who oppose such standardized assessment will identify with Finland. The simple truth is that we have too many variables and not enough countries for this kind of approach ever to yield much in the way of useful insights.

What we can do, however, is look for things that we know affect how much students learn and see if there are any systematic differences in these factors between the more successful and the less successful countries. One obvious factor is the time students spend studying.

The number of hours that students spend studying each week is remarkably similar across most rich countries. Journalists routinely report that Finland's students spend less time studying at school than other countries, but at 24.2 hours a week, a typical Finnish student's working week is not that much shorter than that of a student in the United States (27.7 hours a week)—about forty minutes a day. Finding out how much time students spend studying outside school is more difficult. What is harder still is finding out what students are doing in this extra time. Most published studies do not distinguish between homework and formal supplementary instruction outside school time. They also rely on students' self-reports about how much time they are studying, which are notoriously inaccurate.

The data are therefore far from ideal, but the broad picture is that on average, students in the Far East spend a similar amount of time studying as students in the United States. Combining in-school and out-of-school study time, US fifteen-year-olds spend about forty-eight hours each week studying, compared with fifty in Korea, forty-eight in Taiwan, forty-six in Hong Kong, and fifty-one in Singapore. The outliers are Finland (thirty-six hours), Japan (forty-one hours), and, at the other extreme, the four Chinese provinces participating in PISA (Beijing, Guangdong, Jiangsu, and Shanghai), where students spend fifty-seven hours studying each week.

The number of hours students spend studying is less important than how this time is spent, especially for out-of-school study. For example, as a result of China's one-child policy, parents invest much more heavily in ensuring their child gets the best possible education, and, in Shanghai, like many other parts of the Far East, this means private tuition and supplementary schooling. Employers who move factories to China may not care whether the high levels of achievement in Shanghai's workers are the result of better schools or parental investment in education; if the students have the skills, who cares how they got them? But if we want to learn the reasons for these high levels of achievement, we had better be sure we are looking at the right things, and it is clear that private tuition and supplementary schools are a significant element in the success of many countries on the western rim of the Pacific Ocean. In Korea, for example, one estimate suggests that without the effects of private tuition and supplementary schools, achievement would be below that of the United States.[16]

Finally, it is worth noting that cultural factors have a large effect on education achievement. John Jerrim looked at the scores obtained by Australian students on PISA and found that Australian children of Chinese heritage actually scored higher than those in Shanghai.[17] It seems that it was not the education system students attended that was the key ingredient in their success. Rather it was the "tiger mothers" who made sure that homework and violin practice were done before their children were allowed anywhere near their computer games or TV.

## Even If We Figure Out Why Other Countries Do Well, Could We Do It Here?

From the foregoing, it should be clear that it is hard, and may in fact be impossible, to identify exactly why some countries perform better than others in international comparisons such as PISA, TIMSS, and PIRLS. But there is an even greater problem with trying to improve education by copying other countries, and that is that even if we are right about the reasons for a country's success, whether the same success could be reproduced in another country is far from clear.

Pasi Sahlberg is a visiting professor at Harvard University. He was at one time the chief inspector of schools in Finland, until the Finnish government decided that schools did not need such surveillance. He now spends much of his time dispelling myths about why Finland's fifteen-year-olds did so well on international comparisons like PISA.

He acknowledges the benefits of having teaching as a high-status profession, which makes it easier to get high-quality teachers. He also realizes that the fact that Finnish is written as it is pronounced makes it easier for young children to learn to read. But in his view, probably the main reason that Finland does so well in education is that Finns are voracious readers, they take out more library books, own more books, and read more newspapers than any other country.

> Reading is part of our culture. At one time, you couldn't marry unless you could read. If you belonged to the Lutheran state church, you had to go to camp for two weeks before confirmation, as I did. I had to read the Bible and other religious books to the priest and answer questions to show I understood them. Only then could I be confirmed and only if I was confirmed could I get a license to marry in church. That is still the case. Now, of course, you can get married anywhere, but 50 years ago there were very few options other than marrying in church and, 100 years ago, none at all.[18]

He is also skeptical that Finland's teachers would be effective if they worked in the United States. He imagines what would happen if a group of Finnish teachers who were fluent in English spent five years teaching in the United States.

> Education policies in Indiana and many other states in the United States create a context for teaching that limits (Finnish) teachers to use their skills, wisdom and shared knowledge for the good of their students' learning. Actually, I have met some experienced Finnish-trained teachers in the United States who confirm this hypothesis. Based on what I have heard from them, it is also probable that many of those transported Finnish teachers would be already doing something else than teaching by the end of their fifth year—quite like their American peers.[19]

While comparing the performance of different countries does not provide much in the way of clues to improving educational performance, there is actually one common factor in those countries that are doing well, and that is stability in the political control of education.

In Finland in the late 1960s, there was an often-acrimonious debate about whether postelementary education should be comprehensive, with all students in a locality going to the same school, or whether the selective system then in force, with students being directed to academic or vocational schools, should be retained. In the end, the arguments in favor of a comprehensive system prevailed, and comprehensive schooling was adopted as policy. But perhaps the most interesting thing that happened subsequently was that those who had lost the argument *agreed that they had lost the argument.* Since the 1970s, there has been broad agreement—even consensus—that schooling should be comprehensive. This means that over the last forty years, schools, administrators, and teachers have been allowed to get on with improving education free from political interference.

Similar political stability appears to be a significant factor in the success of Singapore, Hong Kong, Taiwan, and Korea. But if this really is the key to educational improvement, then it is clear that looking at other countries will have little relevance to the United States, because the kind of political stability enjoyed by these countries is unlikely to be achieved here. Although education is meant to be an issue reserved for the states, school districts and states increasingly rely on federal funding to balance their books, and so as power changes hands in Washington, states have to change their priorities. In a similar vein, changes of power at the state level require districts to change what they are doing, and changes in school board composition change policies directly at the school level. We need to find coherent policies that can survive changes in local, state, and federal governments and thus have some chance of being effective over the medium to long term. Looking at other countries may give us ideas. It will never provide us with solutions.

## Conclusion

Looking at how other countries are doing has a valuable role to play in helping us decide what to do to improve education in the United States. We can look at how different factors contribute to, or detract from, student success. We can look at the educational experiments that other countries conduct and see whether the successes might be replicated here. We can also examine whether a failure might have been averted if certain features of the reform had been changed. But the main message of this chapter is that we have to be very careful in doing this because of three main reasons. First, countries that appear to be successful may not be as successful as they seem. Second, even if they are successful, it is not easy, and may in fact be impossible, to determine why the country was successful. Third, even when we are sure of the reasons for a country's success, it may not be possible to reproduce the circumstances that led to that success. Looking at what other countries are doing has its place, but the solutions will have to be home-grown.

---

1  Rickover (1965, p. 16).

2  Husén (1967).

3  It might seem odd to give an approximate figure here, but there are many sensitivities around what counts as a country in PISA. Kosovo participated in 2015, but as of December 1, 2016, was recognized by only 110 of the 193 members of the United Nations. Shanghai participated in 2012, and in 2015 was joined by students from Beijing, Jiangsu, and Guangdong provinces, but Hong Kong and Macau are listed separately, and Taiwan appears as "Chinese Taipei." Macedonia has participated in every PISA, but due to a deadlocked dispute with Greece, is described as "The former Yugoslav Republic of Macedonia." Because of these sensitivities, PISA tends to refer to the performance of jurisdictions rather than countries.

4  TIMSS originally stood for "Third International Mathematics and Science Study," which followed the First International Mathematics Study in the 1960s and the Second International Mathematics Study (1980–1982). Realizing that a fourth such study would have the same initials as the first, the International Association for the Evaluation of Educational Achievement (the organization administering the surveys) decided to change the meaning of the initials to "Trends in Mathematics and Science Study."

5  These estimates are based on the TIMSS assumptions that the standard deviation of student achievement is 100 points and that one year's growth is around 0.4 standard deviations, as estimated by Rodriguez (2004).

6  Downloaded from http://www.bbc.com/news/uk-wales-38147860 on December 5, 2016.

7   Astala, Kivelä, Koskela, Martio, Näätänen, and Tarvainen (2005).

8   For more on the issue of whether tests can ever really be translated from one language to another, see Wiliam (2008).

9   Loveless (2013).

10  The system is actually called the *huji* system, with a *hukou* being an individual record within the *huji* system, but the term *hukou* is now widely used to describe the system as well as an individual record.

11  Programme for International Student Assessment (2001).

12  Programme for International Student Assessment (2004).

13  See, for example, Bonsall (2015).

14  Organisation for Economic Co-operation and Development (2016b).

15  Greene (2012, p. 72).

16  Choi (2012).

17  Jerrim (2014).

18  Wilby (2013).

19  Sahlberg (2013).

CHAPTER 7

# Expanding School Choice

Parents in the United States have less choice about the schools their children attend than those in many other rich countries, and therefore, it is not surprising that expanding school choice has been widely advocated as a way of improving student achievement. In many rich countries, religious organizations play a major role in elementary and secondary education, but in the United States, the constitutional requirement for the separation of church and state makes greater involvement of religious organizations much more difficult. As a result, attention has focused on two main mechanisms for increasing parents' choices in how their children are educated: charter schools and vouchers.

A total of forty-three states, and the District of Columbia, permit the establishment of charter schools, but the laws governing the establishment, operation, and funding of charter schools vary greatly from state to state. As a result, US charter schools are very diverse, and comparing their performance to traditional public schools is difficult.

The best evidence that we have suggests that the initial enthusiasm for charter schools resulted in more concern for creating new charter schools than for how effective they would be, and many states, for many years, gave little thought to how less effective charter schools might be closed. The result was that for the first twenty years of their operation charter schools on average probably reduced student achievement slightly across the United States—about half of all charter schools performed about as well as comparable traditional public schools, about one-third performed worse, and about one-sixth performed better. However, as states became more effective in closing less effective schools, the quality of charter schools across the United States has improved. Currently, performances of students in charter schools and comparable traditional public schools are similar, with charter schools perhaps performing slightly better.

However, it is important to note that the most effective chains of charter schools are part of charter management organizations (CMOs) that are very careful to maintain the quality of their schools, and none of these CMOs are contemplating rapid expansion of their schools. Charter schools may offer parents greater choices in how their children are educated, but their impact on national levels of educational achievement over the next fifty years will be too small to detect.

The other widely advocated mechanism for expanding school choice is to give parents vouchers for the cost of educating their child in a public school, which the parents can then use to offset the cost of attendance at a private school or to support home tuition. Because students attending private schools are not required to take state-mandated tests, good evidence on the performance of students in private schools is limited. However, the evidence that we do have suggests that while some private schools are exceptionally good, many are not, and the same student would probably learn more in a typical public school than a typical private school. Neither charter schools nor educational vouchers are likely to have much impact on average levels of educational achievement in the foreseeable future.

Within the United States, over the last thirty years or so, one of the most widely promoted and widely adopted mechanisms for attempting to increase student achievement has been to give parents more choice in the schools their children attend.

To many observers from outside the United States, the reaction to these developments is, "What took you so long?" For those living in other countries, one of the most surprising things about education in America is how little choice most parents have in the school their children attend, unless of course they are willing to pay to send their child to a private school. In the Netherlands and the Republic of Ireland, more than half of all students attend government-supported private schools, and such schools are a significant part of the education landscape in Australia, Denmark, Korea, Luxembourg, and Spain. In other countries, such as England and Sweden, the majority of schools are supported by government funding, but parents are still given substantial choice about which schools their children attend.

The idea of giving parents choice about which schools their children attend is attractive on many levels. Of course, home schooling is an option in all fifty states of the United States, but the regulations vary considerably from state to state, and the Supreme Court has consistently upheld the rights of states to regulate home schooling.[1] Moreover, no state grants to parents the right to opt out of paying taxes solely on the grounds that they are not making use of public schools. For many, perhaps most, parents, home schooling is not an option because of time and cost.

Many people believe that governments should not be telling parents how or where their children should be educated. Some parents want to ensure that the education their children receive is consistent with their religious or other beliefs. Others may wish to choose a school that can meet their child's particular interests or needs. And of course, there is a widespread belief that competition improves performance, so if schools have to compete for students, by offering parents what they want, schools will improve.

However, two features of the organization of education in the United States have made it difficult to provide parents with genuine choice in the public schools their children attend. The first is a widespread belief that education should be funded primarily from local taxes, and specifically, from property taxes.[2] The second is that American school districts are, in terms of population at least, small. Of the 13,491 school districts that existed in the United States in 2014, around 20 percent enrolled fewer than three hundred students, and 85 percent enrolled fewer than five thousand students.[3] These two reasons are, of course, related. Funding schools from local taxes provides taxpayers with a relatively greater say in how their schools are run, and this influence would be weakened in larger districts.

The small size of many American school districts means that many have just a single high school, a single middle school, and perhaps four to six elementary schools. Providing parents with a choice of middle school or high school would entail sending students to a different school district. Districts are, understandably, reluctant to provide education for students from another district unless those students come with extra cash, and districts are reluctant to fund schools in other districts, even if those other districts are educating students for whom the district would have to pay to educate somewhere. In this context, it is worth noting that in England, parents can choose to send their children to any public school that will take them, and if the school is in another district, the district where the family lives has to send the district receiving the child the money they would have spent on the education of the child had she or he attended a school in the district in which they lived. While many states allow districts to choose to participate in such schemes, only a few, such as Colorado and Florida, mandate that funding must follow the student.

At the elementary level, choice is generally easier to provide than at the secondary level, but even there, due to the low population densities of many American school districts, sending your child to any school other than the nearest one may entail having your child spend an extra hour or more traveling each day. But there is a more fundamental problem with school choice as a way to improve education, and that is that the differences between schools are much smaller than people imagine.

## How Much of a Difference Do Good Schools Make?

At the Julia R. Masterman School, a public school in Philadelphia, the average composite score on the ACT in 2015 was 29.[4] This means that in 2015 the *average* student at this school had a shot at getting into an Ivy League college.[5] At West Philadelphia High School, in the same district, the average score was 14. Only one in every five hundred students here reached the same level as the *average* student at Masterman.[6] The SAT scores tell a similar story. At Masterman, the students averaged 650 in reading and 678 in math (the highest in the whole of Pennsylvania). At West Philadelphia, the scores were 348 and 344, respectively.

So Masterman must be a much better school, right? Could be. But before we draw any conclusions about the quality of the two schools, we need a little more information. And the most important thing to know about Masterman is that it is a magnet school, with a highly selective admissions policy. In fact, students have to score in the top 12 percent of their age cohort even to be considered for a place.

In the United States, this is particularly important because many people seem to believe that schools that get good results must be good schools. Newspapers and magazines print lists of top schools, realtors quote SAT scores when extolling the virtues of particular neighborhoods, and schools are pilloried when half of their students are not reading at grade level. But before we can make sense of a school's results, we need to know about the students going to that school. Many schools that get good results are not particularly effective at teaching, but they are very good at recruiting smart students. And many schools that appear to be doing terribly are in fact making extraordinary progress with their students.

As a result of the groundbreaking work of Betty Hart and Todd Risley, we now know that there are enormous differences in how well children are prepared for school. Over two and a half years, Hart and Risley and their colleagues spent an hour each week in the homes of forty-two Kansas families with a young child. During that hour, they recorded every word spoken between parent and child. What they found was that, by the age of three, in the most affluent homes, adults had spoken around 35 million words to their children. In the families of those on welfare, the figure was 10 million—a 25 million–word gap.[7] Clearly, if a school is recruiting students from affluent families, they are going to find it a lot easier to ensure students are reading at grade level than if they have a substantial number of children from families on welfare. This is why choosing a school on the basis of test scores makes no sense at all. It is like choosing to have open-heart surgery in a local clinic because no one has died there recently.

In fact, the comparison with hospitals is instructive. While some people believe that publishing mortality statistics for hospitals is useful, there are two major problems with doing so. The first is that the results can be misleading. A specialist hospital may have high mortality rates because it is the hospital of last resort; it takes patients who are so sick that less specialized hospitals cannot do anything for them. And another hospital might claim that it has the lowest mortality rates in the state but only because it didn't accept any patients who were really sick. High mortality rates may just indicate that hospitals take a lot of people when they are very unwell. The second problem is that publishing raw mortality statistics can lead doctors to refuse to take on patients for whom the outcomes are not promising. That is why most systems for making public mortality statistics on hospitals available to the public use what are called *risk-adjusted mortality rates*. The mortality statistics for a hospital are adjusted to take into account how sick the patients were when they were admitted.

And when we do something similar for schools, we find that American schools are remarkably similar. American schools differ greatly in the achievement of their students, but they also vary greatly in the achievement of the students when they *started* at the school and how much support they get from parents and caregivers. When we look at the numbers, it turns out that the most important factor in a school's results is how much the students knew when they started at the school. In fact, the *school effect* for American schools is around 8 percent.[8] That means that around 8 percent of the variation in test scores that students get depends on the school they go to, while the other 92 percent is outside the school's control.

Another way to think about this is by considering the likelihood that a student would achieve a certain threshold such as reaching proficient on a state test, passing an end-of-course examination in algebra, or getting a score of 4 or higher on the Advanced Placement examination. There is no point comparing the most effective and least effective schools because they aren't usually alternatives—the most effective school could be at one end of the state and the least effective at the other. And, of course, in rural areas, there is usually no choice at all. However, for the sake of illustration, let us consider parents who have a choice of five schools that are within reasonable traveling distance of their home. If they could, with twenty-twenty hindsight, pick the school that in retrospect would have been the most effective school for their child, it turns out that that will make a difference to whether a student reaches the threshold just 10 percent of the time.[9] For 10 percent of students, the difference between a school chosen at random and a school that would be perfect for them is the difference between reaching the threshold and failing to reach it. For the other 90 percent, however, they were either so far below the required standard that the best school wouldn't get them there or they were so far above the required standard that they still reach it even with a randomly chosen school.

Now, this does not mean that all American schools are the same. They vary hugely in their support for athletics, music, dance, drama, and many other things. So when parents ask me about how to choose schools for their children, I ask them about their child's interests. Schools like the Julia R. Masterman School in Philadelphia may be a good fit for children who are passionate about science and mathematics, irrespective of how effective the school is in terms of student achievement. It also matters greatly whether children will feel—and be—safe at school.[10] There is also evidence that students do better in schools where there are a substantial number of other students who share their heritage or ethnicity. Every American school is unique in all kinds of ways. But American schools are remarkably similar in how much progress their students make.

Many people find this hard to accept. They see schools where students get good results, and they believe that their child will also get good results if he or she goes to that school. They will, if they are like the students who are already going to that school. But not otherwise. Whichever school a child goes to, she or he will still be the same child, with the same parents or caregivers, and these are far more powerful influences than the choice of school.

The main reason that the school effect is so small in the United States is related to the issue of teacher quality discussed in chapter 2. We saw there that teacher quality is very variable—some teachers are much more effective than others—but as we saw in chapter 3, we cannot tell with any reliability which individual teachers are the most effective. The result is that teacher quality is fairly randomly distributed in the United States. If it were possible to reliably figure out who the best teachers were, you can be sure that the richest school districts would hire them all. But they can't, so every school has some highly effective teachers and some less effective teachers. To give some idea of the range of teaching quality in a typical American school, even if we assume that the high scores gained in international tests by students in Singapore and Shanghai were caused entirely by the fact that their teachers were better (rather than the effects of private tutoring, for example), then the average difference in teacher quality between Singapore and the United States is only one-tenth of the range of teacher quality within a single school in America.

Nevertheless, there are many people who believe that the key to improving education in the United States is by expanding school choice with charter schools and vouchers. Let's look at the evidence.

## Charter Schools

Ray Budde was born in St. Louis, Missouri, and graduated from St. Louis University with a bachelor's degree and then served in the US Navy in the Pacific during World War II. After the war, he taught in East Lansing, Michigan, spent some time as an administrator in the same district, and then, in 1966, joined the faculty at the University of Massachusetts Amherst. In 1973, he left the University of Massachusetts Amherst to take up the post of director of the Blackstone Valley Educational Collaborative in Upton, Massachusetts.

During his time at the University of Massachusetts, Budde had become increasingly interested in the idea that groups of teachers should be able to establish their own schools, and in 1974, he presented a paper at the annual meeting of the Society for General Systems Research titled *Education by Charter*.[11] As he recalled twenty years later, when he shared the idea with his colleagues in the mid-1970s, there was little interest.[12] While many people thought that there were real problems with education, none of them thought that such radical solutions were needed.

Ten years later, education reform was back on the agenda, not least because of the publication of *A Nation at Risk* (mentioned in chapter 1). Among the more memorable quotes in that report was the following:

> We report to the American people that while we can take justifiable pride in what our schools and colleges have historically accomplished and contributed to the United States and the well-being of its people, the educational foundations of our society are being undermined by a rising tide of mediocrity that threatens our very future as a Nation and a people. What was unimaginable a generation ago has begun to occur—others are matching and surpassing our educational achievements.[13]

Judging that the climate might now be more receptive to suggestions for school reform, he expanded his ideas, and in January 1988, published a book-length proposal. Rather than just circulating the book to friends and colleagues, Budde sent copies to "anyone who might be interested in the reorganization of public education at the local level."[14] Two months later, Al Shanker, president of the American Federation of Teachers, proposed the creation of new kinds of schools, along the lines that had been proposed by Ray Budde, and on July 10 in his "Where We Stand" column in the *New York Times*, Shanker formally proposed calling these schools *charter schools*.

In October the same year, Shanker was invited by the Minneapolis Foundation to address the Itasca Seminar on the topic of charter schools. Two legislators attending the seminar, Senator Ember Reichgott and Representative Ken Nelson, were impressed by Budde's ideas and tried unsuccessfully for two years to enact laws to make charter schools possible in Minnesota. Finally, with the help of Representative Becky Kelso, a compromise proposal was agreed and the act was signed into law by Governor Arne Carlson on June 4, 1991.[15]

Since then, forty-two states have enacted legislation permitting charter schools, and the number of charter schools has grown steadily, from fewer than two thousand in 1999 to over six thousand in 2014. In 2013–2014, the latest year for which data are available, just over 2.5 million students attended charter schools, which is approximately 5 percent of the US school population.

As it turned out, few of these charter schools were the sort of schools that Budde and Shanker imagined, but the US charter scene is diverse, and as a result, in many areas, parents have a real choice about the schools their children attend. Many charter schools are what are sometimes called *no excuses* schools. These tend to serve disadvantaged students but require that students meet high academic standards, and provide substantial additional support for the students to do so, exemplified by Geoffrey Canada's idea that schools should do "whatever it takes" to ensure all students succeed.[16] The first of the no excuses charter schools appear to have been two middle schools opened by the Knowledge Is Power Program (KIPP) organization in 1995, one in Houston, Texas, and the other in New York City.

KIPP had been created a year earlier by Mike Feinberg and Dave Levin, two fifth-grade teachers in Houston. Starting with forty-seven fifth graders, Feinberg and Levin decided that five features (what they termed the *five pillars*) would be essential for their students to be on track for college:

- High expectations: All students are expected to reach high standards of achievement and behavior, with rewards for success.

- Choice and commitment: Students and their parents have to actively choose to attend a KIPP school and commit to making the time and effort needed to succeed.

- More time: To ensure that students have the time needed to reach high academic standards and participate in a range of extracurricular activities, KIPP schools have longer school days, weeks, and years.

- Power to lead: Leaders of KIPP schools are given control over budgets and personnel so that they can respond quickly to ensure resources are used most effectively.

- Focus on results: The main goal of the program is unashamedly to provide students with the academic preparation to succeed at the country's leading high schools and colleges.

The success of the first two schools led to national interest (including a feature on CBS's *60 Minutes* in 1999), and in 2000, the KIPP Foundation was set up to train principals to open and run new KIPP schools. Currently, KIPP runs two hundred schools across the United States, which serve almost eighty thousand students. Other chains of schools with similar, but not identical, philosophies are Uncommon Schools, which began in 1997, and Democracy Prep Public Schools, which opened its first school in 2006.

The popularity and successes of some charter schools have led many people to argue that expanding charter schools is the best chance of raising educational achievement in the United States. However, it is important to note that no matter how well charter schools perform relative to other public schools, the impact on the average level of achievement in the United States is likely to be small. Even if charters continue to grow at their current rate (expanding by approximately 250,000 students per year) fewer than half of all American students would be enrolled in charter schools in the year 2100.

Given that charter schools are likely to serve only a minority of students for the next few decades, they would need to be substantially better than other public schools to have any impact on average student achievement across the country. And they are not.

## Do Students Learn More in Charter Schools?

For some, whether charter schools get better test scores than traditional public schools is irrelevant. The important thing is that parents get to make choices about which schools their children attend, and it is clear that parents care about a lot more than test scores when choosing schools. Indeed, unless the test scores are particularly bad, test scores may not even be the most important factor in their choice of schools.[17]

However, if charter schools are to play a part in improving the educational achievement of American students, then we need to know whether they are any better than traditional public schools and, if so, by how much.

For most of the last twenty years, there has been very little evidence that charter schools were any better, on average, than traditional public schools. While it is clear that some charter schools are relatively ineffective, it is clear that others, such as the KIPP schools, are highly effective, although demonstrating this is far from straightforward.

One criticism that is often leveled at charter schools is that they cherry-pick their students. If those schools are selecting students who are already achieving at high levels, then their students' scores are likely to be higher, even if the schools are no more effective. To overcome this problem, the respected research organization Mathematica in Princeton, New Jersey, conducted an analysis of those KIPP schools where, because there were more parents wanting to send their children than places available, those who had applied were selected by lottery. They then compared test scores for students who applied to the KIPP schools and were admitted with those who applied but were unsuccessful.[18]

Scientists call such studies *intention to treat studies*—a term that comes from medical research. If the survival rates for patients who did receive a surgical procedure are higher than for those who did not, this may be because those who did not get the procedure were too sick to be operated on. A fair evaluation of the surgical procedure would take a group of people for whom the procedure was suitable, and give the procedure to some and not others in the group, ideally at random, and compare outcomes. The comparison is fairer because we restrict the analysis to those we intend to treat.

What Mathematica found was that students who had spent three years in a KIPP school were almost nine months ahead of students who had applied to the KIPP schools but ended up going to regular public schools—a 25 to 30 percent increase in the rate of learning.[19] Moreover, these results appear to be sustained: 94 percent of students attending KIPP schools graduate high school and 81 percent go to college.[20]

This is a substantial increase in achievement, but it is important to bear in mind that students spend a lot more time in school if they attend a KIPP school. The typical school day at a KIPP school is over nine hours long, with over five hours each day spent on the core subjects of math (eighty minutes), English language arts (ninety-five minutes), social studies (sixty-five minutes), and science (sixty-five minutes). On average, each student attends additional classes on a Saturday once a month, and the school year is two weeks longer than the US average. In total, KIPP students spend 45 percent more time in school than those attending traditional public schools, so while the achievement is higher, there appears to be an element of diminishing returns: 45 percent more time for 30 percent more learning.

Some researchers have suggested that one of the reasons for the superior performance of KIPP schools is that less successful students leave and return to a traditional public school, thus increasing the average scores in the KIPP school and lowering them at the public school they move to.[21] For advocates of public schools, this is a problem, because the students at KIPP schools are no longer representative of the whole population. For those who think giving parents a choice is important, on the other hand, this is not a problem but a feature. While the no excuses approach might not be suitable or effective for all students, allowing parents to choose a rigorous academic preparation for their child, if that is what suits their child best, seems less contentious. In effect, the no excuses charter schools offer a "shape up or ship out" program. For those for whom the program works, it is a success. And if students and their parents discover that it is not what suits the child best, and the child returns to a traditional public school, then it is hard to see why this is so terrible. Moreover, it is important to note that while the so-called *attrition rates* are somewhat higher than average at KIPP schools, most KIPP schools are located in disadvantaged areas where the attrition rates are higher than average for all students. Within each locality, the attrition rates for KIPP schools appear to be similar to traditional public schools.

Another criticism that is sometimes made is that KIPP schools select more advantaged students, but across all KIPP schools, 88 percent of students are from low-income families and 96 percent are either African American or Hispanic. In this light, the achievements of KIPP schools, particularly in respect of high school graduation and college enrollment, are impressive. However, they are far from typical. And when we look at the performance of charter schools across the United States over the last twenty years, the picture is far from encouraging.

Comparing the performance of charter schools with traditional public schools across a state would be misleading—in most states, the proportion of minority students is greater in charter schools than in traditional public schools, and charter schools tend to be concentrated in high-poverty areas. To provide a fairer comparison, a 2009 study by the Center for Research on Educational Outcomes (CREDO) at Stanford University examined how the progress of students at charter schools in fifteen states and the District of Columbia compared with students attending traditional public schools in the same locality.

What they found was sobering. In 46 percent of the 2,403 charter schools in their sample, gains in math achievement in charter schools were no different from local traditional public schools. Math gains were better than comparison schools in 17 percent of schools and worse in 37 percent of schools. To put it another way, in 2009, around a quarter of a million US schoolchildren had lower achievement in math because they had attended a charter school.[22]

Because of the diversity of the charter sector, it is impossible to be sure why performance was so poor in so many charter schools, but one plausible conclusion is that, in the rush to do something to raise student achievement, many states gave more thought to how to create more charter schools than to how to close poorly performing charter schools down (which seems to have been a particular problem in some states, such as Ohio). The logic appears to have been something like:

"We must do something."

"This is something."

"We must do this."

As more and more states have developed ways of closing down poorly performing charter schools, the performance of charter schools has improved steadily. By 2013, the CREDO team, now including twenty-two states in their survey, found that, on average, the performance of US charter schools was very slightly better than traditional public schools in the same locality. Specifically, in math, performance was higher in 29 percent of charter schools, about the same in 40 percent, and lower in 31 percent of schools. For reading, the figures were 56 percent, 25 percent, and 19 percent, respectively. To put this in perspective, a child attending a charter school in the United States would make an extra eight days' progress in reading per year than if she or he had attended a traditional public school in her or his locality.[23]

As states learn more about the features of effective charter schools, it seems likely that charter schools will continue to improve relative to traditional public schools, but the gains in student achievement that can be achieved through the expansion of charter schools are not large. First, it is worth noting that the most effective charter school organizations are not keen to expand quickly. When Doug Lemov, CEO of the Uncommon Schools charter school organization, was asked about his expansion plans, he saw the group expanding from forty-nine schools currently to sixty schools in five years' time—an expansion rate of just 4 percent per annum.[24] Second, even if we could persuade the most successful organizations to expand, the impact would be small. For example, even if we could instantaneously make all charter schools as good as KIPP schools, and charter schools continued to expand at their current rate, then it would take until the year 2058 to get an extra three weeks' learning per year across the United States.[25] Of course, the expansion of charter schools could be accelerated, but this would likely reduce the quality of the charter schools and thus reduce their performance relative to traditional public schools.

Expanding charter schools may be popular with some parents and politicians and does give parents more choices for the education of their children. They may therefore be an important part of the American educational system. However, as a solution to the challenge of raising the achievement of all American school students, their impact will be small.

Charter schools are, of course, public schools. In most states, they are closely regulated, and their students have to take state tests. Another way to provide parents with greater choice is to give the money that the school district would have used to pay for places in district schools and let the parents spend the money wherever they wish, through the provision of educational vouchers.

## School Vouchers

School vouchers, in one form or another, have been a feature of American education for many years. As noted above, many US school districts are small, and some, such as Rocky Hill, New Jersey, are so small that they do not have any schools at all. Instead, local property taxes are used to purchase places at schools in neighboring districts. As noted above, the use of public money to buy places in private schools is a well-established principle in many countries, most especially the Netherlands, where over 70 percent of students attend government-funded private schools.[26] However, in the United States, the idea of school vouchers is most widely associated with Milton Friedman, who suggested educational vouchers in his book *Capitalism and Freedom*.[27]

For those who are not quite ready to say that the government should get out of the business of K–12 education entirely, vouchers represent a reasonable compromise. The idea is that parents get a voucher, equivalent to what the state would have spent on providing schools for their child, and can use that voucher to educate their child wherever they please (and in some voucher proposals, could even keep the cash and educate their children at home).

A voucher scheme certainly expands parental choice, but for many, the attractive thing about vouchers is that because student achievement is higher in private schools, vouchers are often viewed as a way of increasing student achievement rapidly.

The logic is attractive because student achievement in private schools in the United States really is higher than in public schools. Most private school students do not take state-mandated standardized tests, but private school students in the United States do participate in the PISA testing program, and the evidence is clear.

As noted in the previous chapter, PISA scores are reported on a scale where the international average is set to 500. In 2012, US fifteen-year-olds scored 481 in math, 498 in reading, and 497 in science.[28] In math, the United States' score was different enough from the international average to be taken seriously (*statistically significant* in the scientific jargon), while in the other two subjects, the differences were small and therefore possibly due to random fluctuation—within the margin of error, as we would say for opinion polls.

Performance in private schools in the United States was much higher: fifteen points higher in math, twenty-one points higher in science, and twenty-nine points higher in reading.[29] To put these figures in perspective, one year's growth on PISA is around thirty to forty points,[30] so in the United States, fifteen-year-olds attending private school are ahead of their peers in public schools by around four months in math, six months in science, and almost nine months in reading.

Of course, as noted above, we cannot conclude that these differences are the result of superior instruction in private schools, because the students attending private schools in the United States are different from their public school peers in many ways, not least that they are more affluent. In order to take account of this, the PISA researchers collect a range of background data on the students participating in PISA and use these to construct what they call the *PISA index of economic, cultural and social status*. This index combines information on parents' employment and education, measures of the family's wealth, and home educational resources (such as the number of books in the family home).

When we do an apples-to-apples comparison on student achievement, in math, for example, by taking into account differences in students' backgrounds, we find that students attending public schools in the United States actually perform better than their private school peers by seven points (equivalent to an extra two months' learning).[31] In other words, the same child going to the typical private school in the United States would actually make less progress than if he or she had gone to a public school.

Another factor that makes it harder to compare the performance of private schools and public schools is the contribution that peers make to a child's learning. When there are many highly motivated students in a class, the achievement of other students is increased. Researchers have debated why exactly this is—it could be that it becomes cool to be academically successful, students may learn from their peers, and it may make it easier for the teacher to create an academic ethos in the classroom. No one knows for sure. But we do know that the effect is real and substantial.

For parents, this is largely irrelevant. Who cares whether an increase in a child's academic achievement was caused by the presence of higher-achieving peers or by better instruction? Better results are better results. But if we want to understand the effects of widespread use of voucher programs, we need to understand the reasons behind the differences in performance in private and public schools because our existing private schools are largely elite institutions. It is far from clear that the same results would be found if private schooling expanded to cover the whole achievement range. As we saw earlier, in math, on an apples-to-apples comparison, students in private schools actually did worse than students in public schools. When we also take into account the social status of the schools, and thus control for the effects of peers, private schools in the United States fall even further behind, with public school students outperforming private school students by twenty-seven points.[32]

Like charter schools, school vouchers are certainly likely to increase the choice available to parents, and this is, to many people, reason enough to pursue their expansion. Charter schools and private schools may not be, on average, any better than traditional public schools. But for a particular child, a particular charter or private school may be a better fit than the local traditional public school. And while parents may not always make the best decisions for their children, it is hard to argue that a bureaucrat will get the decision right more often. That is why I have a lot of sympathy with those who see charter schools and school vouchers as an important element of educational policy.

However, those who think that charter schools and school vouchers will have any appreciable impact on levels of educational achievement are deluding themselves. The numbers simply don't stack up. The best charter schools are superb, but this is in large part because of the careful training their leaders received. Expanding charter schools rapidly is likely to lead to a drop in quality, resulting in charters that are no better than traditional public schools. As for private schools, the data from PISA show that when we do an apples-to-apples comparison, we find that in the United States, the same child would get higher test scores by attending a public school than a private school. And if all schools were private schools, then private schools would be substantially worse than they are now.

Advocating expanding school choice as a way of increasing student achievement in the United States is the educational equivalent of rearranging the deck chairs on the *Titanic*. Yes, it makes things better. But not much. And there are other things we can do that will have a much greater impact on how much our children learn.

---

1    See, for example, *Runyon v. McCrary*, 427 U.S. 160 (1976).

2    Although parents like the idea that education is funded locally, over the last fifty years, federal and state funds have become more and more important in school finance. In some rural counties in Florida, for example, only 25% of the education budget comes from local taxes.

3    National Center for Educational Statistics *Digest of Educational Statistics*, table 214.20, downloaded from https://nces.ed.gov/programs/digest/d15/tables/dt15_214.20.asp.

4    Data on ACT and SAT scores in Pennsylvania are from Pennsylvania Department of Education (2016).

5    According to University Language Services (2013), the middle 50 percent of students admitted to Brown University scored between 29 and 34 on the ACT.

6    This is based on the assumption that students' scores in each school are normally distributed and uses the estimate of the standard deviation for the ACT composite provide by ACT.

7    Hart and Risley (1995, p. 198).

8    Organisation for Economic Co-operation and Development (2007, Table 4.1a).

9    Wiliam (2010).

10   Interestingly, a study of Virginia high schools found that while there were more incidents of bullying in larger high schools, this was only because they were larger. The chances of being bullied are actually lower in a large high school than a small one (Klein & Cornell, 2010).

11   Budde (1974).

12   Budde (1996).

13   National Commission on Excellence in Education (1983, p. 5).

14   Budde (1996, p. 72).

15   Laws of Minnesota for 1991, Chapter 265, H.F.No. 700.

16   Tough (2008).

17   Brasington and Hite (2012).

18   Tuttle, Gill, Gleason, Knechtel, Nichols-Barrer, and Resch (2013).

19   The effect size over the three years, averaged across math, reading, social studies, and science, was 0.28 standard deviations, which, using the norms provided in Bloom et al. (2008), equates to an extra nine months learning over the three-year period, or an increase of 25% in the rate of learning.

20  Source: http://www.kipp.org/schools.

21  See, for example, Miron, Urschel, and Saxton (2011).

22  This figure is obtained by taking 17% of the approximately 4,700 charter schools in the US in 2009 and assuming an average enrollment of 300 students per charter school (the national average at the time, using the national charter school population of 1.4 million given in the 2009 CREDO report).

23  Center for Research on Education Outcomes (2013, p. 63).

24  Roberts (2016).

25  Assuming the creation of 250,000 more charter school places each year, each of which has students making 30% more progress each year and a growth rate in the US school population of 0.7% per year.

26  Ritzen, van Dommelen, and De Vijlder (1997).

27  Friedman (1982).

28  Programme for International Student Assessment (2013b, Table I.A, p. 19).

29  Programme for International Student Assessment (2013b).

30  The PISA scores are standardized to have a standard deviation of 100, so assuming one year's growth to be 0.4 standard deviations, then one year's growth would be equivalent to 40 points.

31  Programme for International Student Assessment (2013a, Table IV.4.7, p. 390).

32  Ibid.

# SECTION 3

CHAPTER 8

# Moving Forward

In previous chapters, we have looked at a number of ideas that are being advocated in the United States to improve educational achievement. Some, as we have seen, such as trying to get smarter people into teaching, are likely to have little or no effect. Others, such as firing bad teachers, would, obviously, improve student achievement if we could implement the policy effectively, but we can't because right now it is not possible to identify bad teachers reliably, and even if we could, their replacements might not be any better. Still others, such as expanding school choice, are likely to have a positive effect, at least in the long term, but even with the most optimistic projections, they aren't going to have enough of an effect on enough students to make an appreciable difference to average student achievement across America.

There are other ideas that we could have discussed. Some people believe that greater use of computers in classrooms will improve education, but overall, the evidence is not encouraging. There have been a number of successes, but in general, these are the result of lengthy periods of development and focus on very specific skills. For example, Carnegie Learning's Cognitive Tutor for Algebra focuses on certain aspects of ninth-grade algebra, and students using this computer program learn algebra more quickly—equivalent to having a teacher in the top one-sixth of teacher quality.[1] But this program took over thirty years to develop and deals with less than half of the content of just one high school course. Overall, the impact of computers on educational achievement today remains as it was a decade and a half ago; in the words of Stanford University professor Larry Cuban, computers have been "oversold and underused."[2]

There are other things that would improve performance if they could be done, but we don't know how to do them. We know that lifting children out of poverty would improve student achievement, but no country has figured out how to do this, let alone how to create the political support that would be needed. We know that the involvement of parents makes a huge difference to how much children learn, but changing how parents support their children seems to be very difficult. We know that funding education in a way that does not depend on local property values would improve student achievement, but this is unlikely ever to be proposed by any politicians. As Jean-Claude Juncker, former president of Luxembourg, once said, "We all know what to do, we just don't know how to get re-elected after we've done it."[3]

However, rather than try to list all the possible things we might do, in this chapter, I want to make three proposals about how we might think about *any* ideas that are suggested for improving education, to help school board members, superintendents, principals, teachers, parents, and others become more critical consumers of educational research.

The first proposal is that we get away from the idea of *what works* in education, and instead ask, "How well does it work?" For most of the twentieth century, researchers in various fields of science examined the results of their experiments by investigating how likely it was that the results that were actually observed in fact arose by chance or were the result of some systematic difference between groups. For example, if someone flips a coin ten times and gets seven heads and three tails, it would not be reasonable to conclude that the coin is biased. Getting seven or more heads in ten flips of a fair coin happens about 16 percent of the time—not the most likely outcome but not really evidence of bias either. If we toss the same coin one hundred times and get seventy or more heads, then it *would* be reasonable to conclude that the coin is biased, because the chance of getting seventy or more heads out of one hundred flips with a fair coin is very small indeed (the odds are around one in twenty-five thousand). In the scientific jargon, we say that, compared with the result we would expect if the coin was fair, the result is *statistically significant*.

The problem is that the word *significant* in this context means nothing more than the result is unlikely to be a fluke. It doesn't mean that it is a big difference. A result can be significant but not important.

For example, one experiment looked at whether air pollution affects students' performance in examinations. The researchers found that when the level of fine particulate matter in the air (defined as the number of particles smaller than 2.5-millionths of a meter, or about one-thirtieth of the diameter of a human hair) was higher, then student performance on examinations was lower. But not much. They found that on average, taking an exam in the city rather than the suburbs would reduce your score by around one-fortieth of 1 percent.[4] Of course, you could be taking the examination on a day when the pollution in the city is particularly bad, or you could be someone who is so close to the passing score that a tiny change in your score is the difference between passing and failing, but all these are highly unlikely. The result is *statistically significant* because the effect is real, but it's a tiny effect. Now, of course, this doesn't mean that pollution isn't a serious problem and that, all other things being equal, we shouldn't look for ways in which we can reduce pollution and its effect. But there are other things to worry about, things that will have a far greater impact on student achievement. When someone says that some new way of teaching has a significant impact on students' results, the first question we should ask is, "By how much?"

At this point, many people point out that if we insist on doing only those things for which we know the likely impact on student achievement, then we are missing out on a lot of potentially useful innovations. That is true. There are many ideas, such as the process of lesson study that is used by math and science teachers in Japan, that look promising but haven't enough evidence to draw any firm conclusions about the benefits. And if we were already doing everything known to improve student achievement, then experimentation with promising but unproven ideas might be a good idea. But the problem is that right now, we are still not doing the things that we know are likely to work. We don't know everything, but we know enough to make smart choices about priorities.

The second proposal is that in evaluating interventions, as we saw with class size reduction programs in chapter 5, we also need to take into account the cost of interventions. The problem with class size reduction programs is not that they don't work—they often do. Rather, the problem is that class size reduction programs cost a lot to implement, and we should look at what else we could have done with the money.

This kind of cost-benefit calculation seems to be hardwired into people when they are making decisions such as purchasing a refrigerator. If one model costs $800 and another model costs $1,200, the first question most people ask is, "What am I getting for the extra four hundred dollars?" And yet we often fail to ask the same question when purchasing educational programs. Sometimes a modest impact on student achievement can be highly cost effective.

For example, READY4K! is a text messaging program that is designed to help parents of preschoolers prepare their children for kindergarten. Three days a week (Monday, Wednesday, and Friday), parents are sent text messages to remind them to undertake literacy activities with their children, and these generally follow the same structure.

Monday:     FACT—Bath time is great for teaching your child important skills for K. Start by asking: What are the things we need for bath time? Why?

Wednesday:  TIP—When you're bathing your child, point out the letters on shampoo bottles. Ask your child to name them & the sounds they make.

Friday:   GROWTH—Keep using bath time to prepare your child 4K!
Ask: What rhymes with tub (cub, rub), soap (rope, hope), &
bubble (double, trouble)?[5]

The effects of the program were modest. Some aspects of literacy were unaffected, while in others, the children made an extra month or two of progress.[6] However, given the cost of the program—a few dollars per child—the program is very cost effective. Costs and benefits are meaningless if studied separately. Any educational policy needs to be evaluated in terms of the balance of benefit to cost.

The third proposal is that even when a school district has ideas that appear to be supported by good evidence, and that also appear to be cost effective, it is important to be sure that those ideas are likely to be as effective when implemented in that particular district. In chapter 4 ("Paying Good Teachers More"), we saw an example from India where teachers were paid bonuses simply for turning up for work. If teachers are not turning up for work, paying them to do so might make sense. If they are already turning up for work, then there isn't much point in providing incentives for doing so.

This might seem obvious, but many educational innovations work in small-scale settings but when rolled out on a wider scale are much less effective. In one study of supporting teachers to use assessments to track their students' progress, a pilot study found that the scheme did increase student achievement by a wide margin. However, a wider rollout turned out to be much less successful. It turned out that one of the factors behind the success of the pilot was geographical proximity. In the pilot, when the researchers were working with local schools, it was easy to maintain informal contact between the schools and the researchers, and the researchers were able to provide on-site support easily. When the project was scaled up, these informal links were less common, and so the project was less successful.[7] Another good example of this is the national rollout of the National Literacy and Numeracy Strategies in England in the early 2000s. While a small-scale pilot had shown a big impact on student achievement, the national rollout found only half as much impact on student achievement, and the costs were substantial.[8]

Trawling through all the available educational research to find what can be done to have the biggest impact on student achievement sounds like a daunting task, not least because there are now hundreds of journals devoted to research in education and no one has the time to read them all, let alone do anything with the results.

Fortunately, from the point of view of a district leader or school board member, there is no need, nor is there any point, in trying to keep up with the latest research because individual research studies don't mean very much. In fact, a recent review of one hundred research papers published in top psychology journals found that fewer than 40 percent of the studies gave similar results when the same experiments were run again but by a different team.[9] Chasing the latest fads is likely to result in trying to implement ideas that turn out to be ineffective even in the laboratory, let alone in real school settings.

Perhaps more important, over the last twenty years, a great deal of progress has been made in finding ways of accumulating research from different settings in a systematic way, in order to provide robust evidence about what we can do to have the greatest impact on student achievement.

## Systematic Reviews of Research

The first attempts to carry out large-scale systematic reviews of research took place in medicine. While medical researchers conducted research, and periodically other researchers tried to collect together what was known in a particular field by doing formal reviews of research, this process was rarely carried out in a systematic way. As a result, the reviews of research often missed important studies and sometimes reflected the biases of the researchers more than the balance of the evidence. Most important, because the results of many experiments failed to produce results that were statistically significant, they were just regarded as inconclusive. Researchers would conclude that more research was needed.

One reason that the findings weren't more definitive is that researchers were, in effect, counting studies, by looking at the number of studies that found a positive effect for some treatment and comparing that number with the number that had a negative effect or no discernible effect one way or the other.

It is as if, going back to the coin flipping example, a person flipped a coin ten times and got the following result:

H T H H H T H T H H

As we saw earlier, getting seven heads and three tails happens about 16 percent of the time, so we can't conclude there's anything wrong with the coin. But if another person flips the same coin ten times and gets the following sequence

H H T H H H H T H H

then the idea that the coin is actually fair seems less likely.

Suppose now that another eight people each toss the same coin ten times, and we get the following results.

| Person 1 | H T H H H T H T H H |
| Person 2 | H H T H H H H T H H |
| Person 3 | H H T H H T H H T T |
| Person 4 | T H T T T H T H H H |

| Person 5 | H H H H H T H H H H |
| Person 6 | H H H T T H H H T T |
| Person 7 | H T H T H H H H H T T |
| Person 8 | H T H H H H H H H H H |
| Person 9 | H H H H T T H H H T T |
| Person 10 | H H H T H H H H T H H |

Each person, on the basis of her or his own data, cannot conclude that the coin is biased. If, however, these ten people pooled their results, then they would see that they had seventy heads and only thirty tails, and the chance of a result like this happening with a fair coin is very unlikely (approximately one in twenty-five thousand as we saw earlier). The important point about this example is that each individual experimenter does not have enough evidence to conclude that the coin is biased, but if they can find a way of pooling their results, they can see very clearly that the coin is biased.

This is exactly what was happening in medical research in the 1970s and 1980s. Researchers were doing experiments and finding that the results were inconclusive, so people were saying, "More research is needed," but more research wasn't needed. The evidence was already there but scattered over different studies, often in different journals, and sometimes in different countries. What was needed was a way of making sure that the results from different studies were being pooled in a systematic way to reveal the big picture.

One of the most tragic examples concerned the treatment of Americans who suffered heart attacks in the 1970s and 1980s. At the time, it was widely believed that giving these people anti-arrhythmic drugs—drugs meant to control the irregular beating of the heart—would aid recovery. In 1983, Curt Furberg, a doctor and a researcher at the National Institutes of Health in Bethesda, Maryland, looked at the available research evidence. He found a total of fourteen well-designed studies, but the evidence was inconclusive, and his cautious summary of the research was that the benefits of this treatment "had not been realized."[10] Because the evidence was inconclusive and because doctors believed that anti-arrhythmic drugs would help in the treatment of people who had suffered heart attacks, the use of such drugs continued. Ten years later, Furberg and his colleagues reviewed the research again, by which time the number of well-designed studies was up to fifty-one. More important, they used a statistical technique that allowed them to pool the results of different studies to get the big picture. They discovered that giving anti-arrhythmic drugs to people who had suffered heart attacks actually *increased* the risk of death by 14 percent.[11] In 1995, Thomas Moore, a reporter who documented the use of anti-arrhythmic drugs in heart attack patients in a book called *Deadly Medicine*, pointed out that the widespread use of these drugs in the late 1980s probably killed more Americans *each year* than were killed in the whole of the Vietnam war.[12]

Another example concerns the advice given to mothers of newborn babies about whether babies should sleep on their stomachs or on their backs. In early editions of Benjamin Spock's *Common Sense Guide to Baby and Child Care* (i.e., those published from 1946 to 1955), mothers were advised to put their babies to sleep on their backs, but in the 1956 edition, the advice was changed: "I think it is preferable to accustom a baby to sleeping on his stomach from the start if he is willing. He may change later when he learns to turn over."[13]

As we now know, the later advice was wrong. Babies are far more likely to die suddenly in their sleep if they sleep on their stomachs than on their backs. While a lot is still unknown about *sudden infant death syndrome*, as it is called, by the late 1980s it was clear that the best advice to parents was to put their babies to sleep on their backs. As a result, many countries mounted comprehensive campaigns to inform parents about the new findings, and the effects were marked, with some countries seeing a 75 percent reduction in the number of cases of sudden infant death within a few years.[14]

The point of these stories is not to vilify pharmaceutical companies, doctors, and scientists but rather to draw attention to the fact that by the mid-1980s, there was enough evidence in each case about which kinds of drugs were most effective for treating heart attack patients and what sleeping positions were safest for babies. The failure was in collecting and using the results of all the different studies in a systematic way—what one scientist called "the scandalous failure of scientists to cumulate scientifically."[15]

Systematic reviews are now standard across many experimental sciences and have provided a number of surprises.

- *Scared straight* programs in which juvenile delinquents meet incarcerated adults to dissuade them from a life of crime turn out to increase criminal behavior.[16]

- *Brain-training* programs increase performance on the specific tasks used in the training but not on anything else.[17]

- Regular, frequent practice testing does actually improve student achievement.[18]

However, if systematic reviews are to provide reliable and robust findings, there are several issues that need careful attention.

The first is that studies are easier to find if they are published in prestigious journals, and it is far easier to get results published if the results are statistically significant—one estimate is that a researcher is twelve times more likely to get a study published if its results are significant.[19] It is also easier to get results published if the findings are novel or surprising. This gives rise to what is sometimes called the *file drawer problem* in research. Papers with significant results, especially if they are eye-catching, are more likely to get published. The others remain in the researcher's file drawer.

The file drawer problem is a particular problem in pharmaceutical research because if pharmaceutical companies have spent millions of dollars developing their drugs, they want to recoup that investment by selling those drugs. If the company finds that a particular drug works in some experiments but not in others, it is completely free to publish only the successful studies and bury the others.[20] Even if all the trials to date show that the drug does not effectively treat the condition it was intended to treat, company researchers can look to see if the drug improves other aspects of health (what is called *outcome switching*). As economist Ronald Coase pointed out, "if you torture the data long enough, it will confess."[21]

Now, in fact, it is possible to detect whether such statistical shenanigans have occurred because if they have, the most impressive results will be found in the smaller experiments (i.e., those done with fewer people). An experimenter might get lucky twenty times but not two hundred times. The simplest way to do this is with a graph called a *funnel plot* that shows how much impact the drug, or the educational program, has had versus the number of people in the experiment. If there is a tendency for the most impressive results to occur in the smaller experiments, there are a number of ways of adjusting the results to take account of any bias, but the important point is that this is often a matter of judgment rather than an exact science.

A second problem with producing systematic reviews of research in an area is that, in some areas, it is often hard to be sure that you have found all the relevant studies. In medicine, there is widespread agreement about the key words that researchers use to describe their papers to help others find them when searching online. So, for example, any study of the use of anti-arrhythmic drugs in patients suffering heart attacks is likely to have the phrases *anti-arrhythmic drugs* and *myocardial infarction* as key words (and probably in the title too). In education, there is no such agreement. Papers might talk about *testing* or *assessment* or *evaluation*, and if the tests are used to modify instruction, then the researcher might avoid these words entirely and instead talk about *responsive teaching*.

A third problem is that it is sometimes difficult to be sure that we are doing an apples-to-apples comparison when we combine studies. The chapter on class size reduction described a number of studies that investigated the impact of smaller classes on student achievement. However, to pool the results from all these studies together, we have to be careful. In some of the studies, class size may have been reduced by only 10 percent, while in others they may have been reduced by 30 percent or even 50 percent. If we take an average across the different studies, that may be misleading because it costs a lot more to reduce class size by 50 percent than it does to reduce class size by 10 percent, so there are likely to be many more studies that involve only modest reductions in class size, because they are less expensive to carry out. The fact that most studies of class size reduction programs find small effects may be nothing more than a reflection of the fact that big reductions in class size are expensive to implement and research.

A fourth problem with systematic reviews is that the statistical techniques that are used to pool the results from different experiments require researchers to make assumptions that may not always be met. The technique that is most widely used is called *meta-analysis*, first developed by Gene Glass, a professor of education at the University of Colorado, in the 1970s.[22] While the use of meta-analysis is now standard across most of the sciences, it is more difficult to use in education because how we measure the results of our experiments is not standard. In medicine, different treatments might be evaluated in terms of how long the patient took to recover, the time taken until the patient was discharged from the hospital, or five-year survival rates. While the policies about when patients are discharged may vary somewhat from hospital to hospital, they are likely to be similar, so results of similar experiments can be compared without too much difficulty. In education, however, even when different experiments are looking at the same thing, comparing the results is much more difficult. For example, if one experiment finds that grouping students by ability for math improves achievement and another finds that it does not, the obvious conclusion would be that it works sometimes and not others. But if the first experiment measured student achievement with teacher-assigned grades and the second used standardized tests, then it might be that the higher performance seen in the first group is caused by differences in assessment methods.

Using meta-analysis to compare the results of different experiments also requires that the thing we are measuring (e.g., student achievement) is spread out roughly the same way in the different experiments. This is an issue when some experiments are done with subgroups of students, such as gifted students or students with special needs. It is also an issue when some experiments are done with younger children and others are done with older children, since, in terms of achievement, older students tend to be more spread out than younger students (when students are older, the gifted students have had more time to pull ahead and the slower students have had more time to fall behind).

What this means is that meta-analysis, for all its advantages over traditional ways of drawing together results from different research studies, is not a panacea, and especially not in education. As well as the technical issues discussed above, if most of the studies included in a meta-analysis were done in laboratories, it is by no means clear that the findings obtained there would apply in real classrooms. And in many branches of psychology, the majority of published experimental studies are indeed laboratory studies. Even if a meta-analysis is restricted to studies actually carried out in schools, if most of the studies included in the meta-analysis were conducted in urban and suburban districts, it is a stretch to assume that the findings would be the same in rural districts.

In short, as I have suggested already, district leaders and school board members have to become *critical consumers* of educational research, and this involves steering a fine line between two extremes. At one extreme are those who reject any study that wasn't done in the state, and perhaps even those that weren't carried out in the district, presumably because of the belief that the district is unique, and what applies elsewhere will not apply in the district.

At the other extreme are those who are always looking for the next big thing, whether it is lesson study, educational neuroscience, mobile learning, personalized learning, or whatever. There is some evidence that each of these might improve student achievement.[23] And, as noted earlier, if districts were already doing everything the research evidence indicates would improve achievement, then there is nothing wrong with looking for the next big thing; although, as we have seen, educational research is full of ideas that looked promising but turned out to be duds.

The reality is that there is now a great deal of well-organized evidence that shows that there are things that every school district could be doing, that have worked in a lot of school districts—rural, suburban, and urban—and that have worked with different state standards. Unfortunately, while these ideas are familiar, old hat even, they are not being implemented consistently in our schools. We need to stop looking for the next big thing and instead focus on doing the last big thing properly. The evidence about what we should be doing is actually pretty clear. We know what we should be doing. We're just not doing it. It's what Stanford management professor Jeffrey Pfeffer calls the *knowing-doing gap*.[24]

The next four chapters look in detail at things that any district could implement that would have a substantial impact on student achievement, at modest cost. Moreover, these measures appear to have greater benefits, at a smaller cost, than anything else that districts might do to improve student achievement. They are ensuring a knowledge-rich curriculum and requiring every teacher to improve.

---

1    What Works Clearinghouse (2016).

2    Cuban (2002).

3    Economist (2007).

4   Lavy, Ebenstein, and Roth (2014).

5   Stanford University Center for Education Policy Analysis (2016).

6   York and Loeb (2014).

7   Goe and Bridgeman (2006).

8   Machin and McNally (2009).

9   Open Science Collaboration (2015).

10  Furberg (1983, p. 32C).

11  Teo, Yusuf, and Furberg (1993).

12  Moore (1995).

13  The original advice, given in Spock (1946) was, "Some say it is a little safer for the baby to sleep on his back in the first six months, so it is better to get him used to that position if you can. There is only one slight disadvantage. A baby on his back tends to turn his head always toward the same side and this may flatten the back of his head on that side. This would not hurt his brains and the head will gradually straighten out as he grows older. If you start early you may be able to get him used to turning his head to both sides by putting his head where his feet were every other sleeping period" (p. 96). The quotation from the 1956 edition (Spock, 1956) is on page 164.

14  Gilbert, Salanti, Harden, and See (2005).

15  Chalmers (2005).

16  Petrosino, Petrosino, and Buelher (2004).

17  Melby-Lervåg and Hulme (2013).

18  Dunlosky, Rawson, Marsh, Nathan, and Willingham (2013).

19  Dickersin and Min (1993).

20  For a detailed analysis of the scale of this issue, the problems it causes, and what can be done, see Goldacre (2012).

21  The quote from Ronald Coase is from Tullock (2001, p. 205).

22  Glass (1976).

23  The potential for lesson study and educational neuroscience to improve student learning is discussed in Wiliam (2016a). Mobile learning may also have a role to play but is currently not well-enough defined for its effects to be evaluated. Most recently, a number of philanthropic organizations have advocated "personalized learning" as a priority for improving education, but the problem is that there is, again, little agreement about what, exactly, it means. Indeed, the term itself is somewhat odd, since all learning is personalized—learning is the mysterious process that happens in students' heads as a result of which they are able to do things they couldn't do before. What most people mean when they talk about "personalized learning" is really "personalized instruction." And while there is some evidence that this may improve learning a little (Pane, Steiner, Baird, & Hamilton, 2015) this evidence is far from convincing (Penuel & Johnson, 2016). Furthermore, as is explained in chapters 9 and 10, many of the assumptions about personalized instructions go against what we know about how we learn best.

24  Pfeffer (2000).

CHAPTER 9

# Why Curriculum Matters

The word *curriculum* is used in a number of different ways in the United States. The first use of the word (at least in English) was in Scottish universities in the early seventeenth century to describe the selection of courses that students chose to follow. Countries that have national statements about what students should be learning often talk about having a *national curriculum*.

In the United States, the word *curriculum* is sometimes used in the way it was used originally in Scotland—the selection of required and elective courses a student follows in high school, for example—but it is also used in other ways and, in particular, in a much more specific sense to describe the textbooks that a district has adopted (as in, "We changed our curriculum," meaning, "We changed our textbooks").

What makes things really confusing, in the United States at least, is that many people assume that standards (whether at the state or federal level) define a curriculum. Now, of course, words can be defined in any way we choose, but it is helpful to distinguish between what we want students to know at the end of certain periods of instruction (standards) and the experiences that schools organize to get them there (curriculum). The standards are the destinations, and the curriculum is the route plan. Obviously, we need to start with the standards. To paraphrase former Yankees catcher Yogi Berra, if you don't know where you're going, you might wind up someplace else.

## What Should Our Children Be Learning?

Over the last half-century or so, as technology has transformed our world, there have been increasingly frequent calls for our school curriculum to change to reflect the changes in society and work. For example, currently there are many voices claiming that students should learn coding (i.e., what used to be called *computer programming*) in school. The arguments seem compelling. Michael Mandel has pointed out that in

2012 in North America (the fifth anniversary of the opening of Apple's App Store), there were over 750,000 people working in the app economy—three-quarters of a million people doing jobs that did not exist five years earlier.[1] Those who have coding skills clearly have a marketable skill. For the moment.

The problem is that we aren't very good at predicting what jobs will be needed in the future. A hundred years ago, rising wealth would have led people to conclude that we needed more blacksmiths because as people got richer, more of them would be able to afford to own their own horses. Five years ago, owning a medallion to operate a New York taxi seemed like a good investment, which is why a single medallion cost over $1 million. Today, because of the extraordinary growth of ride-sharing services such as Uber and Lyft, the value may be only one fourth of that.[2]

But it is important to note that our inability to predict the future goes both ways. Not only are we not very good at predicting which things will disappear, we are also not very good at predicting what will survive.

Anyone who learned computer programming in the 1970s would have learned the cutting-edge computer languages of the day—Fortran, ALGOL, Pascal, BASIC, or APL—and these languages are all but extinct today. On the other hand, someone who learned to program ten years earlier, in the 1960s, would have probably learned Cobol (originally Common Business-Oriented Language, but now just COBOL or Cobol). It might be expected that those who learned the more modern computer languages would be at an advantage, but, in fact, the opposite is the case.

Because of the massive investment in computing in the 1970s, something like 80 percent of the world's daily business transactions today run on computer programs written in Cobol.[3] Cobol programmers were in particular demand in 1999 because many computer programs written in the 1970s had been set up on the assumption that two digits would be enough to record the year of a transaction because no one thought these programs would still be in use twenty years later. As the millennium bug threatened to crash computers all over the world at midnight on December 31, 1999, Cobol programmers were brought out of retirement to check and, if necessary, update, the programs.

Similarly, before any commercial airplane takes off in the United States, the airline prints off a passenger manifest—on a dot matrix printer that is fed with paper that has sprocket holes down the sides—a technology that has been around for fifty years. It might be assumed that this is just because the old technology has lasted, but in fact, the Dutch national airline KLM recently decided to replace all its printers and, after careful evaluation of different options, found that the best machine for the job, because of its dependability and reliability, was a dot matrix printer.[4] As the late Heinz Wolff once said, "The future is further away than you think."[5]

The important takeaway here is that coding is a valuable skill right now, but it is impossible to know for how long this will last. We already have computer programs that write computer programs, and fairly soon, we are likely to have computer programs that write computer programs that write computer programs. In the same way, right now, many humans are employed repairing robots, but we already have examples of robots that can repair other robots,[6] and this, in turn, has led to robots that can design other robots.[7]

This is what makes education today such a fraught process. We are preparing children for a world that no one can imagine. Anyone who says that he or she knows what specific things students need to be learning in school is, in effect, taking a gamble with our children's future. If the guess is correct, then students will be well prepared for whatever is coming. If, on the other hand, the guess is incorrect, then students will have wasted large amounts of time on things that have done them no good. More important, that time will not be available for other things.

The impossibility of knowing what students need has prompted some people to go to the other extreme by saying we cannot possibly know what our children need in the future, perhaps best exemplified by this quotation from Seymour Papert:

> So the model that says learn while you're at school, while you're young, the skills that you will apply during your lifetime is no longer tenable. The skills that you can learn when you're at school will not be applicable. They will be obsolete by the time you get into the workplace and need them, except for one skill. The one really competitive skill is the skill of being able to learn. It is the skill of being able not to give the right answer to questions about what you were taught in school, but to make the right response to situations that are outside the scope of what you were taught in school. We need to produce people who know how to act when they're faced with situations for which they were not specifically prepared.[8]

Now, the main idea here is obviously correct. No matter how much our schools teach our children, it won't be enough, because much of what our children need to know for the rest of their lives hasn't been discovered or invented yet. No one wanted to design apps for smartphones twenty years ago because it wasn't an available option. The idea that our children should, above all else, be learning how to learn is attractive, but there is one major problem with focusing on learning how to learn as the goal of schooling, and that is that it doesn't appear to be possible to learn how to learn without learning *something*. This is particularly clear when we look at what are sometimes called *twenty-first-century skills*.

## Twenty-First-Century Skills

The origins of the term *twenty-first-century skills* are obscure, but in 2002, a group of businesses, not-for-profit organizations, and government agencies created the

Partnership for 21st Century Skills. The aim of the coalition was to provide answers to the question, "How can we best prepare students to succeed in the twenty-first century?"[9]

That, of course, is the goal of every education system in the world. Every country wants its children to succeed. And there are certain trends that seem to be irreversible. The value of physical strength in the workplace has been declining steadily ever since water and animal power gave way to steam and then electricity and the internal combustion engine. As robots become more sensitive to their surroundings, even manual dexterity becomes less and less valuable.

It is tempting, therefore, to conclude that as more and more workers become knowledge workers, different skills will be needed in the workplace, and the driving idea behind the twenty-first-century skills movement is that there are particular skills that will be especially important in the future.

Unfortunately, there is no widely agreed-on definition of what, exactly, the twenty-first-century skills are. Different writers use different labels for the same things, the same labels for different things, and organize the skills in different ways. However, most writers on this subject seem to include the same basic elements—namely, collaboration, communication, creativity, critical thinking, and problem solving.

Now, to be clear, being able to collaborate and communicate with others, to be creative, to think critically, and to solve problems are all valuable things to be able to do. The problem comes when we start calling these things *skills*.

The word *skill* comes from Old Norse—the language spoken in Scandinavia from the ninth to the thirteenth century—and originally, it just meant "knowledge" or "discernment." Someone who was skilled was more knowledgeable or wise than someone who was not. Over the years, the word has come to mean something rather more specific; today, it generally means something that someone is able to do as a result of a sustained period of practice rather than a natural gift.

The problem is that as soon as we start thinking about something like critical thinking as a skill, there is an implication that it is *one* skill, something that, once learned, can be applied widely. In doing so we have slipped from talking about standards (what we want students to learn) to talking about curriculum (how we get our students to learn). Now, this would not be too much of a problem if critical thinking was a skill. Unfortunately, this is not the case. Critical thinking is not a skill. It is a collection of many skills.

For example, there is a well-known mathematical proof that $1 = 2$.[10] The "proof" works by dividing an equation by zero, which is not permitted in mathematics, because the idea of dividing any number by zero has no meaning.

In math class, therefore, students are taught that they must not divide an equation by zero, which seems like easy advice to follow. But sometimes, it is possible to divide by zero without realizing it. For example, in high school algebra, given an equation like:

$$z(x - y) = x(x - y)$$

many students can see that the equation could be simplified by dividing both sides by the common factor $(x - y)$. However, from this point on, the equation holds only if $x$ is not equal to $y$ (because if $x$ ever equals $y$, then you have in effect divided by zero). The careful mathematics student notes that what follows from this point on is true only if $x$ and $y$ are not equal. This is an example of critical thinking in mathematics (and reveals the error in the fallacious proof that $1 = 2$). The important point here is that this skill is learned in mathematics class. Critical thinking in mathematics requires learning, in mathematics class, what it means to think critically in math, and this ability does not transfer from one school subject to another. No amount of training students to think critically in history makes them any better at critical thinking in math.

To a greater or lesser extent, the same applies to the other twenty-first-century skills. While there is some evidence that getting students to work cooperatively in one setting improves their ability to work cooperatively elsewhere, for communication, creativity, critical thinking, and problem solving, the idea that students can learn these skills in one context and apply them in another is attractive but essentially wrong. If we want students to think critically in science, then we have to make this part of science instruction. If we want students to be creative in science, then this too has to be part of science instruction.

Now, this does not undermine the idea that collaboration, communication, creativity, critical thinking, and problem solving are important things for students to be learning. These twenty-first-century skills should be included in our standards. But the fact that these skills do not transfer easily from one context to another does have implications for our curriculum. Each of the twenty-first-century skills has to be taught in each subject. Ultimately, the so-called twenty-first-century skills are best thought of as a way of ensuring that our standards are sufficiently broad. Do our standards for math require students to communicate about mathematics, to work effectively in teams on math problems, to be creative in mathematics, to think critically when doing math, and to solve problems? And the same goes for language arts, and science, and social studies. The twenty-first-century skills provide a way of looking at our standards, to ensure their breadth. They are not, however, skills that can be learned in one subject and applied in another.

This has been known to psychologists for many years. Our brains really do not seem to transfer what we learn in one context to another context. For example, in one experiment, members of a university scuba diving club participated in an experiment in which they were given special masks that allowed them to be taught and tested either at the surface or underwater. The students recalled things they had learned at the surface better when they were at the surface than underwater. But when the students were taught things underwater, they recalled them better underwater than at the surface.[11] Students who are taught things in one room recall them better in that room than they do in a different room.[12] Even one's mood can influence what one remembers. In one experiment, university students were given a campus map and taught a nineteen-item set of instructions for a route around the campus. Half of the students were taught sober, and half were taught after three gin and tonics. After the instruction, all students were tested on their knowledge of the map and the instructions. The following day, students were tested a second time on what they remembered, with half being tested sober and half being tested after three more gin and tonics. The students who were taught sober scored the same the next day if they were tested sober but, as might be expected, did much less well if they were tested when intoxicated (scoring 35 percent lower). Those who were taught when intoxicated scored over 25 percent lower on the second day if they were tested when sober, but if they were tested when intoxicated they did just as well as they had the previous day.[13]

This is why the idea of generic or transferable skills is so misguided. Of course, it would be great if we could teach our students to solve problems in science in a way that would also improve their ability to solve problems in history, but it seems that this is not the way our brains work. And if we are to have our students collaborate, communicate, be creative, think critically, and solve problems in a variety of subjects, we need to understand more about how our brains actually work.

## How Our Brains Work

Most people, if asked to copy the following marks on the page, would take quite a while to do it.

ЖӘШІК

It is likely they would have to do it one character, and perhaps even one stroke, at a time and would look back to the page perhaps a dozen times or more to check it was correct. People who have learned some Russian would find it easier, because four of the characters (Ж, Ш, І, К) would be familiar, although one (Ә) would be unfamiliar and would probably need to be copied carefully. Someone who could read Russian could probably look just two or three times at the marks to copy them correctly. Those who can read Kazakh, however, would be able to do it straight away after a single glance, not only because all the letters are familiar, but also because they would recognize the marks as the Kazakh word for *box*.

This may not seem very surprising, but this task, like many others, reveals something rather profound about the way our brains work. Moreover, a failure to understand what such tasks reveal has caused us to design an education system that is fundamentally incapable of doing what we need it to do.

Of course, no one knows exactly how the human brain works, but, over the years, scientists have developed a number of models that seem to describe pretty well how our brains do what they do, and, importantly, they seem to predict quite accurately what humans find hard and what they find easy.

One particularly powerful model involves regarding memory as being made up of two basic components: short-term memory and long-term memory. Short-term memory (or working memory, or even short-term working memory, as it is sometimes called) is where we hold things that we are working on right now, like when we look up a phone number and hold it in our heads while we are dialing the number. Long-term memory is where we store things like our social security numbers and our dates of birth, our route home from work, and what our children look like.

The important point—the point that in fact should guide the whole of education—is that short-term memory is limited, in both capacity and duration. We can't hold very much in short-term memory, and even what little we can hold doesn't stay there for very long. Most adults can remember a seven-digit phone number long enough to key the number into a phone, but ten minutes later, the number is usually difficult to recall.

I live on the boundary of two area codes, 904 and 352, so sometimes, even though I am making a local call, I have to remember to begin dialing with an area code. Fortunately, I don't have to remember ten different digits because, for the area code, I have to remember only whether it is 904 or 352. In other words, it's one extra thing to remember, not three. And this shows the crucial relationship between long-term memory and short-term memory. If I am making a long-distance call to an unfamiliar number, I have ten digits to remember, but if I am making a local call, my knowledge of the two local area codes, which is in long-term memory, makes my use of my short-term memory more efficient. And this is really important, because of the limited capacity of our short-term memories.

In 1956, George Miller, one of America's leading psychologists, published an article titled "The Magical Number Seven, Plus or Minus Two." In the article, he drew attention to the fact that across a range of different kinds of experiments, humans could hold roughly seven things in their heads at the same time. For example, people were played three different tones to hold in their heads, with the lowest-pitched tone labeled 1, the next labeled 2, and the highest labeled 3. Then they had to identify the tone when played. They never made mistakes. With four different tones, mistakes were rare, but with five or more tones, mistakes were frequent, and this did not seem to vary much whether the tones were similar or very different in pitch. Similar results were found when asking people to identify different degrees of loudness, different intensities of taste, different sizes of square, different degrees of brightness, and different intensities of the same hue.[14]

Miller did find much greater capacity in the ability to remember physical locations along a line—up to ten for most people and fifteen for some—which may be why he settled on seven as the magical number. However, as more research has been done, it seems as if, at least for many human capacities, five is more typical than seven.

One aspect of memory that has been researched in great detail is the ability to listen to a string of single-digit numbers being read at the rate of one per second, and then, once all the numbers have been read, to repeat them, either in the same order or backward. One of the reasons this has been so widely studied is that this ability is tested in two widely used intelligence tests, the Wechsler Adult Intelligence Scale (WAIS) and the Wechsler Intelligence Scale for Children (WISC). It certainly seems as if the ability to hold in memory a string of numbers is a fairly good way of measuring the capacity of short-term memory, but even here, the contents of long-term memory turn out to be important.

## Memorizing Digits

At the age of six, most children can correctly reproduce a string of five digits going forward but only three going backward. The ability improves slowly but steadily as children get older, and by the age of sixteen, most young people can correctly recall seven digits going forward and four or five going backward. After the age of twenty, however, forward digit span begins to decline slowly and is down to six digits by the age of eighty, and backward digit span declines in a similar way, dropping from five at the age of twenty to about four at the age of eighty.[15]

Obviously, some people will be able to memorize more numbers than others, but what is interesting is whether the number of digits someone can hold in his or her head can be improved by the right kind of practice.

Anders Ericsson and William Chase, two psychologists at Carnegie Mellon University, investigated this by recruiting an undergraduate student named Steve Faloon at the end of his junior year to help them in their experiments. Faloon would come into the lab at Carnegie Mellon and practice repeating strings of numbers that had been read to him at the rate of one per second.

After four one-hour sessions, Faloon was reliably recalling seven digits and usually got the eight-digit strings right. However, he was getting only about 50 percent of the nine-digit strings and did not manage to recall a single ten-digit string correctly.

Then, on Friday, the fifth day, Faloon managed to recall an eleven-digit number, two more than he had managed on the previous four days. This began what Ericsson describes as "the most surprising two years of my career."[16] By the sixtieth training session, Faloon was managing twenty digits, and after two hundred sessions, he had managed to recall a string of eighty-two digits perfectly.

This appeared to go against everything that was known about memory training at the time. While memory training experiments had produced small improvements in digit span—typically one or two extra digits—nothing like this had ever been seen before. Psychologists had shown time and time again that short-term memory could not be improved very much, and yet here was someone who was literally off the charts. To give some idea of how extreme this was, it was about as surprising as someone scoring over 2000 on an IQ test, where 100 is average and anything over 140 is regarded as genius.[17]

But, as Ericsson and Chase show in their description of the experiment, Faloon's short-term memory didn't improve very much, if at all.[18] His superior performance was produced by harnessing the power of long-term memory.

Faloon was a keen middle-distance runner and had learned a great deal about national and world records. So when he heard "3 . . . 4 . . . 9 . . . 2," he associated this with a time for an athletic event: "3 minutes 49.2 seconds, near world-record mile time."[19] Other strings might be associated with ages, so "8 . . . 9 . . . 3" was a very old man (89.3 years old) and "1 . . . 9 . . . 4 . . . 4" would be just before the end of World War II. This is what George Miller, in his 1956 paper, called *chunking*—breaking material up into chunks so they can be easily memorized—because each chunk seems to take up roughly the same amount of space in short-term memory as a single number.

That is why the task of copying the Kazakh word for *box* discussed earlier is trivially easy for Kazakh readers, straightforward for Russian readers, and really quite demanding for those unfamiliar with the Cyrillic alphabet. It's one chunk for the Kazakh speaker, five or six for the Russian speaker, and about a dozen for a person unfamiliar with the Cyrillic alphabet. Our abilities to hold things in short-term memory depend crucially on what we have in our long-term memories.

Once Faloon's extraordinary performance showed how associating strings of numbers with the contents of long-term memory could improve performance on the digit span task, improvements were rapid. Just since 2000, the world record has been broken twelve times. The current world record for digit span is held by Lance Tschirhart, from Texas, who, at the 2015 World Memory Championships in Chengdu, China, successfully reproduced a string of 456 digits.[20]

At first sight, this seems implausible. At a rate of one per second, it would take almost eight minutes to recite 456 digits. The idea that anyone could listen to those numbers for that length of time and then recite them back, in order, without a single mistake, is hard to believe. However, like most competitors in memory competitions, Tschirhart is able to produce this incredible performance by associating strings of numbers with visual images. For example, he associates the string 141 with a dart, 251 is an electrical outlet, and 213 is a nutmeg. So, to remember the string "1 . . . 4 . . . 1 . . . 2 . . . 5 . . . 1 . . . 2 . . . 1 . . . 3," he says, "I can imagine throwing a dart into an outlet and sparks shooting out around a nutmeg." The important point here is that the power of short-term memory is increased massively by relying on the contents of long-term memory.

Perhaps nowhere is the importance of long-term memory as a way of improving the performance of short-term memory clearer than in playing chess.

## Memory in Chess

In the 1940s, Adriaan de Groot, a chess player and psychologist, conducted a number of experiments about how expert players played chess, which were summarized in his PhD thesis "Thinking About Chess."[21] One of the tasks that he used was to show a position from the middle of a chess game for a few seconds and then ask players to reproduce what they had seen.[22] In one experiment, four players—a chess grandmaster, a master, a good player, and a novice club player—were each asked to do this for fourteen different chessboards. The grandmaster and the master chess players correctly placed 93 percent and 91 percent of the pieces, respectively. The good player placed 68 percent of the pieces correctly, and the novice managed only 51 percent. From this, it was clear that the best chess players had better visual memories, but it was not clear which was the cause and which was the effect. Did the players with naturally better visual memories become better chess players, or did playing chess a lot improve visual memory?

William Chase—whom we met earlier—and Herbert Simon, another psychologist at Carnegie Mellon, decided to use a version of Adriaan de Groot's task to see if they could figure out how expert chess players were able to memorize the positions of chess pieces so much better than novices.

As in de Groot's original experiment, they showed a situation from a chess game to three chess players, an expert, an intermediate player, and a novice, and the players were, after a few seconds, asked to reproduce what they had seen. Each player did this twenty times, with twenty different layouts. As would be expected, given de Groot's results, the expert was much better than the novice and the intermediate player. The novice player got on average four pieces correctly placed, the intermediate player got around eight pieces correct, and the expert got twelve pieces correct.

Chase and Simon then added a new wrinkle to the task. As well as showing situations from actual games, they also included eight chessboards where the pieces had been placed at random. And here the results were very different. The novice got one or two pieces in the right place, the intermediate player did only slightly better, getting two or three pieces in the right place, and the expert was hardly any better than the intermediate player, getting only three pieces in the correct place. Experts are much better than novices at recalling the placement of chess pieces *only when the boards showed positions from actual games.*

Why this might be is made clear by a second wrinkle that Chase and Simon added to the experiment. Ten of the chessboards used were from the middle part of chess games, typically after about fifteen to twenty moves by each player, with about twenty-five pieces remaining on the board, while ten of them showed later parts of games, after about forty moves by each player, with only twelve to fifteen pieces left. The novice and the intermediate player did equally well on mid-game situations *and* end-game situations. However, experts were much better on mid-game situations than they were on the end-game situations. On end-game situations, the expert was no better than the intermediate player, getting about eight pieces correctly placed. However, on middle games, experts got almost twice as many pieces placed correctly (sixteen for the expert versus nine for the intermediate player).[23]

This last finding is particularly important because it rules out the possibility that the expert player had a better visual memory for chessboard situations. If this were the case, the expert would have been better on end-game positions, where there are fewer pieces on the board to remember, than with mid-game positions. The expert was better on the mid-game positions because they were *familiar.* The positions of pieces early in a game will be familiar to expert players because they will have seen them before, and indeed, many of the standard patterns of early play in chess have specific names, such as the "Najdorf variation of the Sicilian defense." Even when the exact pattern of play is unfamiliar, particularly in the middle of games, the pieces will be in familiar patterns, such as connected pawns, so it is the pattern that is remembered, rather than the individual pieces, just as Kazakh speakers remember a word rather than individual strokes on a page when looking at a Kazakh word.

Chase and Simon estimated that a grandmaster would actually have memorized something like fifty thousand different patterns of chess pieces (*chunks* in George Miller's terminology), and it was the ability to see chunks rather than individual pieces that enabled expert chess players to memorize mid-game situations so effectively. Toward the end of a game, the arrangements of pieces are more disorganized, so the pieces are less likely to fit a recognizable pattern. Again, as we saw with memorizing digits, it is the amount of knowledge that is stored in long-term memory that crucially limits what can be held in short-term memory.

## Talent Versus Practice

We see the same thing over and over again. Expert diagnosticians see things in x-ray films that novices cannot see because novices lack the store of knowledge in long-term memory to be able to see what the expert can see.[24] In team sports such as football and soccer, experts can see patterns in what novices see as a jumble of players moving in different directions because they recognize things they have seen before. They do not have superior processing power—they have more, and better organized, content in their long-term memories. And this is why, in so many areas of human experience, it takes so long to acquire expertise. It takes a long time to build up content in long-term memory.

Now, to be sure, there are some areas where better performance is the result of natural gifts. As David Epstein shows in his book *The Sports Gene*, natural gifts play an important role in elite performance in many sporting activities. He points out that if you are a North American male between the ages of twenty and forty, and you are six foot three, your odds of playing professional basketball in the NBA are around one in two hundred thousand. If you are seven feet tall, the odds are one in six. To be a major-league batter in baseball, you need extraordinary eyesight—the typical major-league batter can see at twenty feet what an average person can only see at eleven feet, and this seems to be the result of more, and more densely packed, light-sensing cells in the retina.[25]

In a similar way, some children have natural advantages when it comes to academic achievement at school. I often ask educators whether they believe intelligence, as measured with a traditional IQ test at the end of elementary school, tells us anything about the grade point average that a child will have by the end of high school. Typically, well over ninety American teachers out of every hundred think that it does not. And they are wrong. Students with higher IQ scores at the end of elementary school do on average have higher GPAs at the end of high school, and the link, while far from perfect, is actually quite strong. Moreover, there is a substantial genetic component of intelligence. In the United States, most people seem to assume that the debate about nature versus nurture—whether some people are just naturally intelligent or whether the ability to do IQ tests is the result of their upbringing—has been settled in favor of nurture. In fact, as might be expected, both are important, but studies of identical twins (who therefore share the same genes) who have been reared apart show remarkable similarities in their intelligence.[26] Moreover, the genetic component is not just random—more intelligent parents have more intelligent children. No one who knows the science behind these findings doubts any of these points, but many people find them unacceptable and, as a result, want to downplay the role of genes in academic success. In fact, we should do just the opposite. To see why, a comparison with physical height is instructive.

Most people have little difficulty in accepting the fact that taller parents tend to have taller children, but of course, other factors, particularly nutrition in childhood, also play a part. While estimates vary, the scientific consensus is that, in rich countries, between 60 and 80 percent of the variation in height is due to genetic factors, and 20 to 40 percent is due to environmental factors, such as nutrition.[27] However, if some children are deprived of key nutrients, such as calcium and vitamins A and D, then how tall they will be as adults will depend on how much calcium and key vitamins they got. Well-nourished children will be taller and poorly nourished children will be shorter. The population would, on average, be shorter, but the *variation* in height will be greater. If, on the other hand, all children have equally good nutrition, then average height would increase, but more variation in height will be genetic, because the environments in which different children are raised aren't that different. Ideally, we would like to reduce the environmental contribution to zero because that would mean that we were doing everything we could in terms of nutrition, and the only remaining source of variation in height would be genetic.

In the same way, if we gave all students a uniformly high-quality upbringing and education, then the average achievement would be higher, but environmental factors would play a smaller role, because the differences in the upbringing and education that children received would be smaller. This means that the genetic contribution to achievement would actually increase. Some students really do find learning school stuff easier than other students, but by minimizing the environmental sources of variation, we create a more equal world, even if the genetic contribution to achievement increases.

In a way, the reluctance of teachers to acknowledge the role of intelligence in academic achievement is perfectly understandable, especially given the use of intelligence tests in the eugenics movement in the United States in the first half of the twentieth century.[28] But as David Hume, the Scottish philosopher, pointed out many years ago, you can't deduce an *ought* from an *is*—the fact that something *is* the case does not mean it *has* to be that way.[29] Accepting that some students are more intelligent than others, accepting that some students find learning school stuff easier than others, does not mean we have to accept that that this is the way things have to be. Indeed, the inventor of the IQ test, Alfred Binet, was primarily interested in how to identify Parisian schoolchildren who might need additional support to be successful in school. He is reputed to have said, "Why measure something if you cannot change it?"

Similar views were expressed by the American psychologist Benjamin Bloom, who pointed out that if the results of students form a "bell curve" of scores, then the education system is not working properly, because the bell curve is what nature gives us. The purpose of education is to destroy the bell curve and make sure that *all* students gain the level of proficiency on their state's standards that they need to live productive and fulfilled lives.

Bloom thought that the best way to ensure that all students were proficient on the academic standards adopted was to find ways of increasing the instructional time for those students who needed it. Now, of course, this is obviously correct. Increased instructional time for those who are failing to reach the standards specified for their grade is undoubtedly an effective way of increasing student achievement. But it is not *efficient*. Increasing instructional time can be difficult and expensive to organize, especially in suburban and rural areas, because of the need to provide additional transportation. Fortunately, there is a less expensive alternative.

As we have seen in this chapter, particularly in areas that do not require physical skill, it seems that what really separates those with high- and low-level performance is the content of long-term memory, and this is why curriculum matters so much in school. The differences in people's intelligence and differences in the capacities of their short-term working memories (which undoubtedly exist) matter very little if they have the same extensive knowledge. Education can't do much for intelligence or working memory,[30] but it can have a massive impact on long-term memory.

The important point—the fact about our brains that should drive our whole education system—is that we cannot create the chunks on the fly. One of the reasons that the digit span task is so challenging is that hearing numbers at the rate of one per second does not allow the numbers to be stored in long-term memory. We can, like Steve Faloon or Lance Tschirhart, use things that are already in long-term memory to improve the efficiency of the way that we use short-term memory, but we cannot move things temporarily from short-term memory to long-term memory when we are engaged in a task. That is not the way our brains work. Once things leave short-term memory, they are gone, and they have to be refreshed. To be useful in expanding the capacity of short-term memory, the chunks have to be already existing in long-term memory.

The big mistake we have made in the United States, and indeed in many other countries, is to assume that if we want students to be able to think, then our curriculum should give our students lots of practice in thinking. This is a mistake because what our students need is more to think *with*. The main purpose of curriculum is to build up the content of long-term memory so that when students are asked to think, they are able to think in more powerful ways because what is in their long-term memories makes their short-term memories more powerful. That is why curriculum matters.

---

1   Mandel (2013).

2   http://www.businessinsider.com/nyc-yellow-cab-medallion-prices-falling-further-2016-10.

3   Beach (2014).

4   Epson Europe (2014).

5   M. Jackson and Wolff (1983).

6   Gaudin (2014).

7   Edwards (2016).

8   Papert (1998).

9   Honey, Fasca, Gersick, Mandinach, and Sinha (2005, p. 4).

10  See, for example, https://en.wikipedia.org/wiki/Mathematical_fallacy#Division_by_zero.

11  Godden and Baddeley (1975).

12  S. M. Smith, Glenberg, and Bjork (1978).

13  Lowe (1980).

14  Miller (1956).

15  Myerson, Emery, White, and Hale (2003).

16  A. Ericsson and Pool (2016, p. 4).

17  On the Wechsler intelligence tests, the mean digit span is approximately 6.5, with a standard deviation of just over 0.5. A digit span of 82 is about 130 standard deviations above the mean, and since the standard deviation of a standardized IQ is generally around 15 points, Faloon's performance is as unexpected as someone getting an IQ score that is $130 \times 15$ points above the mean.

18  K. A. Ericsson, Chase, and Faloon (1980).

19  Ibid (p. 1181).

20  World Memory Sports Council (2016).

21  This was published in English as de Groot (1965/1978).

22  This task had been used by Djakow, Petrovskij, and Rudik (1927) to study players attending the 1925 International Chess Tournament in Moscow, but players had been given over a minute to study the position of the pieces, whereas de Groot's experiments allowed players much shorter intervals (typically two to ten seconds).

23  Chase and Simon (1973).

24  Lesgold, Rubinson, Feltovich, Glaser, Klopfer, and Wang (1988).

25  D. Epstein (2013).

26  For an up-to-date summary of what we know about intelligence, see Ritchie (2015).

27  Lai (2017).

28  See Selden (1999) for an excellent history of the eugenics movement in the United States.

29  The idea that you cannot deduce an *ought* from an *is*—also known at the naturalistic fallacy—was described by David Hume in *A Treatise of Human Nature* (Hume, 1739).

30  See, for example, Hitchcock and Westwell (2017).

CHAPTER 10

# A Knowledge-Rich Curriculum

In the previous chapter, we saw how what is stored in long-term memory is crucial for the effective use of short-term memory. The more children have in their long-term memories, the less important the capacity of short-term memory becomes. That's why a major goal of education is to equip children with knowledge (i.e., rich stores in long-term memory), which is, in turn, why a knowledge-rich curriculum is essential.

People who advocate a knowledge-rich curriculum are often accused of adopting the beliefs of Thomas Gradgrind, the superintendent of the school board in Charles Dickens's novel *Hard Times*:

> Now, what I want is, Facts. Teach these boys and girls nothing but Facts. Facts alone are wanted in life. Plant nothing else, and root out everything else. You can only form the minds of reasoning animals upon Facts: nothing else will ever be of any service to them. This is the principle on which I bring up my own children, and this is the principle on which I bring up these children. Stick to Facts, sir![1]

Now facts are certainly important, but what is even more important, as the following exchange illustrates, is an understanding of the relationship between facts.

Teacher: When was the Treaty of London signed?

Student A: 1604.

Student B: I don't know, but it must have been in the first few years of the seventeenth century, because by 1608, a permanent settlement had been established in Jamestown, Virginia, and previous attempts to establish permanent settlements had failed because they needed regular supplies from England, which were being disrupted by the ongoing war with Spain, and while the defeat of the Spanish Armada in 1588 was important, the war was only finally ended by the Treaty of London.

Student A is correct, while student B does not know the correct answer. However, student B understands why the Treaty of London is important for American history, and, moreover, her response demonstrates two key aspects of historical thinking—chronology and cause and effect. Of course, it would be even better if student B had also known the date of the Treaty of London, but few people would disagree that student B has the kind of understanding of the issues we seek. Facts are important, but what is more important is understanding how facts fit together.

This is why having a properly planned and sequenced curriculum is so important. If we just wanted students to learn facts, then they could be learned in any order. After all, one isolated fact is no more difficult to learn than any other. We could just list all the things that we wanted the students to know, and they could be taught in any order. However, that would not help students see the connection between different aspects of their knowledge. More important, the lack of connection between different aspects of knowledge means that students are less likely to remember what they have learned. Connections between different aspects of knowledge are important both in and of themselves and as an aid to long-term memory.

How much of a difference having the right curriculum makes has become clearer within the last decade or so, as states have begun to collect more systematic data on the textbooks being used in different schools.

In recent years, the whole idea of having textbooks has come under attack. Some argue that textbooks undermine teachers' ability to plan effective instruction for their students. It is certainly possible that the very best teachers would be as effective without textbooks, but given the weak subject knowledge of some American teachers,[2] it seems unlikely that the average teacher could produce better instructional materials each day than the best textbook writers.[3] Others argue that which textbook is the most effective depends on the teachers using them, but this does not seem to be true—textbooks that are more effective on average tend to be more effective for all teachers, irrespective of the teacher's subject knowledge, his or her attitude toward the subject, and the range of achievement in the classes they teach.[4]

Another common criticism of textbooks is that they are rather old-fashioned. In 2015, at the launch of #GoOpen—an initiative to allow states and districts to share instructional materials—Secretary of Education Arne Duncan said, "In order to ensure that all students—no matter their zip code—have access to high-quality learning resources, we are encouraging districts and states to move away from traditional textbooks and toward freely accessible, openly licensed materials."

One specific benefit of digitizing instructional materials that Arne Duncan noted was making available "materials that can be constantly updated and adjusted to meet students' needs."[5] However, as Tim Oates, director of assessment research and development at the University of Cambridge's International Examinations Group, points out, print materials are actually better than online resources in many ways.

- Recent research has shown that scrolling and navigating use up valuable brain capacity so comprehension suffers.

- Referring back to old material is easier with a book than with a collection of websites.

- The Ministry of Education in Singapore found that when their (very well-designed) textbooks were made available electronically, they were less effective, so they went back to books.

- The physical experience of reading a book may be better for developing long-term memory.[6]

Others have pointed out that moving away from textbooks makes it easier for schools to collaborate and share resources. Richard Culatta, who was director of technology at the Department of Education during the Obama administration, has suggested that textbooks should be discarded entirely and replaced with digital materials within the next few years: "So you may have a district that says, 'We're going to pull together a great list of resources for teaching fractions.' You have another district that says, 'We're going to do a similar thing for division.'"[7]

The idea that districts can collaborate and share materials is very attractive, but there is one fundamental flaw with the whole idea. A collection of teaching resources is no more a curriculum than a pile of bricks is a house. If students are to develop knowledge, what is crucial is how one set of materials builds on previous materials and builds the foundations for the next. This is why, to paraphrase Mark Twain, reports of the death of textbooks are greatly exaggerated. Most high-performing countries—even the ones that could afford to give every child a tablet or a laptop—make extensive use of textbooks because they enable every student to get high-quality instructional materials. Increasingly, they are also making use of online resources as well, but textbooks are likely to continue to provide the main learning resource for high-quality instruction for the foreseeable future.

The value of good textbooks was demonstrated in an experiment conducted by Roberto Agodini and his colleagues. In the 2006–2007 school year, 131 teachers in thirty-nine elementary schools were asked to use a particular math textbook with their students, selected at random from four well-known and popular textbooks. Students using *Saxon Math* and *Math Expressions* made about three months' more progress in first grade than students using the other two textbooks (*Investigations in Numbers, Data, and Space* and *Scott Foresman – Addison Wesley Mathematics*).[8]

Because the schools were allocated textbooks at random, it might appear that these results are cut-and-dried. However, closer investigation revealed that the way the textbooks were used differed from school to school. First, the teachers following the *Saxon Math* program spent about one more hour on math each week, so the three months' extra progress the students made with these textbooks might just be the result of more time spent on math. Second, some teachers had more help than others. Approximately half of the teachers using *Investigations in Number, Data, and Space* had access to a coach to help them with the new textbooks, while the figure for those using *Saxon Math* and *Math Expressions* was around 80 percent. Third, when the researchers followed the students through into second grade, they found that those who had followed the *Scott Foresman–Addison Wesley Mathematics* caught up with those using *Saxon Math* and *Math Expressions* (although those following the *Investigations in Number, Data, and Space* continued to make less progress). Some textbooks that appear to be less successful in the short term may in fact be laying sound foundations for future learning.

A fourth problem with evaluating textbooks is that a particular textbook might be well aligned to the standards in one state but less well aligned to the standards in another. A recent study found that the *California Math* textbook series was more effective than other textbooks for elementary school students in California.[9] This is useful information for schools in California, but it is not at all clear that textbooks specifically designed for California's math standards would be as effective in another state. Where states have adopted the Common Core State Standards, then there are likely to be well-aligned textbooks, but for other states, many will not have enough students to make it cost effective for publishers to produce a set of textbooks specifically for that state.

The conclusion here is reminiscent of what we saw in chapter 2 with teachers. There, we saw that some teachers are more effective than others, but it is impossible to tell, with any certainty, which individual teachers are more (or indeed less) effective. In the same way, there is now good evidence that not all textbooks are equally effective. For a particular district, some textbooks are likely to be more effective than others for their students, and the difference is likely to be large (up to an extra three months' learning for each child, each year, on average). Unfortunately, it does not seem to be possible to predict with any certainty which textbooks would be the best choice for a particular district.

This is frustrating, of course, because getting the right textbooks is absolutely the most cost-effective way of raising student achievement there is, if you can figure out which textbooks are the right textbooks. While some textbooks are more expensive than others, the differences are small and entirely negligible compared with the costs of teachers' salaries and school buildings.

However, while we cannot be absolutely certain that a particular curriculum will be the best choice, the existing research shows clearly that it is worth taking textbook choice seriously. In many school districts, teachers decide for themselves which textbooks to use, while in others, the decision is made by a curriculum supervisor or an assistant superintendent. Of course, such a process could lead to good choices, but it seems unlikely that a school board would delegate such a decision to a small number of individuals if they knew the stakes. In a school district with ten thousand students, getting the right textbooks could produce increases in learning that would cost as much as $30 million every year to achieve in other ways.[10]

While we do not know in advance which textbooks will be the most effective, there is some good guidance available, and the remainder of this chapter looks at what districts should take into account in deciding which textbooks to adopt.

## The Low-Hanging Fruit: Alignment

Perhaps the most obvious thing to check when looking at which textbooks to adopt is to see whether the textbooks cover the things that students need to learn. It may be obvious, but in many districts, the match between textbooks, the standards, and the tests students take is not good. In many cases, standardized tests do not cover all the things that students need to be learning, so there can be very good reasons for using textbooks that cover things that are not tested or even things that are not in the standards at all. What is less easy to justify is using textbooks that do not cover things that students need to learn, either to do well on the tests they will be taking or for their future needs. Of course, teachers can always supplement the textbooks with additional material, but such material is time consuming to produce, and even when teachers can do this to a high standard, there is always the issue of opportunity cost—what else could they have done with the time?

Ensuring adequate curriculum coverage may seem obvious, but it is often overlooked. Like many other states, New Jersey requires students to pass standardized tests in English language arts and mathematics in order to graduate high school. In most districts, the mathematics test presents more of a challenge than that for English language arts, and in some districts, only around one-fourth of students were passing the mathematics test on the first attempt. Siobhan Leahy and Christine Lyon, two researchers at the Educational Testing Service in Princeton, New Jersey, worked with a local school district to try to improve graduation rates. They discovered that one of the main sticking points was that teachers were not teaching students some of the content on which they would be tested. The researchers helped local teachers prepare review lessons that ensured that students received instruction on all tested material, and in one year, the pass rate for the mathematics assessment rose from 27 percent to 40 percent—a 50 percent increase in the pass rate just by ensuring good alignment between what is taught and what is tested.[11] What perhaps is most interesting is why teachers weren't teaching the necessary content. When asked, they thought changing what they taught to align with the content of the test would be teaching to the test, which they believed was inappropriate. Of course, teaching to the test can be bad if it means distorting the curriculum by teaching only those things that are tested, even when the tests don't fully reflect the standards. But in every school, students must have the opportunity to learn the material on which they are going to be tested.

Many states have tried to ensure alignment by requiring all textbooks and other instructional materials purchased with public funds to be approved by the states (although there is generally nothing to stop other funds, such as charitable contributions raised locally, from being spent on unapproved materials). While some saw such restrictions as a guarantee of quality, there is little doubt that in most states, the textbook review process focused far more on issues of sensitivity (such as the relative number of males and females depicted) than instructional quality, and state approval processes have been criticized from both sides of the political spectrum.[12]

Partly in response to these criticisms, many states have relaxed the regulations regarding textbook purchases. Many of them, including California, Florida, and Texas, still produce lists of approved textbooks but allow districts to choose the materials they think will suit their students best. Others, such as Louisiana, go further and publish annotated reviews of major textbooks and allocate textbooks and other instructional materials to one of three tiers. Tier 3 materials are those that fail to meet a series of nonnegotiable criteria. In mathematics, Louisiana's nonnegotiable criteria are that all materials should be:

- Focused on the main standards

- Consistent and coherent

- Balanced and rigorous in developing conceptual understanding, procedural skill and fluency, and application

In English language arts, the nonnegotiable criteria include requirements for the texts

- To build content knowledge and reading skill

- To include a range of genres, including literature and informational texts

- In the elementary grades, to build the foundational skills in reading

- To integrate reading, writing, speaking, and listening

Materials that meet these requirements are allocated to Tier 2 or Tier 1, depending on how far they also satisfy additional desirable criteria.[13]

While such state review procedures do generally ensure adequate alignment with the state's standards and tests and provide a good starting point for review, such procedures do not provide a guarantee of quality, for several reasons.

First, what is in the materials matters less than how they are used. Materials that look good may, in practice, be rather ineffective if they are not used in the intended way by teachers, so effective implementation may require a great deal of staff support. Second, they may not capture the interest or imagination of students, which, as any parent knows, is often impossible to predict. Third, and most important, texts and materials that look as if they should be effective may not be, because in many aspects of human performance, the best way to get good at something is by doing something else. People learning to play musical instruments practice scales, even though the scales they are learning are unlikely to feature in any pieces of music they will ever actually be asked to play. Professional football players practice tire runs, in which they run over tires laid out in zigzag patterns, not because this skill will ever be needed—during a real game, there aren't any tires on a football field—but because they develop skills of agility, endurance, speed, and strength. The best things to do to get good at something often do not look like the thing you are trying to get good at. One particularly interesting example of this kind involves a game that Brazilians call "futebol de salão" (literally, "ballroom football" or "hall football").

## Going at Things Sideways: The Case of *Futsal*

As its name suggests, *futebol de salão*, or usually just *futsal*, is an indoor version of soccer. The basics of the game were invented by Juan Carlos Ceriani Gravier. Born in Buenos Aires in 1907, after high school, he studied economics at the North American Academy of Buenos Aires but then spent two years at the International YMCA Training Schools in Springfield, Massachusetts, training to become what the YMCA calls a "secretary general of physical education" (someone who is in charge of physical education at a YMCA branch). Following his postgraduate training, he returned to Buenos Aires, where, from 1928 to 1929, he was director of the physical education department at the Buenos Aires branch of the YMCA.

In 1930, he moved to Uruguay to take up the post of director of the children's department at the YMCA's branch in Montevideo and undertook further study at the Technical Institute of the South American Federation of YMCAs, an organization that had been set up in Montevideo in 1922 to train directors of physical education for YMCAs for the whole of South America.[14] It was there that he hit on the idea of playing soccer on a basketball court to allow children to play in all weather conditions.

The rules he invented for the game were, of course, based on soccer, but the adaptations made to the game to make it work on a smaller playing field drew on a number of other sports that he had studied in Springfield. The number of players on a team (five) and the duration of a game (forty minutes) were taken from basketball, but the role of goalkeeper was modeled on water polo. The size of the playing field was taken from handball, as was the size of the goal.

*Futsal* (*fútbal sala* or *fútbol de salón* in Spanish) caught on quickly in Uruguay, not least because soccer was gaining in popularity as a result of the country's success in international competitions, gaining gold medals in soccer at the 1924 and 1928 Olympic Games and winning the World Cup in 1930. As a result, the game featured strongly in the work of the Technical Institute in Montevideo. And because the Technical Institute was training directors of physical education for the whole of South America, the game spread quickly across the continent.

Two Brazilians, João Lotufo and Asdrubal Monteiro, had graduated from the institute in 1935. When they returned to São Paulo, Brazil, they encouraged the development of the game, and as they rose within the YMCA, their influence increased. By 1948, Lotufo had been appointed as secretary general for the Christian youth ministries for the whole of São Paulo, and Monteiro had taken over as director of physical education. One problem they saw was that while futsal was growing in popularity, there were a number of concerns about the number of injuries sustained by players, so they looked at a number of changes they could make to the rules to make it safer. The changes they proposed essentially defined the modern game.

Lotufo and Monteiro decided that a traditional soccer ball was too large and so tried using smaller balls. The standard futsal ball has a diameter of eight inches, which is the size typically used in soccer with players from eight to twelve years old. It is also heavier than a soccer ball, weighing fourteen to sixteen ounces at the start of a game, whereas a standard soccer ball of the same size would be two or three ounces lighter.

Lotufo and Monteiro also decided that a traditional soccer ball was too bouncy, so they tried filling the balls with sawdust, cork, and even horsehair to deaden the bounce, and this idea has also passed through to the modern game. The standard rules of futsal now specify how bouncy the ball should be: dropped from a height of six feet six inches (i.e., two meters), the first bounce must be at least twenty inches and no more than twenty-six inches (for comparison, a standard soccer ball dropped from the same height would bounce between fifty-three and sixty-one inches[15]). This makes the ball a lot deader than a typical soccer ball—indeed, before the term *futsal* was widely used, the game was known in Brazil as *the sport of the heavy ball*.[16]

From this description of its origins, it should be clear that the game of futsal was never intended as a training program for improving soccer skills. Its entire purpose was as a way of keeping children entertained in the inner city where there weren't any soccer fields. Nevertheless, several features of futsal have obvious benefits in terms of developing the skills needed for soccer.

First, slide tackles and excessive body contact are forbidden, so there is a premium on skill, rather than size, which is important in getting younger children involved. The small size of the playing field means that opposing players can close on the player with the ball quickly, placing a premium on fast thinking and accurate passing. Also, with a smaller playing field, raw speed is less important than ball-control skill. The heavy, and less bouncy, ball helps younger players develop ball-control skills. Also, with only five players on a side, each player gets to touch the ball more times per minute of game time.[17]

Now, of course, the fact that countries in South America that play a lot of futsal also do well in international soccer competitions does not prove that futsal is the cause of that success. But it is worth noting that many of the world's greatest soccer players played futsal in their youth. Moreover, Pele, Lionel Messi, and Ronaldo all credit futsal as being an important part of their development as soccer players. It certainly seems plausible that the kinds of skills required in futsal—good ball control, quick passing, and so on—would be of benefit when playing regular soccer.

The important point for the purpose of the argument being made here is that it might be assumed that the best way to get people to play soccer better is to have them play lots of soccer, on the grounds that practice makes perfect. But in soccer at least, it seems that the best way to get people playing soccer well may be to get them to practice doing something else.

This is an important lesson that we have to take to heart when we move from our standards, whatever they are, to figuring out the best way to help students achieve those standards. In English language arts, for example, if we want students to be able to identify the main idea in a passage, it seems obvious that the best way to do that would be to practice identifying the main idea in lots of different passages. If we want students to be able to solve problems in mathematics, it seems reasonable that the best way to achieve this is for students to practice solving problems in mathematics lessons. If we want students to understand scientific ideas, then wouldn't it be great if students could carry out the scientific experiments that led to those ideas? However, as with soccer and futsal, it seems that things are a little more complex than that.

## Knowledge, Not Skills

In a series of publications, extending over several decades, E. D. Hirsch Jr., now emeritus professor of education and humanities at the University of Virginia, has shown convincingly that many, if not most, of the difficulties that children have in making progress in reading stem not from a lack of reading skill but from a lack of background knowledge about what is being described in the text. Consider this extract from a news item that appeared on the Politico website in 2015:

> The Nebraska Supreme Court just dropped the Keystone XL
> pipeline decision back onto John Kerry's lap. That means the
> secretary of state will have a chance to show just how com
> mitted he is to tackling climate change, environmentalists say,
> just a month after Kerry jetted to Peru to press for the world
> to act.[18]

The reporter has presumably used the phrase *secretary of state* as an example of what writing stylists call *elegant variation* in order to avoid mentioning John Kerry's name three times in the same paragraph. But the effect is to make the paragraph incomprehensible if you do not know that John Kerry is secretary of state. Background knowledge about what is being described is essential to understanding the paragraph.

Most readers of this book will have had little difficulty with the passage above because they knew that, at the time it was written, John Kerry was indeed secretary of state. But people who did not know this fact would have formed a completely different understanding of the paragraph, and, most important, *would not know that their understanding was not what was intended*. The content of long-term memory is always, and instantaneously, influencing what is happening in short-term memory.

In a similar vein, for someone who knows about baseball, the following sentence is perfectly clear: "He got a walk to first, stole second, got bunted over to third, and scored on a sacrifice fly." Someone who is not familiar with baseball might not know the meaning of the word *bunt*, but even if the meaning of this unfamiliar term is explained to them, they would not be able to understand what is being read or spoken because they cannot make sense of what they are hearing or reading quickly enough.

E. D. Hirsch summarizes what is going on in situations like these as follows:

> Comprehension depends on constructing a mental model that makes the elements fall into place and, equally important, enables the listener or reader to supply essential information that is not explicitly stated. In language use, there is always a great deal that is left unsaid and must be inferred. This means that communication depends on both sides, writer and reader, sharing a basis of unspoken knowledge. This large dimension of tacit knowledge is precisely what is not being taught adequately in our schools.[19]

This is a profoundly important insight because it highlights why what is happening in many American classrooms will not achieve what is wanted. All states, in their standards for English language arts, include requirements for students to be able to identify the main idea of a passage of text. As a result, teachers all over the United States spend a great deal of time teaching students about reading comprehension strategies—a set of general skills that students can use when they are reading.

The idea of teaching students general strategies for reading is attractive, because once students have learned the strategies, they can be applied to any reading activity. Moreover, the strategies seem plausible because anyone who can read recognizes in the strategies things that they do when they read. Most people who have come across an unfamiliar word have tried to figure out what the word means by looking at the context in which the word appears. Most readers have had the experience of having one's eyes scan the words on a page but realize that they haven't been taking it in—knowing whether you are, in fact, understanding something when reading is undoubtedly a useful skill. And most readers know that sometimes you have to make connections between different sentences to understand the text, as in the following example from Daniel Willingham and Gail Lovette: "I can't convince my boys that their beds aren't trampolines. The building manager is pressuring us to move to the ground floor."

The two sentences make perfect sense as separate sentences. The parent might not be able to convince her or his children that their beds are not trampolines, and, coincidentally, the building manager might be pressuring the family to move to the ground floor. But the intended interpretation is that the building manager is pressuring the family to move to the ground floor *because* the boys are using their beds as trampolines.[20]

In fact, there is now a great deal of research evidence that shows that teaching these three main reading comprehension strategies—using context to figure out a word's meaning, noticing understanding, and connecting ideas—does improve children's reading.[21] However, to use these strategies sensibly, it is important to understand how they work.

Many people assume that reading strategies are skills, and if they are practiced over and over again, students will get better and better—more skillful, in fact—at them. However, as Willingham and Lovette point out, this cannot be the explanation. To make the connection between the two sentences above, the reader has to supply additional information that is not provided in the text, including the fact that bouncing up and down on beds is noisy or at least creates vibrations, that this is disturbing to neighbors (particularly those on the floor below them), that the building manager wants to respond to the neighbors' complaints, and that if the beds were on the ground floor, the problem would be solved or at least less serious. A general reading strategy (i.e., one that would apply to any passage of text) cannot possibly anticipate all the things that a student might read:

> It can't tell a reader the specifics of how to achieve reading comprehension because comprehension depends on connecting the meaning of sentences, and doing that depends on sentence content. No reading comprehension strategy can offer general guidelines about how to connect sentences; you need to know that the first sentence is about bed trampolines and second sentence is about apartment managers before you know how they relate.[22]

The real reason reading comprehension strategy instruction works seems to be that it helps readers, especially those who are struggling, to see that the purpose of reading is not to get to the end of the paragraph, or page, or book, but rather, that it is to understand what someone else is trying to say. The strategies work because they provide a few pointers when readers are stuck, but that's as far as they go. The most convincing evidence for this is that fifty lessons on reading strategies don't seem to be any more effective than ten.[23] Yes, teachers should teach reading comprehension strategies to their students, but once taught, they do not need to be practiced much. It is important that students are able to identify the main idea of a passage, but getting the main idea does not need to be practiced much because it's not a skill. Getting the main idea of a passage depends on knowing a lot about what is being discussed in the text. And that is why the majority of English language arts instruction should be focused on building knowledge, through reading, speaking, listening, and writing.

The same principles apply in other school subjects, as illustrated by the following mathematical activity that features in the British TV quiz show *Countdown*. In one segment of the show, participants are shown some numbers and have to use the four rules of arithmetic (addition, subtraction, multiplication, division) with all or some of these numbers to get as close as they can to a given target number. Given the numbers shown below and a target number of 127, most adults can find a perfect solution quite quickly.

What is interesting is that most adults find a solution quickly because the fact that 25 multiplied by 4 is 100 just comes into their heads. This is not the way a computer would solve the problem. A computer would try many combinations of numbers until it found one that worked. But for someone who has the fact that $4 \times 25$ is 100 in long-term memory, this fact is rapidly retrieved when they see the 4 and the 25, and they know they need to reach a total of 127. As we saw earlier, it is the content of long-term memory that makes short-term memory efficient. This is why knowing multiplication tables by heart is so useful.

Many people assume that if students do not know their multiplication facts but can work out number facts quickly, then that is just as good. For example, say a student is working on a problem that requires knowing what $6 \times 6$ is. If the student does not know this by heart but does know that $3 \times 6$ is 18 and knows that $6 \times 6$ will be twice that and can calculate this in a second or so, then many people assume this is OK. However, there are two issues with such an approach. The first is that the student has used up valuable space in short-term memory to perform this calculation, whereas the student who just knows that 6 × 6 is 36 has all her short-term memory available for the problem at hand. The second issue is that students who know that 6 × 6 is 36 instantaneously can see connections between numbers in the same way that most adults immediately know that 25 × 4 is 100 when presented with the *Countdown* problem above.

The relationship between long-term memory and short-term memory also has implications for learning more advanced aspects of mathematics. In the early 1980s, an Australian psychologist named John Sweller looked at the best way to help high school and university students solve mathematical problems—a major aim of math instruction. In one of his early experiments, he and his colleagues gave college math majors a starting number and a target number, and the students were asked to get from the starting number to the target number by using just two rules: multiply by 3 or subtract 29. Since the students were all math majors, the students solved the problems quickly, with few failures or false steps. But there was something very surprising about the performance of the students. They didn't get any quicker at solving the problems even after practice. Sweller and his colleagues found this surprising, because every single pair of starting number and target number they used in the experiment had the same solution strategy—students were required to alternate the two arithmetic operations in a fixed sequence. So, if four steps were required to solve the problem, the solution was always ×3, –29, ×3, –29. If six steps were needed, it was always ×3, –29, ×3, –29, ×3, –29. The students were solving the problem, but they weren't *learning* anything.

After a few more experiments of this kind with similar results, Sweller and his colleagues developed a simple but powerful idea, which they called *cognitive load theory*. The main idea of cognitive load theory is that the mechanism that transfers information into long-term memory itself takes up space in short-term memory. If all the capacity of short-term memory is used on the problem at hand, nothing gets learned. In other words, for novices at least, *solving problems is not the way to learn to solve problems*.

As Sweller himself later observed, "It was the worst possible time to be publishing papers calling into question the efficacy of using problem solving as a learning device."[24] In 1980, the National Council of Teachers of Mathematics had published its *Agenda for Action*, which called for problem solving to be at the heart of math instruction.[25] Now, of course, no one would disagree with the idea that a major goal of math instruction is to get students to be able to solve mathematical problems. But very quickly, the focus shifted from problem solving as a *goal* of math instruction to the idea that problem solving should be the *means* of getting there as well, which, as Sweller had shown, was just incorrect. However, for reasons that are now hard to understand, the main reaction to Sweller's careful experimental work was not disagreement. No one tried to find errors in the experiments that had been carried out. Instead, the main response was to ignore the work completely.

Spurred on by the fact that they were finding the same thing over and over again, and no one was finding any conflicting evidence, during the next two decades, Sweller and his colleagues developed their ideas further and showed conclusively that tasks that overloaded short-term memory resulted in less learning. Some of their key findings are shown below.

- For novices, worked examples—where they are taken through the steps of solving a problem by the teacher—are more effective than having the students solve problems themselves. For more expert students, problem-solving tasks work well, because they have some spare capacity in short-term memory so cognitive load is not too great.

- Tasks where students have to split their attention (e.g., between a text and a diagram) are less effective than those where the text and the diagram are integrated.

- Redundant information reduces learning. If a textbook has a diagram of a heart that shows blood flowing from the left ventricle to the aorta, adding text that says, "Blood flows from the left ventricle to the aorta" makes it harder for students to process the information and so reduces learning.

- Where a task requires integrating a number of pieces of complex information, introducing the elements one by one and making sure that each of the individual elements is understood is more effective than presenting information in a more natural format.

In the same way that practicing the skill of getting the main idea does not improve students' ability to identify the main idea of a passage of text very much, practicing problem solving does not improve problem solving very much unless there is a lot of knowledge stored in long-term memory.

Once the principles of cognitive load theory have been understood, these conclusions may seem obvious. However, all over the United States, there are calls for students to be involved in more authentic tasks in classrooms—solving real, as opposed to contrived, problems, learning science concepts by undertaking experiments rather than being formally taught, role-playing historical events, and so on. Where students already have a great deal of knowledge about the subject at hand, practice in applying this is useful. But if the necessary background knowledge is not present, then investigative or authentic tasks are often ineffective. This is particularly true for practical work in science classrooms.

As mentioned in chapter 1, many people believe that we need more students studying science to an advanced level. According to the latest PISA survey, almost two in every five American fifteen-year-olds expect to be working in a scientific field at the age of thirty—ten years ago, the figure was less than one in three. And three-fourths of them believe that studying science will enhance their career prospects. A similar proportion say that they enjoy learning science. So, what's the problem? Most American students think science is important, think it will enhance their career prospects, and say that they enjoy learning science. The problem is that we may have made science learning enjoyable but less effective.

When students are asked what kinds of things they like to do in science lessons, practical activities in laboratories usually come top of the list. Moreover, doing experiments that allow students to see scientific concepts such as angular momentum in action does lead to higher achievement.[26] But—and given the focus of this chapter, this will not be surprising—the role of long-term memory is crucial. Put bluntly, when students do experiments, they often do not have enough content knowledge to understand what they are seeing. While students do seem to prefer inquiry-based instruction, it is generally less effective than teacher-led instruction, at least as far as performance in the most recent PISA survey.

The 2015 PISA survey focused on science literacy and investigated in particular the factors that were associated with student success in science. The two most positive factors were predictable—students from more affluent homes did better, as did students taught by teachers who were able to adapt the lesson to meet their individual needs. The third most significant positive factor was how much teacher-directed instruction took place. The more teacher-led instruction there was in a classroom, the higher students scored on PISA. And, at the other end of the scale, students in classrooms where there was a lot of inquiry-based instruction, where students explored their own scientific ideas, did worse. In fact, inquiry-based instruction had a greater negative impact on student achievement in science than student absence (defined as skipping at least one day of school in a two-week period).[27] To be effective, practical work in laboratories has to be designed to build carefully on students' formal scientific knowledge—what they already have in long-term memory.

These results are surprising to many people, but in fact, they are consistent with a large body of research evidence that has accumulated over the last fifty years or so on the effectiveness of what is sometimes called *direct instruction*.

Direct instruction originated in the efforts of Siegfried Engelmann and his colleagues at the University of Illinois in the 1960s to design a preschool program for students from impoverished backgrounds. The main idea behind direct instruction is an assumption that the differences we see in student achievement are mainly due to poorly designed instruction—the basic belief is that all students can learn with well-designed instruction. In contrast to more exploratory approaches to learning, for example by using authentic tasks, direct instruction involves choosing and sequencing examples carefully and ensuring that students have become fluent in a particular task before moving on to the next step. This approach is clearly consistent with the model of short-term and long-term memory discussed previously. Practicing any task until fluent involves transferring the task to long-term memory, thus freeing up short-term memory for the next step, much as learning patterns of chess pieces allows expert players to see the big picture rather than individual pieces.

Over the last fifty years, although direct instruction has been rather ignored in education policy, a large number of research studies have been carried out and show consistently positive effects on student learning. A recent review of 328 studies on direct instruction, in different school subjects, for students of different ages, found that the impact of direct instruction was comparable to the size of the achievement gap between advantaged and disadvantaged students.[28] While the details of how direct instruction was implemented differ from study to study, there seems little doubt that carefully planned and sequenced and explicit teaching of what we want our students to learn is essential for student success.

To recap, short-term memory is limited, both in capacity and duration, and cannot be increased very much, if at all. The way humans become more capable is not by extending the capacity of short-term memory but by having more content in long-term memory. The major purpose of education, then, is to enrich what students have in long-term memory, in order to make the use of short-term memory more powerful. A good curriculum is aligned to what we want students to learn and builds knowledge carefully, step by step. There is, at the moment, no scientific way to guarantee a curriculum will be effective, but the best curricula focus explicitly on communicating knowledge to students and do so in a direct way, rather than expecting students to discover such knowledge for themselves. There are, however, a couple of other features of the best curricula, and understanding these requires some knowledge about how human memory works.

## How Memory Works

Most people's view of memory is as a kind of recording device, where things that are learned are recorded in some way, and over time, these memories decay. If we cannot remember something, we assume that the memory has decayed so much that it has disappeared.

There is no doubt that things we have learned in the past but do not use frequently are indeed harder to recall, and so it is tempting to think that the memory has vanished, but this is not what has happened. For example, when asked for the first home telephone number they learned as a child, many people cannot remember the number, and they assume they have forgotten it. But, if they are shown five possible numbers, they can immediately identify which one is correct. If the memory really had disappeared, this would not be possible. The number is still stored in memory. What is hard is retrieving it.

Robert Bjork, a professor of psychology at the University of California Los Angeles (UCLA), is one of the world's leading researchers of human memory, and he has pointed out that the fact that things get harder to remember over time is a good thing.

For example, my work involves a lot of travel and a lot of hotel stays. When I am staying in a hotel, most times I can remember my hotel room number, but I generally cannot remember the number of the room I stayed in the previous night, and this is really useful. Since almost everything we have ever learned is stored somewhere in our long-term memory, if all the numbers of all the hotel rooms I had ever stayed in were equally accessible, I would have great difficulty in remembering the number of tonight's hotel room as opposed to last night's hotel room, or even the number of a room I stayed in six months ago. Forgetting is an important part of remembering.[29]

Robert Bjork's research shows that how easy something is to recall on a given occasion depends on two things: storage strength and retrieval strength. Storage strength describes how secure something is in long-term memory, while retrieval strength is a measure of how easy it is to recall the information right now. Anything that has ever been learned thoroughly at any point in the past has high storage strength (it will probably always be there), but whether it can be recalled right now depends on the retrieval strength. So, the first home telephone number that someone learns as a child has high storage strength (most people will never get to a point where they cannot recognize the number) but might have low retrieval strength (they cannot remember what it is at the moment). On the other hand, a social security number generally has both high storage strength (it will always be recognizable) and high retrieval strength (people are generally asked for it often enough for it to be easy to recall). For someone staying at a hotel, a room number has high retrieval strength (during the stay, the number is quite easy to recall) but is unlikely to have high storage strength (six months later, most people would not be able to recognize the number, let alone recall it).

This might seem like an unnecessarily complicated theory, but the crucial point is that we now know that studying something has more impact on long-term memory (i.e., storage strength) when retrieval strength is *low*. Students reading material that is familiar generally feel good because they feel that they know the material, but that is only because retrieval strength is high. A week later, they may well find it impossible to recall because their studying had little impact on how well the material was stored in long-term memory. Studying things when they are *less* familiar has a greater impact on storage strength. This has radical implications for how we design our curricula.

In mathematics, for example, a teacher might allocate three weeks to a unit on equations and graphs, and the students will spend all this time improving their understanding of equations and graphs. By the end of the unit, many students will be pretty good at answering test questions on equations and graphs and so will feel that they have a good knowledge of this topic, but that is misleading. They feel good because they are able to recall the material, but that is not because it has been well learned. Rather, it is because the retrieval strength of this material is high. And that is why, often, six weeks later, they cannot answer any of the test questions. At the end of the unit, *performance* was good but only because the retrieval strength was high. Not very much had been *learned*.

This distinction between learning and performance is very important, because most people assume that if students do well in a learning task, they have learned it, but that is performance, not learning. In fact, Bjork has pointed out that long-term memory is better when learning is harder—when there are, in his words, "desirable difficulties" in learning.[30]

If students spend two lessons on equations and graphs and then study other math topics for two weeks, when they return to the topic of equations and graphs, it feels frustrating because they feel that they have forgotten what they learned, and they have to start again. But this is good, because now retrieval strength for the material on equations and graphs is low, which means that this is the *best* time to re-study the material; it will have a greater impact on long-term memory.

In fact, the benefits of spacing out study—what is sometimes called *distributed practice*—has been found for all aspects of human learning, even in physical skills like accuracy in throwing. There are two clear implications of this research for the design of curriculum. The first is that studying things in big blocks (what is sometimes called *massed practice*) is less effective than spreading practice out over a number of sessions. Students feel frustrated because they do not feel they are making progress, but studying things when they are harder to retrieve leads to better longer-term learning. Massed practice is useful for those situations, such as cramming for a test, where students only need to remember things for a few days, but for building up long-term memory, breaking things up and spreading them out over weeks and months is far more effective.

The second is that practice testing—testing students on the content of their learning—should be a regular part of the curriculum. When students take a test, they are required to retrieve the material on which they are being tested, and this changes the structure of long-term memory so that the material on which students are tested becomes easier to recall in the future. In fact, an hour spent on practice testing has a greater benefit for learning than an hour spent re studying the same material.[31] There is a second benefit of testing, and that is that when students guess an answer but guess wrong, then when they are told the correct answer, they remember the correct answer for longer than if they had guessed correctly in the first place (this is sometimes called the *hypercorrection effect*).[32]

The problem with practice testing, of course, is that students do not like being tested all the time, even though it is good for them. However, the resolution of this dilemma is simple. Students do not gain any additional benefit from testing when a score is entered into a gradebook. Testing improves students' achievement because it provides retrieval practice and capitalizes on the hypercorrection effect. What this means is that the best person to grade a test is the person who just took it. There is a place for formal review testing in the curriculum, but frequent practice testing works best when the students score their own tests and don't have to tell anyone how well they did, unless they want to.

## Conclusion

We are frequently told that young people of today are radically different from those of previous generations. We are told that they are, in Marc Prensky's terms, *digital natives* rather than *digital immigrants*[33] and therefore need to learn in different ways from their predecessors. We are told that they cannot work on one thing for a sustained period of time because they are multitaskers. We are told they love to customize their world (hence the huge market in smartphone ringtones), and so the curriculum needs to be personalized to their interests and needs. We are told that they think and process information differently, and the school curriculum needs to reflect this. All this is plausible, but it is nonsense. For all intents and purposes, the brains of young people today are the same as the brains of young people thirty thousand years ago.

And our brains are rather odd. The human brain's capacity for long-term storage is so large that it might as well be infinite, and yet thinking has to be done with short-term memory that can generally only work with half a dozen or so things at a time.

Attempts to increase the capacity of people's short-term memory have failed, so the only way to make humans more capable in their thinking is to expand the store of things that they have to think with—in other words, to have more knowledge in long-term memory.

This is why curricula have to focus on building knowledge. Teaching skills, such as reading comprehension strategies, can help, but these skills can be learned quickly and don't require much practice. People often see a knowledge-rich curriculum as somehow incompatible with creativity, but for all but the most trivial examples, creativity requires knowledge—someone once described creativity as "making novel selections from well-stocked shelves."

Moreover, far from being oppressive, ensuring that all children get access to what society regards as important to know is profoundly liberating. As E. D. Hirsch points out in his most recent book, *Why Knowledge Matters*, countries that have taken knowledge out of the school curriculum and replaced it with a curriculum that is tailored to some notion of the students' needs have seen inequality in educational outcomes *increase*. Students with well-educated parents can always get this knowledge at home. It is the students from less advantaged homes that lose out when knowledge is taken out of the curriculum.[34]

Hirsch and his colleagues have produced examples of such a curriculum, called the *core knowledge sequence*, but he freely admits that this is just an example of one way that our children can build the knowledge they need to participate effectively in society. We are just at the beginning of understanding what the essential features of a curriculum should be, but we do have some solid starting points.

First, and most obviously, the curriculum must be well-aligned to the aims of education. Second, the curriculum needs to provide a carefully structured sequence for building knowledge. The sequence in which topics are arranged can make a big difference to how easy it is for students to learn things. In most American classrooms, for example, students learn how to calculate the area of a triangle before they learn how to calculate the area of a parallelogram, but students learn quicker if the area of the parallelogram is taught first.[35] Of course, not all subjects will have such strong sequential aspects, but careful sequencing of material to be learned will improve students' progress in all subjects. Third, because of the limited capacity of short-term memory, instructional sequences need to be carefully designed so as not to produce overload because spare capacity in short-term memory is needed to produce changes in long-term memory. Fourth, rather than teaching things in big blocks, material needs to be distributed over weeks, months, and even years, giving students a chance to review material when it is no longer familiar, thus boosting long-term memory. Fifth, and finally, the curriculum should provide regular, frequent opportunities for self-testing, to provide retrieval practice and to take advantage of the hypercorrection effect.

---

1   Dickens (1854, p. 3).

2   See, for example, Zhou, Peverly, and Xin (2006).

3   For evidence of the mathematical knowledge of American teachers versus those in China, see Ma (1999).

4   Agodini and Harris (2016).

5   United States Department of Education (2015).

6   Oates (2016).

7   Schneider (2016).

8   Agodini et al. (2009).

9   Koedel and Polikoff (2017).

10  An extra three months' learning each year, in a district spending $12,000 per student per year (which is the national average) would be worth $3,000 per student, so, with 10,000 students, that's $30 million each year.

11 Leahy and Lyon (2007).

12 For a critique of US textbooks from a liberal perspective, see Loewen (2008). For an equally critical, but more conservative, perspective, see Ravitch (2003).

13 Louisiana Department of Education (2017).

14 Johnson (1964).

15 FIFA specifies that to be approved, a soccer ball must, when dropped from a height of 2 meters, bounce between 135 and 155 cm when the ball is at a temperature of 20°C.

16 Bellos (2014, p. 169).

17 In *The Talent Code*, Daniel Coyle (2009, p. 27) refers to a study conducted at Liverpool University that showed futsal players touch the ball six times more often per minute than those playing the eleven-a-side game. However, the only reference listed is to a study conducted by researchers from the University of Leeds (J. D. Allen, Butterly, Welsch, & Wood, 1998), which compared the number of ball touches for four players playing five-a-side and eleven-a-side soccer. On average, each player touched the ball once every 66 seconds in the eleven-a-side game, and in the five-a-side version, once every 10 seconds. While five-a-side soccer shares many common features with futsal, it is by no means the same game, but the comparison of the frequency of contact does give some idea of how much more intensive ball contact is likely to be in futsal.

18 Restuccia (2015).

19 Hirsch (2009, p. 15).

20 Willingham and Lovette (2014).

21 Willingham and Lovette (2014).

22 Willingham and Lovette (2014).

23 Willingham and Lovette (2014).

24 Sweller (2016, p. 5).

25 National Council of Teachers of Mathematics (1980).

26 Kontra, Lyons, Fischer, and Beilock (2015).

27 Organisation for Economic Co-operation and Development (2016b, p. 228).

28 Stockard, Wood, Coughlin, and Khoury (2018).

29 M. C. Anderson, Bjork, and Bjork (1994).

30 Bjork and Linn (2006).

31 Dunlosky et al. (2013).

32 Huelser and Metcalfe (2012).

33 Prensky (2001).

34 Hirsch (2016).

35 The standard way of justifying to students the standard rule for the area of a triangle (half of the base times the height) is to put two triangles together to make a rectangle, but this only works if the triangles are right angled. The rule for other triangles has to be taught after the area of the parallelogram has been covered. In most countries, the standard sequence is rectangle (don't bother with the square, it's just a rectangle), parallelogram, triangle, trapezoid.

CHAPTER 11

# Improving the Teachers We Have

In previous chapters, we have seen that the amount of progress students make in school depends on a number of factors. Some factors, such as the quality of school buildings, may have some impact, but—at least as far as we know—the effects are very small and could probably be achieved more effectively in less expensive ways. Others, such as poverty, undoubtedly have a major impact on student achievement but are hard to change. Still others, like the time teachers have to prepare instruction, are difficult to evaluate. In almost all the countries where students score higher in international tests than the United States, teachers have more time to prepare lessons and spend less time actually teaching, but we cannot be sure whether the extra time is the cause of those high scores. When looking for ways to improve education, we have to find things that have a substantial impact on student achievement and that we can do something about at reasonable cost. Poverty is important but hard to change, while spending more money on new school buildings is relatively easy to do but doesn't help students very much. Class size reduction does improve student achievement, particularly for the youngest children, but only where there is a plentiful supply of teachers. Moreover, the cost is very high. In the previous two chapters, we saw that curriculum checks all three boxes. Getting the curriculum right has a big impact on student achievement, and there are some concrete things that districts can do to improve their curricula at modest cost. The other factor that—in terms of the available research evidence—seems to have the greatest potential for improving student achievement is investing in the professional development of the teachers already working in our schools, and that is the focus of this chapter and the next.

In this chapter, I suggest that expertise in teaching shares the characteristics of expertise in other areas of human endeavor, so that the research on the nature of expertise in those other areas is likely to apply to teaching also. One of the most important findings in expertise research is that, with ten years of the right kinds of effort to improve practice, almost all people can reach elite levels of performance. In other words, almost all teachers could be as good as the best if they work hard at it for at least ten years. Of course, this will only be true if teachers work on the right stuff, and in the final part of the chapter, I argue that attention to classroom formative assessment is likely to be the most productive focus for teachers to develop.

As we saw in chapter 2, there is now a great deal of research, done in at least a dozen states, that shows that students make more progress in some classrooms than others, and the most important variable is not the size of the class, nor how students are grouped for instruction, but the quality of the individual teacher. Moreover, the differences between teachers are substantial. William L. Sanders, a statistician at the University of North Carolina at Chapel Hill, estimates that having good teachers for three years would bring the achievement of a child from an impoverished background up to that of a child from an affluent home being taught by average teachers.[1] While others have criticized some of the methods used in this research, the basic finding—that the academic progress a child makes depends greatly on the skills of her or his teacher—has been confirmed over and over again.[2] No one who has looked at the data in depth doubts this conclusion. However, knowing that teacher quality matters is one thing. Doing something about it is another.

Particularly in the United States, most initiatives for improving teacher quality have focused on raising the quality of the teachers who are trained and recruited, retaining the most effective teachers, and removing the least effective teachers, replacing them with better ones. However, as we saw in chapters 2, 3, and 4, no matter how aggressively these policies are pursued, the impact on student achievement will be small and will take time to materialize—more time than our children have, because every child needs the best education we can provide *now*.

The reasons that most states are pursuing ineffective strategies is obviously a complex question, but part of the answer probably lies in the way people think about teacher quality. Many people, particularly economists of education, think of teacher quality as being made up of two elements: teacher talent and teacher effort. They also believe that teacher talent is fixed (they think teachers are born, not made), and so they focus on teacher effort. The idea is that if we threaten to fire bad teachers, then those who are just lazy will try harder and therefore become more effective, and those who cannot improve will be fired. At the other end of the scale, paying the best teachers more will provide incentives for them to become even better.

In a way, focusing on teacher effort is understandable, because our efforts to improve teachers to date have been unsuccessful. While many, perhaps most, teachers clearly do improve in their first few years of practice, the improvements are not great and are dwarfed by the natural variation of teacher quality in our schools. Imagine for a moment that we can actually measure exactly how effective every teacher is, and we give a score of 0 to the least effective teacher in the country and 100 to the most effective, with all other teachers given quality scores between these extremes. A teacher who gets a score of 40 at the beginning of her or his career will get a score of around 55 to 60 after twenty years in the classroom.[3] This estimate provides the answer to the question "Are teachers born or made?" The answer is "Both," but right now, we aren't very good at making teachers. That's why the improvement in teachers over a career is much smaller than the variation in the effectiveness of teachers on their first day on the job.

More important, the improvements currently made by teachers seem to be mostly produced by experience, rather than by any training they get on the job. We saw in chapter 4 that paying teachers to gain master's degrees makes little sense, because teachers with master's degrees are no more effective than those without. Many states require teachers to log a certain number of hours of professional development each year, but the requirements for these hours are so lax that almost any educational activity qualifies, whether it is related to that teacher's job or not. It is therefore hardly surprising that our existing efforts to improve teachers through in-service professional development have been largely unsuccessful.

It is also not surprising that people look at our failure to improve our teachers and conclude that teacher talent must be fixed, so the only way to improve teacher quality is by replacing existing teachers with better ones or by getting teachers to try harder.

As we saw in chapters 2, 3, and 4, neither of these strategies will have much impact: removing ineffective teachers is difficult, and improving student performance by paying good teachers more is expensive and has only a small impact on student achievement. Fortunately, the conclusion that teachers cannot improve is incorrect, and to see why, we need to look at the nature of expertise in other aspects of human endeavor.

## Expertise

Many people have heard about the 10,000-hour rule—the idea that 10,000 hours of practice makes someone an expert. Unfortunately, while it contains an element of truth, this idea is fundamentally wrong.

The idea of the 10,000-hour rule comes from Malcolm Gladwell's description of the work of Anders Ericsson—whom we met in chapter 9 through his work on memory with William Chase.[4] Ericsson and his colleagues interviewed violinists at the Berlin Academy of Music and asked them questions about how much practice they had done when they were younger. They found that the most promising students—the ones who had the potential to become solo violinists in top orchestras—had racked up an average of 10,000 hours of practice by the age of twenty. They also found similar figures for professional violinists in local orchestras. Good, but not outstanding, players had only around 8,000 hours by the same age.[5] However, the figure of 10,000 hours should not be relied on for a number of reasons. First, the figure is based on just twenty violinists—ten students and ten professionals. Second, it was an average over these 20 twenty people. Some had less, and some had a lot more. Third, the figure relies on the violinists remembering accurately how much practice they had been doing ten years earlier (and more like thirty years for the professionals). Fourth, while the figure does seem to apply reasonably well to violin and piano, for other orchestral instruments, the average figure is a lot lower.[6] Even with musical instruments, the idea that 10,000 hours is needed to become expert is fairly dubious and certainly a stretch for the other areas of expertise that have been studied, such as chess, x-ray diagnosis, scuba diving, acting, and so on.

Ericsson—now one of the world's leading researchers of expertise—does not think there is anything special about 10,000 hours, but he suggests there is an idea that has a far longer track record, and that is that it takes *ten years* of practice to get really good at something.[7]

Approximately five thousand years ago, in the Mesopotamian city of Uruk, scribes started making marks on clay tablets for bookkeeping. Each mark corresponded to a syllable in the local language, but, presumably to keep things manageable, only around five hundred different marks were used, while there were thousands of different syllables in the language. Each mark could therefore have a number of different meanings, so the marks needed to be interpreted in context. It seems to have taken scribes ten years to learn the system.[8]

In medieval Europe, a young person who wanted to become a craftsman would serve as an apprentice to a master for a period of around seven years, followed by three years working for other masters for pay, which often involved traveling to other towns (hence the name *journeyman*). To become a member of a guild, therefore, generally took ten years.[9]

At the end of the nineteenth century, William Lowe Bryan, professor of psychology at the University of Indiana, and Noble Harter, superintendent of schools for Brookville, Indiana, examined how the performance of wireless telegraph operators improved with experience. Their conclusion was that it took ten years of training to make a seasoned press dispatcher.[10]

This does not preclude the importance of talent. After all, to spend ten years working really hard at something, most people would need to gain some sense of success early on, so natural talent may be important in getting people to put in the time needed to become an elite performer. Also, where you grow up matters. Matthew Syed, a world-class table tennis player, describes how he happened to be brought up in a village where the local village hall had a table tennis table set up, and he and his friends spent hours playing table tennis there.[11] Usain Bolt wanted to be a cricketer, but he was brought up in Jamaica, where sprinting is the national passion. The annual school athletics championships, known as Champs, are held in packed stadiums and are televised nationwide. Anyone in Jamaica with any talent for sprinting is channeled into the sport, whereas in the United States, the same child would probably be pushed toward football, baseball, or basketball.

But, as the studies of expertise that have been collected together in the nine-hundred-page *Cambridge Handbook of Expertise and Expert Performance* show, whatever natural talents people have, in most areas, on top of that, ten years of practice is needed.

And not just any old practice. One of the most interesting things about the study of violinists carried out by Ericsson and his colleagues was not just differences in the amount of practice but also differences in the *kind* of practice. As noted above, by the age of twenty, the best violinists had completed about 2,000 hours more practice, but what seems to be more important was that the good, but not outstanding, players spent a lot of time playing the things they could already play, while the best players spent most of their practice time trying to play things they could not yet play well. The quality of the practice appears to be at least as important as the quantity of practice. Most American adults have well over ten years of driving practice, but they are generally no better, and often a lot worse, than they were after just a year or two of driving. The practice they are doing is just repetition. It is not designed to improve performance, and it doesn't do so. Simple repetition makes performance less demanding, but it doesn't make it better. To get better, practice needs to be focused on doing things that the individual cannot yet do, ideally with feedback—what Ericsson calls *deliberate practice*.

Why does this matter? Because David Berliner, a professor at Arizona State University, has shown that expertise in teaching shares the same characteristics as expertise in other areas.

- It is specific and limited. In the same way that grandmaster chess players are generally no better than average at checkers, a teacher can be great at teaching seventh-grade math but much less effective at teaching seventh-grade math to students with special needs.

- It is only weakly related to general ability. Smarter people do play chess better to begin with, but after a few years, it is the amount of practice that matters. After ten years of practice in chess, natural ability is almost irrelevant. In the same way, as we saw in chapter 2, smarter people don't make better teachers.

- It involves seeing meaningful patterns. In the same way that Newell and Simon found that good chess players saw things that novices could not see, novice teachers struggle to see what is going on in their classrooms, while expert teachers seem to have eyes in the backs of their heads.

- It is not reducible to words. The way that chess players see things cannot be put into words. It requires building up the fifty thousand or so chunks in long-term memory, and that is why the right kind of practice is so important. In the same way, well-meaning advice given to novice teachers is usually ineffective because the words don't mean the same thing to novice teachers as they mean to experts.[12]

Now, it is important to acknowledge that the research into expertise in teaching is not as clear-cut as that in areas like chess or medicine, not least because it has not been studied in as much detail. But for these general findings on expertise *not* to be relevant to teaching, it would have to be the case that all of the areas that have been studied are in some way similar to each other but are all different from teaching. Given that the areas that have been studied include acting, soccer, chess, x-ray diagnosis, physics, computer programming, and surgery, this seems unlikely. The obvious conclusion, therefore, is that expertise in teaching is like expertise in other areas and requires ten years of deliberate practice to reach an elite level of performance.

This is important because, as we saw in chapter 2, most teachers improve fairly rapidly in their first couple of years, but then the improvement slows and sometimes stops completely. It seems that very few teachers in the United States are getting the time or the support to put in ten years of deliberate practice. If, as the research suggests, expertise in teaching is like expertise in other areas, we could have almost all our teachers as good as the very best if we created an environment in which every teacher gets at least ten years of deliberate practice, where every teacher commits to improving, not because they are not good enough, but because they can be even better. And when teachers do their jobs better, their students live longer, are healthier, and contribute more to society. There is almost no limit to what our schools can achieve if we just support teachers in the right way.

## What Should Our Teachers Get Better At?

Creating a culture in our schools where all teachers improve, no matter how good they are, is only part of the solution. The other part is getting the focus on the right things. Teachers can change their practice in many ways. Some will benefit students, and some will not, and this is where the research evidence is important. Tailoring instruction to take into account an individual student's learning style takes a great deal of time, and, as we saw in chapter 1, there is no evidence to suggest that students benefit. Trying to use evidence from neuroscience to design more effective instruction looks scientific—teachers are regularly shown scans of brains that claim to show which parts of the brain are doing what—but right now, there is not a single study from neuroscience that provides any guidance about how to make instruction more effective.[13] Research evidence is useful in showing which kinds of changes are unlikely to help our children, but research will never tell teachers, schools, and districts exactly what to do. What research can do is identify which avenues are likely to be dead ends and which will provide the most powerful ways of helping our children make more progress in school.

A clue is provided in the most recent set of PISA results, which were discussed in chapter 9. The biggest impact on student achievement in science was the socioeconomic status of the parents. The second biggest was the ability of teachers to adapt instruction to meet student needs. Now, this finding was based on just three questions in the PISA survey, so we should not place too much weight in this single finding, but in fact, this finding echoes hundreds of research studies on what happens in classrooms, going back at least fifty years.

In 1968, David Ausubel, one of America's leading educational psychologists, wrote:

> If I had to reduce all of educational psychology to just one principle, I would say this: The most important single factor influencing learning is what the learner already knows. Ascertain this and teach him accordingly.[14]

This sounds obvious, but all over the country, teachers are saying to students things like, "You should know this. You're in fifth grade." Quite apart from the fact that this is not a particularly helpful thing to say—if the students don't know it, they don't know it—in most states, the way a student gets into fifth grade is to start in fourth grade and have a birthday. Teachers need to start from where their students are, not where they would like them to be. And the problem with *that* is that our children do not always learn what they are taught.

This is a profoundly important point. If students always learned what they were taught, we would never need to assess our children. We could just make a list of all the things the teacher had covered. But as anyone who has spent more than a few minutes in schools knows, the relationship between what the teacher has taught and what the student has learned is complicated. That is why Ausubel's advice is so important. Good instruction has to start from where the student is, and because that is unpredictable, assessment is at the heart of effective instruction. While we are used to assessing students at the end of a period of instruction, by then, it is usually too late to use the result to do anything more than tell the students how well they have done. The most important assessment happens *during* the instruction, so teachers and students can make adjustments to what they are doing to make the instruction more effective. This is why assessment is the bridge between teaching and learning. It is only by assessing our students that we can find out whether the instruction they have received has been effective.

The idea that assessment can improve instruction, as well as just measuring its results, has been around for a long time. In the 1960s, Benjamin Bloom and his colleagues talked about the value of *formative evaluation*. In the 1970s, the influential Instructional Theory into Practice model of teaching developed by Madeline Hunter, a professor of education at UCLA, emphasized the importance of frequent *checks for understanding* during instruction. However, in recent years, the most common term for this idea in the United States is *formative assessment*.

## Formative Assessment

In most US school districts, the term *formative assessment* is used to describe a process in which students are assessed on a regular basis, and teams of teachers look at the resulting data to check that students are making sufficient progress. Where the data show that students are not making sufficient progress, the teachers then plan what kind of intervention they are going to make to get the students back on track. Perhaps the most remarkable thing about formative assessment in the United States is that, for most of the last century, it was comparatively rare. Teachers taught, and the first hint that a student was not ready for the next grade came at the end of the year. However, over the last twenty years, largely through the work of former Illinois school superintendent Richard DuFour, many US school districts have implemented formal formative assessment systems to ensure student progress.

The first, and perhaps most important, step in DuFour's model is that teachers use common assessments. If different third-grade teachers in the district use different assessments, then it is impossible to determine which students need help. The scores of one teacher might be consistently lower than others in the district, not because she is an ineffective teacher, but because she has pitched her assessments at a more demanding level. In order for the third-grade teachers in a school or a district to have meaningful conversations about data, they must be using the same assessments— assessments that assess what the third-grade teachers agree they want their students to learn.

Once the students have taken the assessments and their work has been scored, teachers can look at the data and see whether some students are not making the required progress, so additional support can be provided where needed. Also, the data may show that some teachers are more effective overall, or more likely, some teachers are more effective on some subjects than others or, more likely still, on some aspects of a subject. Where one teacher appears to be especially effective at teaching, say, fractions, that teacher might be asked to share her teaching approaches with others, leading to improvement for all the teachers for that grade, or to take over the teaching of students who are struggling with the concepts.

Those outside education may be surprised that such a process has not been universal for years. Every successful business is able to monitor its progress toward its goals, whether it is in terms of production targets, sales, or cash flow, and, if things are not on track, then some corrective action is taken. The kind of formative assessment system that DuFour advocates should be a feature of every school.[15] But on its own, it is not enough.

In the United States, the groups of teachers who meet to look at instructional data are often called *professional learning communities* (PLCs). Research on these PLCs by Stanford education professor Claude Goldenberg and his colleagues shows that over two to three years, students do make more progress in schools where student progress is rigorously monitored and, where necessary, follow-up action is taken. The increase in progress is equivalent to an extra fifteen points on PISA or an extra month or two of learning per year in elementary schools.[16] Now, this is worth having, and, in terms of the effort required, it is a very effective use of teachers' time. However, even greater increases in student achievement are possible if, in addition to monitoring student progress, formative assessment is used to improve regular instruction.

As noted above, teachers might learn about new approaches to teaching particular units through participation in instructional data teams, but this is a by-product of the process. The major focus of these teams is this year's students. Focusing on this year's students is important, of course, but if that is the only focus, then there will be just as many problems with next year's students because the teachers won't have improved very much. As well as ensuring that this year's students are making progress, every school needs to carve out some time for teachers to work on improving their classroom practice so that next year's students get a *better* deal.

This is particularly important because when teachers improve, however small the improvement, it works like compound interest. Even if a teacher just gets better by 1 percent this year, then that 1 percent improvement will benefit every student that teacher teaches in the future. And if that teacher improves by 1 percent the following year, then every student taught from then on will get the benefit of a 2 percent improvement in that teacher's performance.

The research to date suggests that using formative assessment as a part of regular classroom instruction—on a minute-to-minute and day-to-day basis—has approximately twice as much impact on student learning as the use of common formative assessments pioneered by DuFour.[17] We need periodically to review whether students are learning what they need to be learning (what we might call *long-cycle formative assessment*), but we also need to make better use of assessment as part of regular classroom instruction (what we might call *short-cycle formative assessment*).

Different writers emphasize different aspects of teaching in their approach to short-cycle formative assessment, but there seems to be a reasonable consensus that there are five main features of effective short-cycle formative assessment:

1. Ensuring that students know what they are meant to be learning

2. Finding out what students have learned

3. Providing feedback that improves student learning

4. Having students help each other learn

5. Developing students' ability to monitor and assess their own learning

For each of these five elements, there is a substantial amount of research that shows it can benefit learning. Together, they appear to be a uniquely powerful combination, as some recent research from England shows.

The Education Endowment Foundation, based in London, was asked to provide advice to schools in England on how some additional funding they had been given to tackle achievement gaps might be spent most effectively.

To help schools make smarter choices, researchers at the University of Durham looked at studies from all over the world on how best to improve student achievement, especially for low-achieving students. They looked at thirty-three possible strategies for improving achievement, from arts participation to teachers' aides. For each of the strategies, they reviewed the available research evidence using a *best evidence* approach as described in chapter 8. They then estimated how many additional months of learning would be produced by thorough implementation of each strategy and also estimated how much the strategy would cost to implement. Finally, they produced a judgment about the quality of the available research evidence, so schools could take this into account in deciding where to invest their efforts.[18]

The three most cost-effective strategies (meaning the strategies with the greatest improvement in student achievement for the least cost) for which there was good evidence were:

- Feedback

- Self-regulated learning

- Collaborative learning

These, of course, are three of the five strategies of short-cycle formative assessment listed above, and the other two strategies are necessary precursors to these three. You can't give feedback until you find out what the students have learned, and you don't know what information to collect until you are clear about what it is you want students to learn. What this means is that, as far as we know right now, nothing else is likely to have as much impact on student achievement as the five strategies of short-cycle formative assessment. They form a minimum set of the highest impact strategies that we can implement in classrooms.

There are a number of books for teachers that provide practical advice on practical techniques they can use immediately to implement the five strategies of formative assessment, and a selection of these is included in the appendix. The appendix also lists books that provide guidance to leaders about how to support these efforts in their own schools.

The main point is that it doesn't matter whether we look bottom-up from the research on feedback and formative assessment or top-down at all the things we might do to improve student achievement. Getting teachers to make greater use of minute-by-minute and day-by-day formative assessment is likely to have a greater impact on how much our children learn in schools than anything else. Districts that are serious about improving the achievement of their students need to make short-cycle formative assessment their main policy priority.

## Conclusion

Previous chapters have shown that many things affect how quickly our children learn. As we saw in chapter 9, there are individual differences in how easy children find it to learn, and some curricula are significantly more effective than others. Smaller classes can help too, especially for younger students, provided the additional teachers recruited are as good as those already working in our schools, and expanding school choice may produce some small improvements in educational achievement. However, as a huge body of research now shows, the quality of the individual teacher is one of the most significant variables in every education system, particularly in the United States, where the best teachers are four times as effective as the least effective.

This is why improving teacher quality should be the main focus of most school improvement efforts, but as we saw in chapters 2, 3, and 4, we cannot predict who will be good teachers. Furthermore, we cannot reliably identify good and bad teachers once they are teaching, even if we use classroom observations, student surveys, and standardized test scores, either individually or in combination. For the foreseeable future, improving teacher quality requires investing in the teachers we already have—what my friend Marnie Thompson calls the *love the one you're with* strategy.

To be most effective, however, that investment must be focused on the things that benefit students most, and the available research evidence suggests that is using assessment to adjust instruction to better meet students' needs. Many schools are already using common assessments to monitor students' progress, and this should be standard operating procedure in every district. But in addition, every district needs also to develop the ability of their teachers to assess their students and adjust their instruction minute-by-minute and day-by-day.

The challenge here, of course, is that changing what teachers do in their classrooms is extremely difficult because classrooms are such complex places. Teachers need to keep a clear focus on their instructional objectives, must respond to students' instructional and other needs, manage classroom behavior, keep a focus on equity, and do all this in real time when there is literally almost no time to think. If we are to realize the power of short-cycle formative assessment to improve student achievement, we need to understand how to support teachers in changing their classroom habits, and that is the subject of the next chapter.

---

1   Sanders and Rivers (1996).

2   Hanushek (2011).

3   This is based on the assumption that, compared with an average teacher, the least effective teachers produce one year's average learning in two years, and the most effective produce a year's learning in six months. The range of the 0 to 100 scale therefore corresponds with a difference in learning of 18 months, so an increase of ten points on the scale represents an extra 1.8 months each year. If the average improvement in teachers over their careers is an extra three months learning per year, that would be equivalent to approximately 17 points (= 10 × 3 ÷ 1.8).

4   Gladwell (2008).

5   Ericsson, Krampe, and Tesch-Römer (1993).

6   Jørgensen (1997).

7   Ericsson, Prietula, and Cokely (2007).

8   Bernstein (2013). The reference to the time needed to become an expert scribe is at 5'41".

9   Epstein (1991).

10  Bryan and Harter (1899).

11  Syed (2010).

12  For a summary of the research on expertise, in teaching and in other areas, see chapter 5 of Wiliam (2016a).

13  As Sergio Della Sala and Mike Anderson point out in their introduction to *Neuroscience and Education*, it is cognitive science, rather than neuroscience, that does the intellectual "heavy lifting" (M. Anderson & Della Sala, 2011, p. 3).

14  Ausubel (1968, p. vi).

15  For a good guide to implementing common formative assessments, see DuFour, DuFour, Eaker, and Many (2010).

16  This estimate is based on the research of Saunders, Goldenberg, and Gallimore (2009). The details of the conversion into months of learning can be found in Wiliam (2016a).

17  For a review of the research on formative assessment, see chapter 4 in Wiliam (2016a).

18  For the full list of the strategies they investigated, see Education Endowment Foundation (2018).

CHAPTER 12

# Creating a Learning
# Environment for Educators

In the previous chapter, we saw that long-cycle formative assessment—regular monitoring of the progress made by students through the use of common formative assessments, followed up with meetings of instructional data teams to look at the data from these assessments—can increase student achievement. We also saw that if, in addition to this long-cycle formative assessment, teachers also increase their use of assessment during regular instruction—short-cycle formative assessment—much greater increases in student achievement are possible.

In the United States, most of the work on formative assessment has focused on long-cycle formative assessment, and therefore, the power of formative assessment to improve student achievement has been only partly realized. The reasons for this are complex, but one of the reasons is undoubtedly because getting teachers to look at data and talk about what to do about those data is much easier than getting teachers to change classroom practice. One of the most important things I have learned in thirty years as a teacher educator is that it is much easier to change what teachers do when students are not present than it is to change what they do when students are present.

This is not because teachers are resistant to change (although some may be). It is because learning how to analyze data and identifying students who need additional support is fundamentally different from changing classroom practice. When one is analyzing data and figuring out which students need extra support and of what kind, one has the luxury of focusing on one thing at a time. The same is not true when one is in the classroom with students.

Lee Shulman, one of America's leading professors of education and former president of the Carnegie Foundation for the Advancement of Teaching, summarizes his experience of studying classroom practice like this:

> The more time I spend in classrooms with teachers—talking with them, observing, watching videotapes, talking some more, reflecting on my own teaching—the more I peel off layer upon layer of incredible complexity. After some 30 years of doing such work, I have concluded that classroom teaching—particularly at the elementary and secondary levels—is the most demanding, subtle, nuanced, and frightening activity that our species has ever invented. In fact, when I compared the complexity of teaching with the much more highly rewarded profession, "doing medicine," I concluded that the only time medicine ever approaches the complexity of an average day for a classroom teacher is in an emergency room during a natural disaster. . . . When 30 patients want your attention at the same time, only then do you approach the complexity of the average classroom on an average day.[1]

Because classrooms are such complex places, there really isn't time to think. Teaching involves continually making snap judgments about what to do next. Over time, teachers get better at reacting in ways that help their students, and these patterns of behavior get them through the day. Indeed, this ability to make the right call most of the time is a teacher's greatest asset. But it is also a liability, because the routines that teachers develop in order to do this are hard to change. This was neatly illustrated by a conversation I had with a fifth-grade teacher in New Jersey some years ago.

I had been working with a group of elementary school teachers on a variety of techniques for improving their use of short-cycle formative assessment. One teacher had decided that allowing students to raise their hands to show they had an answer to a question was limiting the information she was getting. She knew that she should call on students who had not raised their hands, but the eagerness of the students with hands raised made that difficult. She decided to ask her students to raise their hands only if they had a question. When the teacher was asking questions, the students would keep their hands down, and the teacher would decide who to call on for a response—*cold calling* as Doug Lemov, author of *Teach like a Champion*, describes it.[2]

At one of our monthly meetings, she confessed that this wasn't going as well as she had hoped. She said, "Every time I ask a question, I always say, 'Does anyone . . . ?' or 'Has anyone . . . ?'" With tears in her eyes, she asked, "Why am I finding it so hard to change the way I ask questions?" Although she was asking the students not to raise their hands to indicate they had a response, she was asking questions in a way that encouraged volunteers.

We sat down, and we figured out that she had been teaching just over twenty-two years. I estimated that so far in her teaching career, she had asked well over half a million questions in her classroom. When you've done something one way half a million times, you'll be pretty good at it, but doing it a different way is going to be challenging.

This seems to me the major problem with most of the professional development that teachers in America have been getting since states started requiring teachers to undertake periodic recertification. We seem to have decided that teachers lack knowledge, and if we only give them the knowledge they lack, they will somehow be better teachers. We have, in effect, been treating teacher professional development as a process of knowledge acquisition. With more knowledge, teachers will be more effective.

Now, of course, knowledge is important. You need to understand what you are teaching at a very deep level if you are going to be an effective teacher, and there is no doubt that some teachers do not know enough of the material they are teaching to be effective. For these teachers, gaining more knowledge of their subject is likely to be the best way of improving their students' achievement, but these teachers are in the minority.

Teachers also need to know about teaching techniques, but what is most important is not knowing them, it's actually using them. For example, most teachers know about the research of Mary Budd Rowe, who looked at the "wait time" that teachers allowed at the end of a question—how much time did teachers allow students to respond to a question before providing a hint of some kind, asking another student, or providing the answer themselves? Rowe found that in US middle school science classrooms, the typical teacher wait time was around one second, and if teachers just increased their wait time to three to five seconds, students would learn more.[3]

The important point here is that all the teachers I have met know that they do not wait long enough after asking a question. They don't need more knowledge. They know what they should be doing. What they need is help in changing what they do in classrooms. In other words, they need help in changing their *habits*.

## Helping Teachers Change Classroom Habits

We actually know quite a lot about how to help people change habits, but most of this research comes from health education and medicine. Telling smokers about the harmful effects of smoking has little impact on smoking behaviors because most smokers already know that smoking is harmful to health. They do not need more information. They need help in changing habits. We know that the spread of antibiotic-resistant infections such as VRSA and MRSA would be controlled if we could get medical practitioners to wash their hands at least 90 percent of the time they should, but in many hospitals and clinics, the compliance rate is below 50 percent.[4] Telling medical practitioners that they need to wash their hands more often does not help much, because they already know what they should be doing. They are just not doing it. Jeffrey Pfeffer's knowing-doing gap again.

Pfeffer points out that most businesses that go bust do not fail because they had the wrong plans. They had the right plans but went out of business because they weren't actually doing what they knew they should be doing.[5] Fortunately, there is now a great deal of good research on habit change, and this research is very well summarized in Chip and Dan Heath's book *Switch: How to Change Things When Change Is Hard*.[6]

For schools, perhaps the most important first step is creating the right climate for improvement by giving up on trying to figure out who the good teachers are and who the bad teachers are. As we saw in chapters 2, 3, and 4, we can't measure teacher effectiveness with any accuracy. There are certainly some very ineffective teachers, but what we should do with them is not clear. As we saw in chapter 2, the least effective teachers improve more rapidly than other teachers, so the key in determining whether to terminate a teacher is whether they are likely to make sufficient improvements for investment in that teacher to make more sense than replacement. Some teachers may be so far below the bar that they will never be able to reach a satisfactory level of performance, so removal would be appropriate. Others may be reasonably effective, but if they do not think they need to improve, there is also a strong argument for termination, because these teachers are usually a corrosive influence. These are the teachers who always blame the students (or the students' parents!) for low test scores. The most important question for any teacher is "Do you need to get better?" If the answer is "Yes," then he or she is probably worth investing in. If the answer is "No," no matter how good he or she is, there may be an argument for removal. However, as noted in chapter 2, all these decisions need to take into account the availability of replacement teachers. Removing bad teachers in order to replace them with even worse teachers is a guaranteed recipe for lowering student achievement.

Instead, schools and districts need to focus on the idea that all teachers need to get better, not because they're not good enough but because they can be even better. Moving the focus from evaluation to improvement also changes working relationships in a building. Where teachers are in competition, either because they are seeking scarce bonuses or to avoid sanctions, then they are unlikely to help each other. In contrast, when it is expected that all teachers improve, cooperation is encouraged and even expected.

The benefits of teacher collaboration have been convincingly demonstrated by John Papay and Matthew Kraft. They have developed an index of the professional environment in schools by combining several elements that previous research has shown are associated with more successful schools.

- Order and discipline: Do administrators consistently enforce rules to help teachers maintain an orderly classroom?

- Peer collaboration: Do teachers routinely collaborate to improve their teaching practices?

- Principal leadership: Do school leaders address teachers' concerns?

- Professional development: Are teachers given time and other resources to enhance their instructional abilities?

- School culture: Does the school environment feature mutual trust, respect, openness, and a press for student achievement?

- Teacher evaluation: Does teacher evaluation focus on feedback that is focused on improving teachers' instruction?

Using data on all students from third grade to eighth grade in Charlotte-Mecklenburg Schools, North Carolina, from 2001 to 2010, they produced an average measure of the professional environment in each school, ranging from 0 to 100. They then looked to see whether student progress was greater in schools with better professional environments, and they found that it was. In fact, they found that where there was a strong professional environment (equivalent to a score of 75 out of 100), teachers improved their effectiveness by 38 percent more than teachers in an average school over a ten-year period. Another way to think about this is that in schools with a strong professional environment, teachers achieve as if they have three or four more years' experience.[7] While this may seem a modest increase, in this particular study, no account was taken of the quality of the collaboration. Just creating the right environment for teachers to collaborate improves student achievement.

The second step, as the study by Kraft and Papay shows, is to give teachers time to improve. As we saw in earlier chapters, American teachers spend more time in front of their students than those in just about every other country, so finding time for teachers to meet together to support each other is challenging. Some districts have experimented with late starts or early dismissals, others have non-contact periods, and others pay teachers stipends on top of their regular salaries for attending additional training sessions outside their contracts. How this is done is not particularly important. What is important is that teachers' professional development becomes part of the contract, so that it is an expectation that teachers will meet regularly, and ideally once a month, for at least seventy-five minutes, to hold each other accountable for making improvements in their classroom practice and to get the support of their colleagues.

The third step is what Chip and Dan Heath call *scripting the critical moves*. Left to their own devices, teachers may well engage in professional conversations. However, too often these are not rigorously focused on the things that are likely to have the greatest benefit for students. For the time that teachers spend collaborating to have the maximum benefit for students, their meetings need to be highly structured.

Now, obviously, there are many different meeting structures that could be used, but through an extensive process of rapid prototyping and experimentation with groups of teachers all over the United States, my colleagues and I settled on a meeting structure with six components. This structure has now been used by well over two thousand teacher groups all over the world, and while the structure might be improved in the future, the fact that the current design has been successful wherever it has been tried suggests that for most US school districts, the model is worth trying out as it stands.

Here are the six parts.

1. Getting started (5 minutes): The teacher responsible for running the meeting outlines the aims for the meeting, including sharing with the participants the learning intentions and criteria for success.

2. Warm-up (5 minutes): Particularly where meetings take place at the end of a working day, teachers may need time to focus on their own learning. Asking teachers to contribute something to a group discussion helps the participants de-pressurize. Possible prompts include asking teachers to share something that a student said that made them smile, something a colleague did to support them, something they are looking forward to in school, and so on. We have also found that in schools in challenging circumstances, it can be therapeutic to give each teacher thirty seconds to sound off about all the things that bug them about their job; getting such issues aired at the start of the meeting makes it less likely that they come up later on and derail the meeting.

3. Feedback (25 minutes): This is the most important phase of the meeting. Each teacher describes what he or she promised to try out in the previous month's meeting and what progress he or she has made putting the idea into practice in the classroom. Even though each teacher has just two minutes, time and again, teachers have told us that it was the fact that they knew that they were going to have to report back to their colleagues that made them prioritize working on improving their classroom practice.

4. New learning about formative assessment (20 minutes): In order to create some variety in each meeting, it is valuable to provide some input for teachers. This could be a book study, where each month the group reads a chapter of a book ahead of time and then in the meeting discusses the relevance for their own teaching. Alternatively, teachers can watch and discuss videos of classroom practice, taken from the internet or produced by teachers at the school. There are commercially produced agendas for such meetings, although many schools have produced their own materials. The important point here is that there is something novel about formative assessment at each meeting, to prevent things from getting stale.

5. Action planning (15 minutes): In this phase of the meeting, each teacher gets time to plan what he or she is going to do over the coming month.

This is essential because given teachers' schedules, most teachers have little time to think. When they are at school, there are colleagues and students making demands on their time, and at home, there is always a family member who needs their time. The purpose of this part of the meeting is to give teachers time to think about how they are going to be a better teacher the following month than they were the previous month.

6. Wrap-up (5 minutes): In the final phase of the meeting, participants review the learning intentions for the meeting, and if they have not been met, they plan what action to take.

In order to keep the agenda on time, it is essential that someone takes responsibility for leading the meeting, but we have found that it is actually more effective if those leading the meetings are not experts. In fact, we have seen teachers in their second year of teaching being outstanding leaders of these groups because they know they do not have the answers. The leader's job is not to be the expert dispensing wisdom but rather the person who creates an environment where like-minded professionals can support each other's growth.

When people learn about this model, they tend to raise two immediate concerns. The first is that having the same structure for each meeting is likely to create boredom. However, when the structure is changed each month, teachers spend the first part of the meeting trying to figure out what they are meant to be doing. When the structure is familiar, teachers arrive at each meeting knowing what is expected of them. As the structure fades into the background, the teachers' own professional learning comes into the foreground.

The second concern is that left to their own devices, teachers will not use their time productively, and that it is therefore better to use external facilitators to run the meetings. Indeed, some academics have gone as far as to claim that external support is essential to school improvement efforts. Now, it is certainly true that many school improvement efforts have been considerably enhanced by the availability of external expertise, and others have failed because such outside support was lacking. However, for the particular purpose of helping teachers improve their classroom practice, our experience has been that teachers really can do it for themselves. Moreover, there are at least three additional advantages of having meetings run by teachers for teachers.

First, many districts in the United States spend a considerable amount of money each year on coaches for their teachers, and there is no doubt that coaching can be an effective way of improving teachers' performance.[8] However, in many parts of the country, good coaches are hard to find, so districts end up taking good teachers out of the classroom to serve as coaches. Where the coaches are better as coaches than they were as teachers, then obviously things are likely to improve. However, good teachers are not always effective as coaches, so the net effect is to lower achievement because the gain in student achievement produced through the coaching is less than the loss generated by replacing a good teacher with an average one.

Second, coaching is very vulnerable to changes in funding. Where education funding is dependent on local property taxes, as it is in most US districts, then a sudden drop of tax income leads to a need to cut expenditure quickly. In such circumstances, money for coaches may be one of the first things to get cut. Given the way that education is financed in the United States, any model for school improvement that requires hiring additional personnel is unlikely to be sustainable, especially in less affluent districts.

Third, coaches are often regarded as lacking credibility as practitioners. Even when teachers come from the district, as soon as they stop teaching and become coaches, many teachers regard the coaches as being out of touch with the realities of teaching. Support from others who are teaching the same students, working in the same buildings, supervised by the same administrators is very different from someone telling you how to do your job.

All this may seem too good to be true. It does seem unlikely, at first sight, that giving teachers just seventy-five minutes once a month—to meet with their colleagues, report back on the changes they tried out in their classroom over the previous month, get ideas from those colleagues, and make commitments about what they are going to do the next month—can make a real difference, but the focus on classroom formative assessment is particularly powerful, for a number of reasons.

First, the focus on adapting instruction to meet student needs appears to be especially important. As noted in the previous chapter, the most recent PISA survey found this to be the most important influence on student learning after the socioeconomic status of the child's family, a finding that is supported by hundreds of research studies from all over the world.[9]

Second, skills of classroom assessment can be applied universally. Increasing teachers' subject knowledge in a particular area of the curriculum is likely to improve their ability to teach that area but is unlikely to be useful for teaching other areas. When we develop teachers' ability to use real-time assessment to adapt their instruction to their students' learning needs, those skills can be applied in all their teaching.

Third, focusing on classroom assessment seems to be a smart place to begin the conversation with teachers. Asking teachers to administer common assessments to generate data on student achievement seems, to many teachers, to be serving the agenda of administrators and bureaucrats by making teachers accountable for their students' progress. On the other hand, all teachers in America would probably agree that it is part of their day job to find out whether students have learned what they have been taught.

Fourth, and perhaps most important, wherever these ideas have been implemented, they have worked. While we do not yet have evidence from randomized-control experiments, schools and districts are finding that using evidence about what students have learned to adapt instruction just works. There is literally nothing else, as far as we know, that can increase student achievement by so much for so little cost.

## Conclusion

Previous chapters have shown that many things affect how quickly our children learn. As we saw in chapter 9, there are individual differences in how easy children find it to learn, and some curricula are significantly more effective than others. Smaller classes can help too, especially for younger students, provided the additional teachers recruited are as good as those already working in our schools, and expanding school choice may produce some small improvements in educational achievement. However, as a huge body of research now shows, the quality of the individual teacher is one of the most significant variables in every education system, particularly in the United States, where the best teachers are four times as effective as the least effective.

This is why improving teacher quality is the main focus of most school improvement efforts, but as we saw in chapters 2, 3, and 4, we cannot predict who will be good teachers. Furthermore, we cannot reliably identify good and bad teachers once they are teaching, even if we use classroom observations, student surveys, and standardized test scores, either individually, or in combination. For the foreseeable future, improving teacher quality requires investing in the teachers we already have.

To be most effective, however, that investment must be focused on the things that benefit students most, and that is using assessment to adjust instruction to better meet students' needs. Many schools are already using common assessments to monitor students' progress, and this should be standard operating procedure in every district. But in addition, every district needs also to develop the ability of their teachers to assess their students and adjust their instruction minute-by-minute and day-by-day. Since this involves changing what teachers do in their classrooms, it is best thought of as a process of habit change rather than knowledge acquisition, which is most likely to be achieved through regular meetings where teachers promise to their peers what they are going to try out in their classrooms and are held accountable for making those changes.

As a result of development work in eight states and extensive implementation all around the world, we now know one seventy-five-minute meeting once a month, led by teachers, with a standard agenda, can produce substantial improvements in our teachers' skills and our students' achievements. There is indeed no limit to what our teachers can achieve if we just support them in the right way.

---

1    Shulman (2004, p. 504).

2    Lemov (2010).

3    Mary Budd Rowe's original research can be found in Rowe (1986). The effect on student achievement of getting teachers to increase their wait time is reported in Tobin (1987).

4    For more on this, see New York surgeon Atul Gawande's excellent book *Better* (Gawande, 2007).

5    Pfeffer (2000).

6    Heath and Heath (2010).

7    Kraft and Papay (2014).

8    A particularly effective distance coaching model has been developed by Robert Pianta and his colleagues at the University of Virginia (J. P. Allen, Pianta, Gregory, Mikami, & Lun, 2011).

9    A comprehensive review of the research in this area can be found in Wiliam (2016a).

CHAPTER 13

# Pulling It All Together

In 1998, my colleague Paul Black and I published an article in *Phi Delta Kappan* magazine titled "Inside the Black Box."[1] The argument we made there was that most educational reforms paid too little attention to what happens inside the black box of the classroom. State and federal agencies measure outputs, such as test scores and graduation rates, and sometimes even inputs, for example, when they try to estimate the value added by teachers, but too often, what actually happens in classrooms gets little attention. While things have improved a little since then, the emphasis is still on grand visions about transforming our schools, which have yielded little or no success.

Despite the aims stated in the 1994 Educate America Act, US schools did not lead the world in math and science by the year 2000. In 2014, to no one's surprise, there were still students failing to reach proficiency on their state standards, twelve years after the No Child Left Behind Act was signed into law. The 2009 American Recovery and Reinvestment Act funded a number of initiatives such as Race to the Top ($4.35 billion) and the School Improvement Grants program ($3 billion) that, as far as the education department's own evaluations of these programs are able to tell, have had no impact on student achievement.[2]

Now, this is not to deny the importance of federal and state programs, not least because they usually provide significant additional funds for districts to use to improve the education they provide. However, decisions at the state and federal levels are unlikely to improve education very much because the people who make the decisions know little about what Friedrich von Hayek called "the particular circumstances of time and place."[3] Solutions to the problem of improving education for our children require each school district to make smart decisions about what will make the most difference in their district.

The danger in all this is that while it is right to reject a one-size-fits-all solution for improving education, it is important to not swing to the other extreme and conclude that anything goes. Some courses of action are much less likely to be successful than others, and this is largely predictable as a result of what we do know about schools, teachers, and students.

Expanding school choice may please parents, but currently, charter schools and private schools are, on average, no better than traditional public schools. As states learn more about the characteristics of the most effective charter schools, it may be possible to get to a point where charter schools are consistently better than traditional public schools, but the evidence is they won't be that much better, and there won't be enough of them, to have any appreciable effect on the average achievement of American students. Moreover, in rural areas, the idea of expanding choice is an irrelevance—just getting to the nearest school often requires students to spend hours each day traveling.

Reducing the size of classes does work, particularly for children in the early grades, but the effects depend on the availability of good teachers, and the costs are very high. For many districts, the use of teachers' aides may be more appropriate, especially as new research highlights which classroom roles absolutely require a good teacher and which can be delegated to a well-managed assistant.

We also know that the quality of the teachers in our classrooms is one of the most important determinants of how much children learn in those classrooms, with the very best teachers generating four times as much progress for their students as the least effective. However, it is also clear from the latest high-quality research that we are not able to measure with any accuracy the effectiveness of an individual teacher—at least not in a reasonable period of time. We cannot use observations because good teachers have bad days and bad teachers have good days, and even if we conduct a large number of observations, so that these variations average out, teachers look more effective when they are teaching motivated, high-achieving students. We cannot use test scores, even if we control for the prior achievement, because every teacher builds on the foundations laid by those who taught their students previously.

We can be reasonably sure that a teacher who looks very, very bad is not, in fact, very, very good. And we can be reasonably sure that a teacher who looks very, very good is not, in fact, very, very bad. But that's about it. A teacher who looks very, very good may, in fact, be below average. And one who looks very, very bad may, in fact, be above average. If we rated all teachers on a scale, with 0 being the very worst and 100 being the very best, the margin of error is at least sixty points. While we may, in the future, be able to measure the effectiveness of individual teachers more accurately than this, such a day is a long way off. For the foreseeable future, however implausible it may seem, we have to accept that no one can reliably identify good teachers. That is why it makes far more sense for districts to focus their efforts on the *love the one you're with* strategy—investing in the teachers already in the district's schools.

As new initiatives come along, the framework provided in chapter 8 should be useful in evaluating their suitability for the district. How much of an impact will the initiative have if it is implemented as designed? How much will it cost to implement it? Will it be possible to implement the initiative in the district? If those proposing initiatives are unable to answer such questions, then this would suggest that adopting the initiative is a risky venture.

Right now, however, the available research suggests there are two particularly powerful levers that districts can use to improve student achievement. The first is to ensure that the curriculum, including whatever textbooks are adopted, is one that is explicitly focused on developing knowledge, because the amount of knowledge in long-term memory determines a student's ability to think. The more knowledge is stored in long-term memory, the more effective the use of short-term memory becomes. This does not refer to rote memorization of facts. Rather, it means ensuring that what students know is richly connected to other knowledge, so that they can solve problems, be creative through making new connections, and have studied areas in enough depth to think critically about them.

The second is to establish, within the district, a culture where all teachers improve, not because they are not good enough, but because they can be even better. Moreover, the focus of each teacher's improvement needs to be what has the greatest benefit for students. Currently, from all the available research, that seems to be short-cycle classroom formative assessment—teachers routinely collecting evidence about student learning in real time so that they can rapidly adjust the instruction to better meet students' needs.

Once these two things are in place, then districts can turn to other initiatives, where the evidence is less clear or where the benefits are smaller or more expensive to secure. Until then, however, the major role of school board members, superintendents, other administrators, parents, and other interested citizens must be to focus the work of the district inside the black box of the classroom—on the things that make the greatest difference to their students.

Today in America, the biggest problem with education is not that it is bad. It is that it is variable. In hundreds of thousands of classrooms in America, students are getting an education that is as good as any in the world. But in hundreds of thousands of others, they are not. By ensuring that every child has access to a high-quality curriculum, we can reduce the differences in student achievement that are due to the students' home backgrounds and help them build the knowledge they will need to participate effectively in society. And by creating a culture where every teacher improves, we can create a teacher workforce where almost all teachers are as good as the very best we have right now. That is a goal we can actually achieve, and our children deserve nothing less.

---

1    Black and Wiliam (1998).

2    Dragoset et al. (2016); Dragoset et al. (2017).

3    Hayek (1945, p. 521).

# APPENDIX

## Practical Advice for Implementing Classroom Formative Assessment

The books listed below contain a large number of practical techniques and strategies that teachers can implement immediately to develop their use of classroom formative assessment.

Clarke, S. (2001). *Unlocking formative assessment*. London, UK: Hodder & Stoughton.

Clarke, S. (2003). *Enriching feedback in the primary classroom*. London, UK: Hodder & Stoughton.

Clarke, S. (2005). *Formative assessment in the secondary classroom*. London, UK: Hodder & Stoughton.

Clarke, S. (2008). *Active learning through formative assessment*. London, UK: Hodder Murray.

Duckor, B., & Holmberg, C. (2017). *Mastering formative assessment moves: 7 high-leverage practices to advance student learning*. Alexandria, VA: ASCD.

Fennell, F. S., Kobett, B. M., & Wray, J. A. (2016). *The formative 5: Everyday assessment techniques for every math classroom*. Thousand Oaks, CA: Corwin.

Keeley, P. (2008). *Science formative assessment: 75 practical strategies for linking assessment, instruction, and learning*. Thousand Oaks, CA: Corwin.

Keeley, P., & Tobey, C. R. (2017). *Mathematics formative assessment volume 2: 50 more practical strategies for linking assessment, instruction, and learning*. Thousand Oaks, CA: Corwin.

Wiliam, D. (2018). *Embedded formative assessment* (2nd ed.). Bloomington, IN: Solution Tree.

Wiliam, D., & Leahy, S. (2015). *Embedding formative assessment: Practical techniques for K–12 classrooms*. West Palm Beach, FL: Learning Sciences International.

## Resources for School Leaders

The following resources provide everything a district needs to begin work on improving classroom formative assessment practices in every building. The book

*Leadership for Teacher Learning* provides background material that expands on the ideas presented in this book, and the *Embedding Formative Assessment Professional Development Pack* provides everything a school needs for two years of monthly Teacher Learning Community meetings together with videos of classroom practice and interviews with teachers and students.

Wiliam, D. (2016). *Leadership for teacher learning: Creating a culture where all teachers improve so that all learners succeed*. West Palm Beach, FL: Learning Sciences International.

Wiliam, D., & Leahy, S. (2014). *Embedding formative assessment professional development pack*. West Palm Beach, FL: Learning Sciences International.

# REFERENCES

Aaronson, D., Barrow, L., & Sander, W. (2007). Teachers and student achievement in the Chicago Public High Schools. *Journal of Labor Economics*, *25*(1), 95–135.

Abramson, P. (2016). *The state of school construction: A look at what happened in 2015.* Chatsworth, CA: 1105 Media.

Agodini, R., & Harris, B. (2016). How teacher and classroom characteristics moderate the effects of four elementary math curricula. *Elementary School Journal*, *117*(2), 216–236. doi: doi:10.1086/688927

Agodini, R., Harris, B., Atkins-Burnett, S., Heaviside, S., Novak, T., Murphy, R., & Pendleton, A. (2009). *Achievement effects of four early elementary school math curricula: Findings from first graders in 39 schools* (Vol. NCEE 2009-4052). Washington, DC: United States Department of Education, Institute of Education Sciences (National Center for Educational Evaluation and Regional Assistance).

Allen, J. D., Butterly, R., Welsch, M. A., & Wood, R. (1998). The physical and physiological value of 5-a-side soccer training to 11-a-side match play. *Journal of Human Movement Studies*, *34*(1), 1–11.

Allen, J. P., Pianta, R. C., Gregory, A., Mikami, A. Y., & Lun, J. (2011). An interaction-based approach to enhancing secondary school instruction and student achievement. *Science*, *333*(6045), 1034–1037.

Amabile, T. M., Phillips, E., & Collins, M. A. (1994). Person and environment in talent development: The case of creativity. In N. Colangelo, S. G. Assouline, & D. L. Ambroson (Eds.), *Talent development: Proceedings of the 1993 Henry B. and Jocelyn Wallace National Research Symposium on Talent Development* (pp. 265–279). Dayton, OH: Ohio Psychology Press.

Amelinckx, A. (2016, December 12). Rise of the (cow milking) robots. *Modern Farmer*. Retrieved January 13, 2017, from http://modernfarmer.com/2016/12/rise-cow-milking-robots/

Anderson, M. C., Bjork, R. A., & Bjork, E. L. (1994). Remembering can cause forgetting: Retrieval dynamics in long-term memory. *Journal of Experimental Psychology: Learning, Memory, and Cognition*, *20*(5), 1063–1087. doi: 10.1037/0278-7393.20.5.1063

Anderson, M., & Della Sala, S. (2011). Neuroscience in education: An (opinionated) introduction. In S. Della Sala & M. Anderson (Eds.), *Neuroscience in education: The good, the bad and the ugly* (pp. 3–12). Oxford, UK: Oxford University Press.

Arnold, M. (1869). *Culture and anarchy: An essay in political and social criticism.* London, UK: Smith, Elder & Co.

Astala, K., Kivelä, S. K., Koskela, P., Martio, O., Näätänen, M., & Tarvainen, K. (2005, August 31). The PISA survey tells only a partial truth of Finnish children's mathematical skills. *Matematiikkalehti solmu [Knot Mathematics Journal].* Retrieved December 22, 2016, from http://matematiikkalehtisolmu.fi/2005/erik/PisaEng.html

Atteberry, A., Loeb, S., & Wyckoff, J. (2013). *Do first impressions matter? Improvement in early career teacher effectiveness.* Washington, DC: Center for Analysis of Longitudinal Data in Educational Research.

Ausubel, D. P. (1968). *Educational psychology: A cognitive view.* New York, NY: Holt, Rinehart & Winston.

Autor, D. H., Katz, L. F., & Krueger, A. B. (1998). Computing inequality: Have computers changed the labor market? *Quarterly Journal of Economics, 113*(4), 1169–1213. doi: 10.1162/003355398555874

Autor, D. H., Levy, F., & Murnane, R. J. (2003). The skill content of recent technological change: An empirical exploration. *Quarterly Journal of Economics, 118*(4), 1279–1333.

Backes, B., & Hansen, M. (2015). *Teach for America impact estimates on nontested student outcomes.* Washington, DC: Center for Analysis of Longitudinal Data in Educational Research.

Bacolod, M. P. (2007). Do alternative opportunities matter? The role of female labor markets in the decline of teacher supply and teacher quality 1940–1990. *Review of Economics and Statistics, 89*(4), 737–751.

Baumert, J., Kunter, M., Blum, W., Brunner, M., Voss, T., Jordan, A., . . . Tsa, Y.-M. (2009). Teachers' mathematical knowledge, cognitive activation in the classroom, and student progress. *American Educational Research Journal, 47*(1), 133–180.

Beach, G. (2014, October 2). Cobol is dead. Long live Cobol! *CIO Journal.* Retrieved December 23, 2016, from http://blogs.wsj.com/cio/2014/10/02/cobol-is-dead-long-live-cobol/

Begley, S. (2007, October 1). The real Sputnik story. *Newsweek.* Retrieved January 3, 2017, from http://www.newsweek.com/real-sputnik-story-103299

Bellos, A. (2014). *Futebol: The Brazilian way of life* (2nd ed.). New York, NY: Bloomsbury.

Berliner, D. C., & Biddle, B. J. (1995). *The manufactured crisis: Myths, fraud and the attack on America's public schools.* New York, NY: Perseus.

Bernstein, W. (2013, May 6). Communication, power and the written word. *Econ Talk.* Retrieved December 31, 2014, from http://www.econtalk.org/archives/2013/05/bernstein_on_co.html

Bessen, J. (2015). *Learning by doing: The real connection between innovation, wages, and wealth.* New Haven, CT: Yale University Press.

Bessen, J. (2016). *How computer automation affects occupations: Technology, jobs, and skills.* Boston, MA: Boston University School of Law.

Bill and Melinda Gates Foundation. (2012). *Ensuring fair and reliable measures of effective teaching: Culminating findings from the MET project's three-year study.* Redmond, WA: Bill and Melinda Gates Foundation.

Bjork, R. A. (2011). On the symbiosis of remembering, forgetting, and learning. In A. S. Benjamin (Ed.), *Successful remembering and successful forgetting: a Festschrift in honor of Robert A. Bjork* (pp. 1–22). London, UK: Psychology Press.

Bjork, R. A., & Linn, M. C. (2006). The science of learning and the learning of science: Introducing desirable difficulties. *American Psychological Society Observer*, *19*(3), 29, 39.

Black, P. J., & Wiliam, D. (1998). Inside the black box: Raising standards through classroom assessment. *Phi Delta Kappan*, *80*(2), 139–148.

Blatchford, P., Basset, P., Brown, P., Martin, C., Russell, A., & Webster, R. (2009). *Deployment and impact of support staff in schools: Characteristics, working conditions and job satisfaction of support staff in schools (strand 1, waves 1–3 in 2004, 2006 and 2008)* (Vol. DCSF-RR154). London, UK: Department for Children, School and Families.

Bliesener, T. (1996). Methodological moderators in validating biographical data in personnel selection. *Journal of Occupational and Organizational Psychology*, *69*(1), 107–120.

Blinder, A. (2009). How many U.S. jobs might be offshorable? *World Economics*, *10*(2), 41–78.

Bloom, H. S., Hill, C. J., Black, A. R., & Lipsey, M. W. (2008). Performance trajectories and performance gaps as achievement effect-size benchmarks for educational interventions. *Journal of Research on Educational Effectiveness*, *1*(4), 289–328.

Bonsall, E. (2015, November 3). Recreating the Finnish miracle. *Harvard Political Review.* Retrieved December 6, 2016, from http://harvardpolitics.com/united-states/recreating -finnish-miracle/

Brasington, D. M., & Hite, D. (2012). School choice and perceived school quality. *Economics Letters*, *116*(3), 451–453. doi: 10.1016/j.econlet.2012.04.022

Bryan, W. L., & Harter, N. (1899). Studies on the telegraphic language: The acquisition of a hierarchy of habits. *Psychological Review*, *6*(4), 345–375. doi: 10.1037/h0073117

Budde, R. (1974). *Education by charter.* Paper presented at the Annual meeting of the Society for General Systems Research.

Budde, R. (1996). The evolution of the charter concept. *Phi Delta Kappan*, *78*(1), 72–73.

Buddin, R., & Zamarro, G. (2010). Teacher qualifications and student achievement in urban elementary schools. *Journal of Urban Economics*, *66*(2), 103–115.

Burute, N., & Jankharia, B. (2009). Teleradiology: The Indian perspective. *Indian Journal of Radiological Imaging*, *19*(1), 16–18.

Carpenter II, D. M., Knepper, L., Erickson, A. C., & Ross, J. K. (2012). *License to work: A national study of burdens from occupational licensing* Arlington, VA: Institute for Justice.

Catalona, W. J., Smith, D. S., Ratliff, T. L., & Basler, J. W. (1993). Detection of organ-confined prostate cancer is increased through prostate-specific antigen-based screening. *Journal of the American Medical Association*, *270*(8), 948–954.

Center for Research on Education Outcomes. (2013). *National charter school study 2013.* Stanford, CA: Center for Research on Education Outcomes.

Centre for Research on the Wider Benefits of Learning. (2006, October). The wider benefits of learning: A synthesis of findings from the Centre for Research on the Wider Benefits of Learning, 1999–2006. Retrieved December 25, 2016, from http://webarchive.national archives.gov.uk/20130401151715/http://www.education.gov.uk/publications/eOrdering Download/RCB05-06.pdf

Chalmers, I. (2005, September 20–23). *The scandalous failure of scientists to cumulate scientifically.* Paper presented at the Ninth World Congress on Health Information and Libraries, Salvador, Brazil. Retrieved January 22, 2018, from http://www.icml9.org /program/public/documents/Chalmers-131528.pdf

Chase, W. G., & Simon, H. A. (1973). Perception in chess. *Cognitive Psychology, 4*(1), 55–81.

Chetty, R., Friedman, J. N., Hilger, N., Saez, E., Schanzenbach, D., & Yagan, D. (2010). $320,000 Kindergarten teachers. *Phi Delta Kappan, 92*(3), 22–25.

Chiang, H., Speroni, C., Hermann, M., Hallgren, K., Burkander, P., & Wellington, A. (2017). *Evaluation of the teacher incentive fund: Final report on implementation and impacts of pay-for-performance across four years.* Washington, DC: National Center for Education Evaluation and Regional Assistance.

Choi, J. (2012). *Private tutoring and educational inequality: Evidence from a dynamic model of academic achievement in Korea.* Philadelphia, PA: University of Pennsylvania.

Clark, M. A., Isenberg, E., Liu, A. Y., Makowsky, L., & Zukiewicz, M. (2015). *Impacts of the Teach for America Investing in Innovation scale-up.* Princeton, NJ: Mathematica Policy Research.

Clotfelter, C. T., Hemelt, S. W., & Ladd, H. F. (2016). *Teaching assistants and nonteaching staff: Do they improve student outcomes?* Washington, DC: Center for Analysis of Longitudinal Data in Educational Research.

Cohen, R. M. (2015, January 5). The true cost of Teach for America's impact on urban schools. *The American Prospect.* Retrieved December 26, 2016, from http://prospect.org /article/true-cost-teach-americas-impact-urban-schools

Cowen, T. (2013). *Average is over: Powering America beyond the age of the Great Stagnation.* New York, NY: Penguin.

Cox, W. M., & Alm, R. (2008). Creative destruction. *Concise Encyclopedia of Economics.* Retrieved November 3, 2015, from http://www.econlib.org/library/Enc/CreativeDestruction.html

Coyle, D. (2009). *The talent code: Greatness isn't born. It's grown. Here's how.* New York, NY: Bantam Dell.

Cuban, L. (2002). *Oversold and underused: Computers in the classroom.* Cambridge, MA: Harvard University Press.

Dabrowski, T., & Klingner, J. (2016, February 3). Steps and lanes: Understanding how Chicago public school teachers get multiple pay raises each year. *Illinois Policy.* Retrieved December 28, 2016, from https://www.illinoispolicy.org/steps-and-lanes-understanding-how-chicago-public-school-teachers-get-multiple-pay-raises-each-year/

Darling-Hammond, L., Holtzman, D. J., Gatlin, S. J., & Vasquez Heilig, J. (2005). Does teacher preparation matter? Evidence about teacher certification, Teach for America, and teacher effectiveness. *Education Policy Analysis Archives, 13*(42).

de Groot, A. D. (1965/1978). *Thought and choice in chess.* Amsterdam, Netherlands: Amsterdam University Press.

Dee, T. S., & Wyckoff, J. (2015). Incentives, selection, and teacher performance: Evidence from IMPACT. *Journal of Policy Analysis and Management, 34*(2), 267–297. doi: 10.1002/pam.21818

Dickens, C. (1854). *Hard times.* London, UK: Bradbury & Evans.

Dickersin, K., & Min, Y.-I. (1993). NIH clinical trials and publication bias. *Online Journal of Current Clincal Trials, 50*(April 28).

Djakow, I. N., Petrovskij, N. V., & Rudik, P. A. (1927). *Psychologie des Schachspiels auf der Grundlage psychotechnischer Experimente an den Teilnehmern des Internationalen Schachturniers zu Moskau 1925* [Psychology of chess on the basis of psychotechnical experiments at the participants of the 1925 International Chess Tournament in Moscow] (W. Brannasky, Trans.). Berlin, Germany: Walter de Gruyter.

Dolton, P., & Marcenaro-Gutierrez, O. D. (2011). If you pay peanuts, do you get monkeys? A cross-country analysis of teacher pay and pupil performance. *Economic Policy, 26*(65), 5–55.

Dolton, P., & Marcenaro-Gutierrez, O. D. (2013). *Global teacher status index.* London, UK: Varkey GEMS Foundation.

Donaldson, M. L., & Johnson, S. M. (2011). TFA teachers: How long do they teach? Why do they leave? *Phi Delta Kappan International.*

Dragoset, L., Thomas, J., Hermann, M., Deke, J., James-Burdumy, S., Graczewski, C., . . . Wei, T. E. (2016). *Race to the top: Implementation and relationship to student outcomes.* Washington, DC: National Center for Education Evaluation and Regional Assistance.

Dragoset, L., Thomas, J., Hermann, M., Deke, J., James-Burdumy, S., Graczewski, C., . . . Wei, T. E. (2017). *School improvement grants: Implementation and effectiveness.* Washington, DC: National Center for Education Evaluation and Regional Assistance.

Duflo, E., Hanna, R., & Ryan, S. P. (2012). Incentives work: Getting teachers to come to school. *American Economic Review, 102*(4), 1241–1278. doi: 10.1257/aer.102.4.1241

DuFour, R., DuFour, R., Eaker, R., & Many, T. (2010). *Learning by doing: A handbook for professional learning communities at work* (2nd ed.). Bloomington, IN: Solution Tree.

Dunlosky, J., Rawson, K. A., Marsh, E. J., Nathan, M. J., & Willingham, D. T. (2013). Improving students' learning with effective learning techniques: Promising directions from cognitive and educational psychology. *Psychological Science in the Public Interest, 14*(1), 4–58. doi: 10.1177/1529100612453266

Economist. (2007, March 15). The quest for prosperity. Retrieved December 29, 2016, from http://www.economist.com/node/8808044

Education Endowment Foundation. (2018). *Teaching and learning toolkit*. Retrieved January 8, 2018, from https://educationendowmentfoundation.org.uk/evidence-summaries/teaching -learning-toolkit

Edwards, C. (2016). Self-repair techniques point to robots that design themselves. *Communications of the Association for Computing Machinery, 59*(2), 15–17.

Epson Europe. (2014). Pre-flight printing. *EPSON case studies*. Retrieved December 23, 2016, from http://assets.epson-europe.com/gb/en/pte_2014/assets/press/other_content/KLM_case_study.pdf

Epstein, D. (2013). *The sports gene: Inside the science of extraordinary athletic performance*. New York, NY: Penguin.

Epstein, S. A. (1991). *Wage labor and guilds in medieval Europe*. Chapel Hill, NC: University of North Carolina Press.

Ericsson, A., & Pool, R. (2016). *Peak: Secrets from the new science of expertise*. Boston, MA: Houghton Mifflin Harcourt.

Ericsson, K. A., Chase, W. G., & Faloon, S. (1980). Acquisition of a memory skill. *Science, 208*(4448), 1181–1182. doi: 10.1126/science.7375930

Ericsson, K. A., Krampe, R. T., & Tesch-Römer, C. (1993). The role of deliberate practice in the acquisition of expert performance. *Psychological Review, 100*(3), 363–406.

Ericsson, K. A., Prietula, M. J., & Cokely, E. T. (2007). The making of an expert. *Harvard Business Review, 85*(7–8), 114–121, 193.

FastBrick Robotics. (2017). Hadrian X: A world first digital construction solution. Retrieved January 13, 2017, from http://fbr.com.au

Federal Reserve Bank of St. Louis. (2016). Manufacturing sector: Real output, index 2009=100, quarterly, seasonally adjusted. *Economic Research*. Retrieved May 10, 2016, from https://research.stlouisfed.org/fred2/series/OUTMS

Flynn, J. R. (2007). *What is intelligence?* Cambridge, UK: Cambridge University Press.

Frey, C. B., & Osborne, M. A. (2013). *The future of employment: How susceptible are jobs to computerisation?* Oxford, UK: University of Oxford.

Friedman, M. (1982). *Capitalism and freedom* (2nd ed.). Chicago, IL: University of Chicago Press.

Furberg, C. D. (1983). Effect of antiarrhythmic drugs on mortality after myocardial infarction. *American Journal of Cardiology, 52*(6), 32C–36C.

Gaudin, S. (2014, May 29). In big step for robotics, one robot repairs another in space. *Computerworld News*. Retrieved December 23, 2016, from http://www.computerworld.com/article/2490001/emerging-technology/in-big-step-for-robotics-one-robot-repairs -another-in-space.html

Gawande, A. (2007). *Better: A surgeon's notes on performance*. London, UK: Profile Books.

Geballe, B. (2005, July 20). Bill Gates' guinea pigs. *Seattle Weekly*, 1–9.

Gershenson, S., & Hayes, M. S. (2016). The implications of summer learning loss for value-added estimates of teacher effectiveness. *Educational Policy, 32*(1), 55–85. doi: 10.1177/0895904815625288

Gilbert, R., Salanti, G., Harden, M., & See, S. (2005). Infant sleeping position and the sudden infant death syndrome: Systematic review of observational studies and historical review of recommendations from 1940 to 2002. *International Journal of Epidemiology, 34*(4), 874–887. doi: 10.1093/ije/dyi088

Gladwell, M. (2008). *Outliers: The story of success.* New York, NY: Little, Brown.

Glass, G. V. (1976). Primary, secondary, and meta-analysis of research. *Educational Reseacher, 5*(10), 3–8.

Glass, G. V., Cahen, L. S., Smith, M. L., & Filby, N. F. (1982). *School class size: Research and policy.* Beverly Hills, CA: Sage.

Godden, D. R., & Baddeley, A. D. (1975). Context-dependent memory in two natural environments: On land and underwater. *British Journal of Psychology, 66*(3), 325–331.

Goe, L., & Bridgeman, B. (2006). *Effects of Focus on Standards on academic performance.* Princeton, NJ: Educational Testing Service.

Goldacre, B. (2012). *Bad pharma.* London, UK: Fourth Estate.

Goldhaber, D., & Anthony, E. (2007). Can teacher quality be effectively assessed? National Board certification as a signal of effective teaching. *Review of Economics and Statistics, 89*(1), 134–150.

Goldhaber, D. D., Goldschmidt, P., & Tseng, F. (2013). Teacher value-added at the high-school level: Different models, different answers? *Educational Evaluation and Policy Analysis, 35*(2), 220–236. doi: 10.3102/0162373712466938

Goldin, C., & Katz, L. F. (2008). *The race between education and technology.* Cambridge, MA: Harvard University Press.

Goos, M., & Manning, A. (2007). Lousy and lovely jobs: The rising polarization of work in Britain. *Review of Economics and Statistics, 89*(1), 118–133.

Gray, L., & Taie, S. (2015). *Public school teacher attrition and mobility in the first five years: Results from the first through fifth waves of the 2007–08 Beginning Teacher Longitudinal Study.* Washington, DC: National Center for Education Statistics.

Greene, J. P. (2012). Best practices are the worst. *Education Next, 12*(3), 72–73.

Grissmer, D. (1999). Conclusion: Class size effects: Assessing the evidence, its policy implications, and future research agenda. *Educational Evaluation and Policy Analysis, 21*(2), 231–248.

Hamre, B. K., & Pianta, R. C. (2005). Can instructional and emotional support in the first-grade classroom make a difference for children at risk of school failure? *Child Development, 76*(5), 949–967. doi: 10.1111/j.1467-8624.2005.00889.x

Hansen, M., Backes, B., Brady, V., & Xu, Z. (2014). *Examining spillover effects from Teach for America corps members in Miami-Dade County public schools.* Washington, DC: National Center for Analysis of Longitudinal Data in Education Research.

Hanushek, E. A. (1971). Teacher characteristics and gains in student achievement: Estimation using micro data. *American Economic Review, 61*(2), 280–288.

Hanushek, E. A. (1999). Some findings from an independent investigation of the Tennessee STAR experiment and from other investigations of class size effects. *Educational Evaluation and Policy Analysis, 21*(2), 143–163.

Hanushek, E. A. (2010). *The economic value of higher teacher quality.* Washington, DC: National Center for Analysis of Longitudinal Data in Educational Research.

Hanushek, E. A. (2011). The economic value of higher teacher quality. *Economics of Education Review, 30*(3), 466–479.

Hanushek, E. A., & Woessman, L. (2015). *Universal basic skills: What countries stand to gain.* Paris, France: Organisation for Economic Co-operation and Development.

Harris, D. N. (2009). Would accountability based on teacher value added be smart policy? An examination of the statistical properties and policy alternatives. *Education Finance and Policy, 4*(4), 319–350. doi: 10.1162/edfp.2009.4.4.319

Harris, D. N., & Sass, T. R. (2007). *Teacher training, teacher quality and student achievement.* Washington, DC: National Center for Analysis of Longitudinal Data in Education Research.

Hart, B., & Risley, T. (1995). *Meaningful differences in the everyday experiences of young American children.* Baltimore, MD: Brooks.

Haselkorn, D., & Harris, L. (2001). *The essential profession: American education at the crossroads. A national survey of public attitudes toward teaching, educational opportunity, and school reform.* Belmont, MA: Recruiting New Teachers.

Hayek, F. A. (1945). The use of knowledge in society. *American Economic Review, XXXV*(4), 519–530.

Heath, C., & Heath, D. (2010). *Switch: How to change things when change is hard.* New York, NY: Broadway Books.

Heilbrun, J. (2003). Baumol's cost disease. In R. Towse (Ed.), *A handbook of cultural economics* (pp. 91–101). Cheltenham, UK: Edward Elgar.

Henry, G. T., Bastian, K. C., Fortner, C. K., Kershaw, D. C., Purtell, K. M., Thompson, C. L., & Zulli, R. A. (2014). Teacher preparation policies and their effects on student achievement. *Education Finance and Policy, 9*(3), 264–303. doi: 10.1162/EDFP_a_00134

Heyman, A. (2001, October 4). Doctors complete first transatlantic surgery. *Badger Herald.*

Hill, H. C., Charalambous, C. Y., & Kraft, M. A. (2012). When rater reliability is not enough: Teacher observation systems and a case for the generalizability study. *Educational Researcher, 41*(2), 56–84.

Hirsch Jr., E. D. (2009). *The making of Americans: Democracy and our schools.* New Haven, CT: Yale University Press.

Hirsch Jr., E. D. (2016). *Why knowledge matters: Rescuing our children from failed educational theories.* Cambridge, MA: Harvard University Press.

Hitchcock, C., & Westwell, M. S. (2017). A cluster-randomised, controlled trial of the impact of Cogmed Working Memory Training on both academic performance and regulation of social, emotional and behavioural challenges. *Journal of Child Psychology and Psychiatry, 58*(2), 140–150. doi: 10.1111/jcpp.12638

Honey, M., Fasca, C., Gersick, A., Mandinach, E., & Sinha, S. (2005). *Assessment of 21st century skills: The current landscape (pre-publication draft)*. Tucson, AZ: Partnership for 21st Century Skills.

Huckman, R. S., & Pisano, G. P. (2006). The firm specificity of individual performance: Evidence from cardiac surgery. *Management Science, 52*(4), 473–488. doi: 10.1287/mnsc .1050.0464

Huelser, B. J., & Metcalfe, J. (2012). Making related errors facilitates learning, but learners do not know it. *Memory & Cognition, 40*(4), 514–527. doi: 10.3758/s13421-011-0167-z

Hume, D. (1739). *A treatise of human nature: Being an attempt to introduce the experimental method of reasoning into moral subjects*. London, UK: John Noon.

Husén, T. (Ed.). (1967). *International study of achievement in mathematics: A comparison of twelve countries* (vol. 1). New York, NY: John Wiley & Sons.

Jackson, C. K., & Bruegman, E. (2009). Teaching students and teaching each other: The importance of peer learning for teachers. *American Economic Journal: Applied Economics, 1*(4).

Jackson, M., & Wolff, H. (Directors). (1983). The future is further away than you think, [Television series episode]. In *QED* (UK)/*Living Proof* (US). United Kingdom: BBC TV.

Jagger, C., Matthews, R., Melzer, D., Matthews, F., Brayne, C., & Medical Research Council Cognitive Functioning Aging Study. (2007). Educational differences in the dynamics of disability incidence, recovery and mortality: Findings from the MRC Cognitive Function and Ageing Study (MRC CFAS). *International Journal of Epidemiology, 36*, 358–365.

Jepsen, C., & Rivkin, S. G. (2002). *What is the tradeoff between smaller classes and teacher quality?* (vol. 9205). Cambridge, MA: National Bureau of Economic Research.

Jerrim, J. (2014). *Why do East Asian children perform so well in PISA? An investigation of Western-born children of East Asian descent*. London, UK: Institute of Education, University of London.

John Deere. (2014, August 4). John Deere updates revolutionary cotton picker with CP690 in 2015. *2014 News Releases and Information*. Retrieved January 3, 2017, from https://www.deere .com/en_US/corporate/our_company/news_and_media/press_releases/2014/agriculture /2014aug4_cp690.page

Johnson, P. K. (1964). The Instituto Technico. *Journal of Physical Education, 61*(6), 135–139.

Jørgensen, H. (1997). Time for practising? Higher level music students' use of time for instrumental practising. In H. Jørgensen & A. C. Lehmann (Eds.), *Does practice make perfect? Current theory and research on instrumental music practice* (pp. 123–139). Oslo, Norway: Norges Musikhøgskole [Norwegian State Academy of Music].

Kan, M. (2015, February 27). Robots to take over work at Foxconn factories in three years. *PC World*. Retrieved January 3, 2017, from http://www.pcworld.com/article/2890032/foxconn -expects-robots-to-take-over-more-factory-work.html

Kane, T. J., McCaffrey, D., Miller, T., & Staiger, D. O. (2013). *Have we identified effective teachers? Validating measures of effective teaching using random assignment.* Seattle, WA: Bill & Melinda Gates Foundation.

Kennedy, E. (2002). Higher education and Pell grants. *Congressional record: Proceedings and debates of the 107th Congress second session* (vol. 148 part 7, pp. 9355–9358). Washington, DC: United States Government Printing Office.

Kirschner, P. A., Sweller, J., & Clark, R. E. (2006). Why minimal guidance during instruction does not work: An analysis of the failure of constructivist, problem-based, experiential, and inquiry-based teaching. *Educational Psychologist, 41*(2), 75–86.

Klein, J., & Cornell, D. (2010). Is the link between large high schools and student victimization an illusion? *Journal of Educational Psychology, 102*(4), 933–946.

Koedel, C., & Polikoff, M. S. (2017). Big bang for just a few bucks: The impact of math textbooks in California. *Evidence Speaks Reports (Brookings Institution), 2*(5), 1–7.

Kontra, C., Lyons, D. J., Fischer, S. M., & Beilock, S. L. (2015). Physical experience enhances science learning. *Psychological Science, 26*(6), 737–749. doi: 10.1177/0956797615569355

Kraft, M. A., & Papay, J. P. (2014). Can professional environments in schools promote teacher development? Explaining heterogeneity in returns to teaching experience. *Educational Evaluation and Policy Analysis, 36*(4), 476–500. doi: 10.3102/0162373713519496

Krueger, A. B., & Whitmore, D. (2001). The effects of attending a small class in the early grades on college-test taking and middle school test results: Evidence from Project STAR. *Economic Journal, 111*(1), 1–28.

Lai, C.-Q. (2017). How much of human height is genetic and how much is due to nutrition? *Scientific American*. Retrieved January 17, 2017, from https://www.scientificamerican.com /article/how-much-of-human-height/

Langer Research Associates. (2016, August). Critical issues in public education: The 2016 Phi Delta Kappa survey topline report. Retrieved January 5, 2017, from http://pdkpoll2015.pdki ntl.org/wp-content/uploads/2016/08/PDK2016PollToplineReport.pdf

Lavy, V., Ebenstein, A., & Roth, S. (2014). *The long run human capital and economic consequences of high-stakes examinations.* Cambridge, MA: National Bureau of Economic Research.

Leahy, S., & Lyon, C. (2007). *The Trenton-ETS Partnership and the High School Proficiency Assessment: The effects of review lessons and targeted tutoring on mathematics scores.* Princeton, NJ: Educational Testing Service.

Lebergott, S. (1957). Annual estimates of unemployment in the United States, 1900–1954. In Universities-National Bureau Committee for Economic Research (Ed.), *The measurement and behavior of unemployment* (pp. 211–242). Princeton, NJ: Princeton University Press.

Lemov, D. (2010). *Teach like a champion: 49 techniques that put students on the path to college.* San Francisco, CA: Jossey-Bass.

Lesgold, A. M., Rubinson, H., Feltovich, P. J., Glaser, R., Klopfer, D., & Wang, Y. (1988). Expertise in a complex skill: Diagnosing x-ray pictures. In M. T. H. Chi, R. Glaser, & M. J. Farr (Eds.), *The nature of expertise* (pp. 311–342). Hillsdale, NJ: Lawrence Erlbaum Associates.

Levin, H. M., Belfield, C., Muennig, P., & Rouse, C. (2007). *The costs and benefits of an excellent education for all of America's children*. New York, NY: Teachers College.

Levinson, M. (2016). *Job creation in the manufacturing revival*. Washington, DC: Congressional Research Office.

Levinson, M. (2017). *U.S. manufacturing in international perspective*. Washington, DC: Congressional Research Office.

Limitone, J. (2016, May 24). Fmr. McDonald's USA CEO: $35k robots cheaper than hiring at $15 per hour. *FOX Business*. Retrieved January 3, 2017, from http://www.foxbusiness.com /features/2016/05/24/fmr-mcdonalds-usa-ceo-35k-robots-cheaper-than-hiring-at-15-per-hour.html

Lleras-Muney, A. (2005). The relationship between education and adult mortality in the United States. *Review of Economic Studies, 72*(1), 189–221.

Loewen, J. W. (2008). *Lies my teacher told me: Everything your American history textbook got wrong*. New York, NY: New Press.

Louisiana Department of Education. (2017). Curricular resources annotated reviews. Retrieved January 15, 2017, from https://www.louisianabelieves.com/academics/ONLINE -INSTRUCTIONAL-MATERIALS-REVIEWS/curricular-resources-annotated-reviews

Loveless, T. (2013, October 9). PISA's China problem. *Brown Center Chalkboard Series Archive*. Retrieved December 9, 2016, from https://www.brookings.edu/research/pisas -china-problem/

Lowe, G. (1980). State-dependent recall decrements with moderate doses of alcohol. *Current Psychological Research, 1*(1), 3–8.

Lyons, B. D., Hoffman, B. J., & Michel, J. W. (2009). Not much more than g? An examination of the impact of intelligence on NFL performance. *Human Performance, 22*(3), 225–245. doi: 10.1080/08959280902970401

Ma, L. (1999). *Knowing and teaching elementary mathematics: Teachers' understanding of fundamental mathematics in China and the United States*. Mahwah, NJ: Lawrence Erlbaum Associates.

Machin, S., & McNally, S. (2009, March). *The three Rs: What scope is there for literacy and numeracy policies to raise pupil achievement?* London, UK. http://www.ifn.se/web /pschooling2009.aspx

Mandel, M. (2013, July 8). 752,000 app economy jobs on the 5th anniversary of the App Store. Retrieved April 3, 2015, from http://www.progressivepolicy.org/slider/752000-app -economy-jobs-on-the-5th-anniversary-of-the-app-store/

Mankiw, N. G. (2014). *Principles of economics* (7th ed.). Boston, MA: Cengage.

Mauboussin, M. J. (2012). *The success equation: Untangling skill and luck in business, sports, and investing*. Boston, MA: Harvard Business Review Press.

McNally, S., Ruiz-Valenzuela, J., & Rolfe, H. (2016). *ABRA Online Reading Support: Evaluation report and executive summary*. London, UK: Education Endowment Foundation.

Melby-Lervåg, M., & Hulme, C. (2013). Is working memory training effective? A meta-analytic review. *Developmental Psychology, 49*(2), 270–291. doi: 10.1037/a0028228

Mencken, H. L. (1917). The divine afflatus. In H. L. Mencken (Ed.), *Prejudices: Second series* (pp. 155–171). New York, NY: Alfred A. Knopf.

Miller, G. A. (1956). The magical number seven, plus or minus two: Some limits on our capacity for processing information. *Psychological Review, 63*(2), 81–97.

Mirabile, M. P. (2005). Intelligence and football: Testing for differentials in collegiate quarterback passing performance and NFL compensation. *The Sport Journal, 8*(2).

Miron, G., Urschel, J. L., & Saxton, N. (2011). *What makes KIPP work? A study of student characteristics, attrition, and school finance*. New York, NY: National Center for the Study of Privatization in Education, Teachers College, Columbia University.

Molnar, A., Smith, P., Zahorik, J., Palmer, A., Halbach, A., & Ehrle, K. (1999). Evaluating the SAGE Program: A pilot program in targeted pupil-teacher reduction in Wisconsin. *Educational Evaluation and Policy Analysis, 21*(2), 165–177.

Moore, T. J. (1995). *Deadly medicine: Why tens of thousands of heart patients died in America's worst drug disaster*. New York, NY: Simon & Schuster.

Mosteller, F. W. (1995). The Tennessee study of class size in the early school grades. *The Future of Children (special issue: Critical issues for children and youths), 5*(2), 113–127.

Myerson, J., Emery, L., White, D. A., & Hale, S. (2003). Effects of age, domain, and processing demands on memory span: Evidence for differential decline. *Aging, Neuropsychology and Cognition, 10*(1), 20–27.

National Assessment of Educational Progress. (2013). *Trends in academic progress: Reading 1971–2012, mathematics 1973–2012*. Washington, DC: United States Department of Education.

National Commission on Excellence in Education. (1983). *A nation at risk: The imperative for educational reform*. Washington, DC: United States Department of Education.

National Council of Teachers of Mathematics. (1980). *An agenda for action*. Reston, VA: National Council of Teachers of Mathematics.

National Education Association. (2008). *Class size reduction: A proven reform strategy*. Washington, DC: National Education Association.

No Child Left Behind Act, Pub. L. No. 107-110, 115 Stat. 1425-2094 (2002).

Nyhan, R. C., & Alkadry, M. G. (1999). The impact of school resources on student achievement test scores. *Journal of Education Finance, 25*(2), 211–227.

Oates, T. (2016, April 18). Why ditching textbooks would be to the detriment of learning. *Times Educational Supplement*. Retrieved January 23, 2017, from https://www.tes.com/news/school-news/breaking-views/why-ditching-textbooks-would-be-detriment-learning

O'Neil, C. (2016). *Weapons of math destruction: How big data increases inequality and threatens democracy*. New York, NY: Crown.

Open Science Collaboration. (2015). Estimating the reproducibility of psychological science. *Science*, *349*(6251), 943, aac4716-4711-aac4716-4718. doi: 10.1126/science.aac4716

Oreopoulos, P., & Salvanes, K. G. (2011). Priceless: The nonpecuniary benefits of schooling. *Journal of Economic Perspectives*, *25*(1), 159–184.

Organisation for Economic Co-operation and Development. (2007). *PISA 2006: Science competences for tomorrow's world* (vol. 1). Paris, France: Organisation for Economic Co-operation and Development.

Organisation for Economic Co-operation and Development. (2010). *Education at a glance*. Paris, France: Organisation for Economic Co-operation and Development.

Organisation for Economic Co-operation and Development. (2014). *Education at a glance*. Paris, France: Organisation for Economic Co-operation and Development.

Organisation for Economic Co-operation and Development. (2016a). *PISA 2015 results: Excellence and equity in education* (vol. 1). Paris, France: Organisation for Economic Co-operation and Development.

Organisation for Economic Co-operation and Development. (2016b). *PISA 2015 results: Policies and practices for successful schools* (vol. 2). Paris, France: Organisation for Economic Co-operation and Development.

O'Toole, G. (2016, July 13). It's difficult to make predictions, especially about the future. *Quote Investigator: Exploring the Origins of Quotations*. Retrieved November 30, 2016, from http://quoteinvestigator.com/2013/10/20/no-predict/

Otterman, S. (2011, January 20). Pilot program of teacher bonuses is suspended. *New York Times*. Retrieved November 20, 2016, from http://www.nytimes.com/2011/01/21/nyregion/21bonuses.html?scp=1&sq=bonuses schools suspended&st=cse

Pane, J. F., Steiner, E. D., Baird, M. D., & Hamilton, L. S. (2015). *Continued progress: Promising evidence on personalized learning*. Santa Monica, CA: RAND Corporation.

Papay, J. P., & Kraft, M. A. (2015). Productivity returns to experience in the teacher labor market: Methodological challenges and new evidence on long-term career improvement. *Journal of Public Economics*, *130*, 105–119.

Papert, S. A. (1998, June 2). Child power: Keys to the new learning of the digital century. Colin Cherry Memorial Lecture, London, UK, Imperial College.

Pashler, H., McDaniel, M., Rohrer, D., & Bjork, R. A. (2008). Learning styles: Concepts and evidence. *Psychological Science in the Public Interest*, *9*(3), 105–119.

Pate-Bain, H., Boyd-Zaharias, J., Cain, V. A., Word, E., & Binkley, M. E. (1997). *STAR follow-up studies 1996–1997*. Lebanon, TN: Heros.

Pennsylvania Department of Education. (2016). SAT and ACT scores. Retrieved January 4, 2017, from http://www.education.pa.gov/K-12/Assessment%20and%20Accountability/Pages/SAT-and-ACT.aspx

Penuel, W. R., & Johnson, R. (2016). *Review of continued progress: Promising evidence on personalized learning*. Boulder, CO: National Education Policy Center.

Petrosino, A., Petrosino, C. T., & Buelher, J. (2004). *'Scared Straight' and other juvenile awareness programs for preventing juvenile delinquency*. Oslo, Norway: Campbell Collaboration.

Pfeffer, J. (2000). *The knowing-doing gap: How smart companies turn knowledge into action*. Cambridge, MA: Harvard Business School Press.

Piketty, T. (2014). *Capital in the twenty-first century* (A. Goldhammer, Trans.). Cambridge, MA: Harvard University Press.

Piketty, T., Saez, E., & Zucman, G. (2016). *Distributional national accounts: Methods and estimates for the United States*. Cambridge, MA: National Bureau of Economic Research.

Pink, D. H. (2009). *Drive: The surprising truth about what motivates us*. New York, NY: Riverhead.

Pittet, D. (2001). Improving adherence to hand hygiene practice: A multidisciplinary approach. *Emerging Infectious Diseases*, *7*(2), 234–240.

Prensky, M. (2001). Digital natives, digital immigrants part 1. *On the Horizon*, *9*(5), 1–6.

Programme for International Student Assessment. (2001). *Knowledge and skills for life: First results from PISA 2000*. Paris, France: Organisation for Economic Co-operation and Development.

Programme for International Student Assessment. (2004). *Learning for tomorrow's world: First results from PISA 2003*. Paris, France: Organisation for Economic Co-operation and Development.

Programme for International Student Assessment. (2013a). *PISA 2012 results: What makes schools successful? Resources, policies and practices* (vol. IV). Paris, France: Organisation for Economic Co-operation and Development.

Programme for International Student Assessment. (2013b). *PISA 2012 results: What students know and can do. Student performance in mathematics, reading and science* (vol. 1). Paris, France: Organisation for Economic Co-operation and Development.

Puma, M., Bell, S., Cook, R., Heid, C., Broene, P., Jenkins, F., . . . Downer, J. (2012). *Third grade follow-up to the Head Start Impact Study: Final report* (OPRE Report 2012-45). Washington, DC: United States Department of Health and Human Services.

Ravitch, D. (2003). *The language police: How pressure groups restrict what students learn*. New York, NY: Vintage Books.

Reshoring Initiative. (2016, March 28). Reshoring initiative data report: Reshoring and FDI boost US manufacturing in 2015. Retrieved December 29, 2016, from http://reshorenow. org/blog/reshoring-initiative-data-report-reshoring-and-fdi-boost-us-manufacturing-in-2015/

Restuccia, A. (2015, January 9). Keystone ruling puts John Kerry back in hot seat. *Politico*. Retrieved January 10, 2015, from http://www.politico.com/story/2015/01/john-kerry-keystone-xl-climate-change-114118.html

Rickover, H. G. (1965, January 31). Has education failed nation? *Monroe Morning World*, p. 16.

Ritchie, S. (2015). *Intelligence*. London, UK: John Murray Learning.

Ritzen, J. M. M., van Dommelen, J., & De Vijlder, F. J. (1997). School finance and school choice in the Netherlands. *Economics of Education Review, 16*(3), 329–335. doi: http://dx.doi.org/10.1016/S0272-7757(96)00078-7

Rivkin, S. G., Hanushek, E. A., & Kain, J. F. (2005). Teachers, schools and academic achievement. *Econometrica, 73*(2), 417–458.

Roberts, R. (Contributor). (2016, November 28). *Doug Lemov on reading.* Retrieved from http://www.econtalk.org/archives/2016/11/doug_lemov_on_r.html

Rockoff, J. E. (2004). The impact of individual teachers on student achievement: Evidence from panel data. *American Economic Review, 94*(2), 247–252.

Rodriguez, M. C. (2004). The role of classroom assessment in student performance on TIMSS. *Applied Measurement in Education, 17*(1), 1–24.

Ross, R. (1999, May 26). How class-size reduction harms kids in poor neighborhoods. *Education Week.* Retrieved November 15, 2016, from http://www.edweek.org/ew/articles/1999/05/26/37ross.h18.html

Rothstein, J. (2010). Teacher quality in educational production: Tracking, decay, and student achievement. *Quarterly Journal of Economics, 125*(1), 175–214.

Rowe, M. B. (1986). Wait-time: Slowing down may be a way of speeding up! *Journal of Teacher Education, 37*(January–February), 43–50.

Sahlberg, P. (2013, May 15). What if Finland's great teachers taught in U.S. schools? *Washington Post.* Retrieved November 24, 2014, from http://www.washingtonpost.com/blogs/answer-sheet/wp/2013/05/15/what-if-finlands-great-teachers-taught-in-u-s-schools-not-what-you-think/

Sanders, W. L., & Rivers, J. C. (1996). *Cumulative and residual effects of teachers on future student academic achievement.* Knoxville, TN: University of Tennessee Value-Added Research and Assessment Center.

Sartain, L., Stoelinga, S. R., Brown, E. R., Luppescu, S., Matsko, K. K., Miller, F. K., . . . Glazer, D. (2011). *Rethinking teacher evaluation in Chicago: Lessons learned from classroom observations, principal-teacher conferences, and district implementation.* Chicago, IL: Consortium on Chicago School Research.

Sass, T. R., Hannaway, J., Xu, Z., Figlio, D. N., & Feng, L. (2012). Value added of teachers in high-poverty schools and lower poverty schools. *Journal of Urban Economics, 72*(2–3), 104–122. doi: http://dx.doi.org/10.1016/j.jue.2012.04.004

Saunders, W. M., Goldenberg, C. N., & Gallimore, R. (2009). Increasing achievement by focusing grade level teams on improving classroom learning: A prospective, quasi-experimental study of title 1 schools. *American Educational Research Journal, 46*(4), 1006–1033.

Schacter, J., & Thum, Y. M. (2004). Paying for high- and low-quality teaching. *Economics of Education Review, 23*, 411–430.

Schloss, D. F. (1891). Why working-men dislike piece-work. *Economic Review, 1*(3), 312–326.

Schneider, S. (2016, May 12). So long textbooks? Former education official pushes for digital teaching tools. *Morning Edition*. Retrieved January 23, 2017, from http://wesa.fm/post/so -long-textbooks-former-education-official-pushes-for-digital-teaching-tools - stream/0

Schumpeter, J. A. (1942). *Capitalism, socialism and democracy*. New York, NY: Harper & Row.

Selden, S. (1999). *Inheriting shame: The story of eugenics and racism in America* (vol. 23). New York, NY: Teachers College Press.

Shulman, L. S. (2004). *The wisdom of practice: Essays on teaching, learning, and learning to teach*. San Francisco, CA: Jossey-Bass.

Slater, H., Davies, N., & Burgess, S. (2008). *Do teachers matter? Measuring the variation in teacher effectiveness in England* (vol. 09/212). Bristol, UK: University of Bristol Institute of Public Affairs.

Smith, A. (2016, March 10). Public predictions for the future of workforce automation. Retrieved January 13, 2017, from http://www.pewinternet.org/2016/03/10/ public-predictions-for-the-future-of-workforce-automation/

Smith, S. M., Glenberg, A. M., & Bjork, R. A. (1978). Environmental context and human memory. *Memory and Cognition*, 6(4), 342–353.

Snow, P. B., Smith, D. S., & Catalona, W. J. (1994). Artificial neural networks in the diagnosis and prognosis of prostate cancer: A pilot study. *Journal of Urology*, *152*(5 part 2), 1923–1926.

Spock, B. (1946). *The common sense book of baby and child care*. New York, NY: Duell, Sloan, and Pearce.

Spock, B. (1956). *The common sense guide to baby and child care*. New York, NY: Duell, Sloan, and Pearce.

Springer, M. G., Ballou, D., Hamilton, L., Le, V.-N., Lockwood, J. R., McCaffrey, D., . . . Stecher, B. M. (2010). *Teacher pay for performance: Experimental evidence from the project on incentives in teaching*. Nashville, TN: National Center on Performance Incentives at Vanderbilt University.

Stanford University Center for Education Policy Analysis. (2016). Ready4K—Text messages to help you prepare your child for kindergarten. *Understanding Behavior Barrier in Education*. Retrieved December 13, 2016, from https://cepa.stanford.edu/cepalabs/ready4k

Stecher, B. M., & Bohrnstedt, G. W. (Eds.). (2002). *Class size reduction in California: Findings from 1999–00 and 2000–01*. Sacramento, CA: California Department of Education.

Steinberg, M. P., & Garrett, R. (2016). Classroom composition and measured teacher performance: What do teacher observation scores really measure? *Educational Evaluation and Policy Analysis*, *38*(2), 293–317. doi: 10.3102/0162373715616249

Stockard, J., Wood, T. W., Coughlin, C., & Khoury, C. R. (2018). The effectiveness of direct instruction curricula: A meta-analysis of a half century of research. *Review of Educational Research*. doi: 10.3102/0034654317751919

Sweller, J. (2016). Story of a research program. In S. Tobias, J. D. Fletcher, & D. C. Berliner (Eds.), *Acquired wisdom: Lessons learned by distinguished researchers* (10th ed., pp. 1–19). Tempe, AZ: Arizona State University.

Syed, M. (2010). *Bounce: Mozart, Federer, Picasso, Beckham, and the science of success.* New York, NY: HarperCollins.

Teo, K. K., Yusuf, S., & Furberg, C. D. (1993). Effects of prophylactic antiarrhythmic drug therapy in acute myocardial infarction: An overview of results from randomized controlled trials. *JAMA, 270*(13), 1589–1595. doi: 10.1001/jama.1993.03510130095038

Texas Education Agency. (2005). *Professional development and appraisal system: Teacher manual.* Austin, TX: Texas Education Agency.

Timmer, M. P., Azeez, A. R., Los, B., Stehrer, R., & de Vries, G. J. (2014). Slicing up global value chains. *Journal of Economic Perspectives, 28*(2), 99–118.

Tobin, K. (1987). The role of wait time in higher cognitive level learning. *Review of Educational Research, 57*(1), 69–95.

Toledo Blade. (1946, October 9). Lie hints he may enter atomic control dispute. *Toledo Blade,* p. 2. Retrieved from https://news.google.com/newspapers?nid=8_tS2Vw13FcC&dat=19461009&printsec=frontpage&hl=en

Tough, P. (2008). *Whatever it takes: Geoffrey Canada's quest to change Harlem and America.* New York, NY: Houghton Mifflin.

Tullock, G. (2001). A comment on Daniel Klein's 'A plea to economists who favor liberty.' *Eastern Economic Journal, 27*(2), 203–207.

Tuttle, C. C., Gill, B. P., Gleason, P., Knechtel, V., Nichols-Barrer, I., & Resch, A. (2013). *KIPP middle schools: Impacts on achievement and other outcomes (Final report).* Princeton, NJ: Mathematica Policy Research.

United States Bureau of Labor Statistics. (2015, July 8). Data retrieval: Labor force statistics (CPS). Retrieved December 29, 2016, from https://www.bls.gov/webapps/legacy/cpsatab4.htm

United States Bureau of Labor Statistics. (2016a, December 2). All employees: Manufacturing. *Current Employment Statistics Establishment Survey.* Retrieved December 12, 2016, from http://research.stlouisfed.org/fred2/data/MANEMP.txt

United States Bureau of Labor Statistics. (2016b, March 15). Employment projections. Retrieved December 29, 2016, from http://www.bls.gov/emp/ep_chart_001.htm

United States Department of Education. (2015, October 29). U.S. Department of Education launches campaign to encourage schools to #GoOpen with educational resources. *Press Releases.* Retrieved January 23, 2017, from https://www.ed.gov/news/press-releases/us-department-education-launches-campaign-encourage-schools-goopen-educational-resources

University Language Services. (2013, May 20). Ivy League average ACT scores. Retrieved January 4, 2017, from https://www.universitylanguage.com/blog/28/ivy-league-act-scores/

Wainer, H., & Zwerling, H. S. (2006). Evidence that smaller schools do not improve student achievement. *Phi Delta Kappan, 88*(4), 300–303.

Weisberg, D., Sexton, S., Mulhern, J., & Keeling, D. (2008). *The widget effect: Our national failure to acknowledge and act on differences in teacher effectiveness.* Brooklyn, NY: New Teacher Project.

What Works Clearinghouse. (2016). *Cognitive Tutor Algebra I.* Washington, DC: United States Department of Education Institute of Education Sciences.

Wilby, P. (2013, July 1). Finland's education ambassador spreads the word. *Schools: The profile.* Retrieved December 10, 2016, from https://www.theguardian.com/education/2013/jul/01/education-michael-gove-finland-gcse

Wiliam, D. (1992). Special needs and the distribution of attainment in the national curriculum. *British Journal of Educational Psychology, 62,* 397–403.

Wiliam, D. (2008). International comparisons and sensitivity to instruction. *Assessment in Education: Principles, Policy & Practice, 15*(3), 253–257.

Wiliam, D. (2010). Standardized testing and school accountability. *Educational Psychologist, 45*(2), 107–122.

Wiliam, D. (2016a). *Leadership for teacher learning: Creating a culture where all teachers improve so that all learners succeed.* West Palm Beach, FL: Learning Sciences International.

Wiliam, D. (2016b, April 28). Learning styles: What does the research say? *Deans for Impact blog.* Retrieved June 21, 2016, from http://deansforimpact.org/post_Learning_styles_what_does_the_research_say.html

Willingham, D. T. (2009). *Why don't students like school: A cognitive scientist answers questions about how the mind works and what it means for your classroom.* San Francisco, CA: Jossey-Bass.

Willingham, D. T., & Lovette, G. (2014, September 26). Can reading comprehension be taught? *Teachers College Record.* Retrieved October 15, 2014, from http://www.tcrecord.org/content.asp?contentid=17701

Winters, M. A., & Cowen, J. M. (2013). Who would stay, who would be dismissed? An empirical consideration of value-added teacher retention policies. *Educational Researcher, 42*(6), 330–337. doi: 10.3102/0013189x13496145

World Memory Sports Council. (2016). World memory statistics. Retrieved July 9, 2016, from http://www.world-memory-statistics.com/disciplines.php

York, B. N., & Loeb, S. (2014). *One step at a time: The effects of an early literacy text messaging program for parents of preschoolers.* Cambridge, MA: National Bureau of Economic Research.

Zhou, Z., Peverly, S. T., & Xin, T. (2006). Knowing and teaching fractions: A cross-cultural study of American and Chinese mathematics teachers. *Contemporary Educational Psychology, 31*(4), 438–457. doi: 10.1016/j.cedpsych.2006.02.001

# INDEX